San Francisco Architecture

San Francisco Architecture

The Illustrated Guide to Over 1,000 of the
Best Buildings, Parks, and Public Artworks
in the Bay Area

Sally B. Woodbridge and John M. Woodbridge

Design and Illustration / Chuck Byrne

Editing / Elizabeth Douthitt Byrne

Chronicle Books, San Francisco

Library of Congress
Cataloging-in-Publication Data

Woodbridge, Sally Byrne.
   San Francisco architecture : the illustrated
guide to over 1,000 of the best buildings, parks,
and public artworks in the Bay Area / Sally B.
Woodbridge and John M. Woodbridge ; editing,
Elizabeth Douthitt Byrne.
   272 p.   cm.
   ISBN 0-87701-897-9 (pb)
   1. Architecture--California--San Francisco--
Guidebooks. 2. Parks--California--San Fran
cisco--Guidebooks. 3. Public art--California--
San Francisco--Guidebooks. 4. San Francisco
(Calif.)--Buildings, structures, etc. I. Wood-
bridge, John Marshall. II. Byrne, Elizabeth
Douthitt. III. Title.
NA735.S35W64 1992
720'.974'61--dc20   92-10027
                                        CIP

Printed in The United States of America.

Distributed in Canada by Raincoast Books
112 East Third Ave.
Vancouver, B.C. V5T 1C8

Chronicle Books
275 Fifth Street
San Francisco, CA 94103

Photography
© 1992, Rik Clingerman,
p. v, 22, 40, 56, 76, 92, 108,
122, 134, 148, 180, 198, 206,
216, 226, 236, 246
© 1992, Chuck Byrne, p. 160
© 1992, All others,
Sally B. Woodbridge and
John M. Woodbridge

Illustration
© 1992, Chuck Byrne
Cover and Maps

The design, illustration and
typography, as well as the photo-
graphic reproduction, done in
preparation for the printing of
this book were executed using a
Macintosh computer.

Contents

Introduction

Most of the entry photographs for this book were taken over the last thirty years while exploring and researching the rich architecture of San Francisco and the Bay Area. In the previous three guides that we have published, we tried to be as inclusive as possible in the areas we covered. In this one we have treated the densely urbanized areas of San Francisco inclusively and the outlying areas more selectively in order to keep the book to a usable size. We have been most selective in Berkeley and Oakland because several guides exist for the East Bay. In the less urbanized areas visibility diminishes because of California's way of producing vegetation as fast or faster than buildings. In reviewing our earlier guides we noted that much of what we listed twenty and thirty years ago is no longer visible and that suburban architecture often duplicated what could be seen better in the cities. Still, many Bay Area communities are fascinating in their own right, and so we have arranged tours of some of them to give a sense of the place and its more visible landmarks. The curious can explore further on their own.

We have also included tours of three North Bay cities: Petaluma, Sonoma, and Napa, which present such a good picture of early California settlement that they seemed to deserve fairly comprehensive treatment, especially Petaluma, which is a textbook example of small town America in the late 19th and early 20th centuries. We hope by this means to provide the maximum of interest with the minimum of frustration and to avoid the disappointments of driving a long winding road to see a house that, in the end, was not visible.

All of the buildings listed in this guide are visible from a public thoroughfare. In no way does the listing of any building imply that anyone has the right to trespass on private property or that the building is open to visitors. Houses, museums, and monuments that are open to the public are so indicated in the listings. Their hours should be checked by telephone.

Finally, we strongly recommend consulting a good road map, particularly for the tours outside San Francisco, because the maps presented here are taken out of the larger context and meant for use within the subject area.

Visitors to San Francisco often remark on its sparkling Mediterranean look, the result of sunlight reflecting off the patchwork of low, pastel-colored buildings marching over the hills, their bay windows looking out to sweeping views that seem to be at the end of every street. But compared to Mediterranean cities, even to eastern U.S. cities, San Francisco is young. Still, its 140-odd years of urban development are nearly all well represented and so present a wide range of architectural history. Although Chicago, Boston, or New York have more architectural landmarks, San Francisco has an impressive number of good buildings that live well together and repay repeated viewing. In spite of its terrain—even because of it—this is a great city for walking and browsing, which is what we recommend.

To look backward from present-day San Francisco to the barren fog-swept headlands that greeted Juan Bautista de Anza and his little band of Spanish settlers in the spring of 1776 requires an enormous leap of the imagination. Only a trip to the still-wild sections of the Point Reyes peninsula can suggest why the Indians shunned the San Francisco peninsula and the Spaniards considered it a hardship post. The scenic topography that seems so glamorous to us was an obstacle exacerbated by the scarcity of water and the almost total absence of tree-cover to give shelter from the biting winds from the sea and the bay.

For nearly 60 years after the presidio and the mission were established hardly any other settlement existed. About 1835 when William A. Richardson, an Englishman, built his house near what is now Portsmouth Square, the village that was to become the city began. By 1846, when the Treaty of Guadalupe Hidalgo made California part of the United States, the village of Yerba Buena had attracted about 500 North Americans. In 1847 Jasper O'Farrell surveyed as far west as Hyde Street and, prophetically, out into the bay to the east. In the wake of the Gold Rush the grid was imposed over the hills with more enthusiasm for real-estate development than any logic based on the terrain. The panoramic views could hardly have been appreciated since the heights were inaccessible to horse and wagon.

Scarcely discouraged by devastating fires and a few warning earthquakes, development pushed more or less evenly westward through the remainder of the century. By 1906 the area bounded by Divisadero Street on the west, the bay on the north and east, and 30th Street to the south was well settled, mainly with closely packed two- and three-story wooden houses that are such a distinguishing feature of the city today. Nob Hill and Pacific Heights and the grand boulevards of Van Ness and Dolores were the choice sites for grand mansions. The flatter lands—the Western Addition and most of the Mission district—were built up speculatively by builders using more or less standard plans with an almost endlessly inventive array of facades.

By 1906 the structure of downtown had evolved through a series of disastrous fires to something very similar to what it is today. Shopping was concentrated near Union Square, finance and business along Montgomery Street. Most business buildings had four to eight stories. Typically the frames combined heavy timbers and cast-iron columns; the walls were brick sometimes clad with stone, but more often with iron cast in varying degrees of elaboration that imitated stone. Such structures had none of the resistance to earthquakes that either the residential wooden balloon-frame or the new steel frame offered. Nor were they fireproof, which proved an equal drawback since the real disaster of 1906 was not the earthquake, but the fire. Because the earthquake ruptured most of the water and gas lines, the fires that ignited everywhere defeated the firefighters. By the time the conflagration was finally contained by dynamiting Van Ness Avenue, the fire had destroyed all of the downtown business district and much of the nearby residential areas.

Even though the great Chicago architect, Daniel H. Burnham, had providentially completed a new plan for the city in 1904 that embodied the precepts of the City Beautiful Movement, the 1906 disaster was more of a trauma than a turning point in the city's development. The drive to rebuild was about as impetuous and greed-inspired as the gold-fever that had produced the early city. Things were put back pretty much as they had been before, but since the value of the fire-proofed steel frame had been proven by the survival of the new skyscrapers, the post-fire business buildings used this structural system to increase their size and height.

The area adjacent to downtown became a zone of low- to mid-rise apartment buildings. Many were built in haste to rehouse the homeless; many more were built soon thereafter to accommodate the crowds expected for the Panama Pacific International Exposition of 1915 that was to celebrate the opening of the Panama Canal and the city's rebirth. Single-family houses dominated the streetcar suburbs and the older enclave of Russian and Telegraph Hills.

Assisted by improved transportation, the growing population pushed the limits of development south and west in the post-fire decades. After 1918 when streetcar service through the Twin Peaks tunnel became available to those residing in the

Sunset Area, development pushed farther west over the sand dunes. Although the exclusive, planned developments of St. Francis Wood and Forest Hill were started, most of the housing in the Sunset and the Richmond districts was built for those of more modest means. Because of cheap land and low construction costs, builders could build and sell for less, thereby serving the growing demand for suburban living fed by the now-affordable automobile. The flat terrain was carpeted with boxy bungalows; their stuccoed facades were as varied as their 19th-century counterparts but derived from current Hollywood images based on Mediterranean prototypes and contemporary styles such as the Moderne.

Little development took place during the Depression; in fact, the skyline remained virtually unchanged from 1930 to 1960. World War II brought all non-defense building to a halt but produced major social upheavals that changed the social character of some of the city's older residential and commercial areas. One example was the Western Addition, where large numbers of defense workers occupied what was already a transitional area, continuing the decline of its housing and commercial stock. Serious overcrowding was typical of the poorer parts of the city. Because of the flight to the rural suburbia of Marin County and the San Francisco Peninsula, fine Victorian houses were selling for under $15,000.

The 1950s brought urban renewal—or at least the planning for it. Redevelopment areas: the Golden Gateway, the Western Addition, Diamond Heights, and Yerba Buena were approved, cleared, and left like bombed-out wastelands, which have taken decades to refill. The 1960s saw the beginning of the boom in highrise office building, which continued more or less until the 1980s anti-growth initiatives and, finally, the adoption of the Downtown Plan in 1985, which limits development. Downtown has at last crossed Market Street, the proverbial "slot" that seemed an unbridgeable barrier in the 19th and most of the 20th centuries. The resident population has declined, becoming both richer and poorer and less family-based. On the positive side, as far as preservation is concerned, the high cost of land and of new construction has encouraged the trend toward rehabilitating older buildings so that, today, a tour of the city's older residential and commercial areas—a sobering experience 30 years ago—is full of pleasant discoveries.

For the visitor with limited time to explore, downtown and the hills immediately around it show San Francisco's image and origins best. Here, the juxtaposition of hills and water, highrise and low buildings, mansions and shanties, along with the compactness of it all combine to make a kind of urbanity that exists in few other places in this country. The cityscape is so rich and varied that any guide to individual buildings should not be taken as the sum total of architectural interest. The city is full of happy accidents where minor buildings play major roles. So we urge you to walk, even at the pain of your leg muscles, to enjoy the surprises offered by this improbable conjunction of man and nature: the green of Angel Island seen at the end of a street, the cascade of little wooden houses tumbling down Telegraph Hill into the skyscraper canyon of lower Montgomery Street, or the fog making those often too solid towers ethereal and translucent.

Acknowledgments

The authors wish to thank Elizabeth Douthitt Byrne for her conscientious editing and Rik Clingerman for many of the photographs that introduce the sections of the guide.

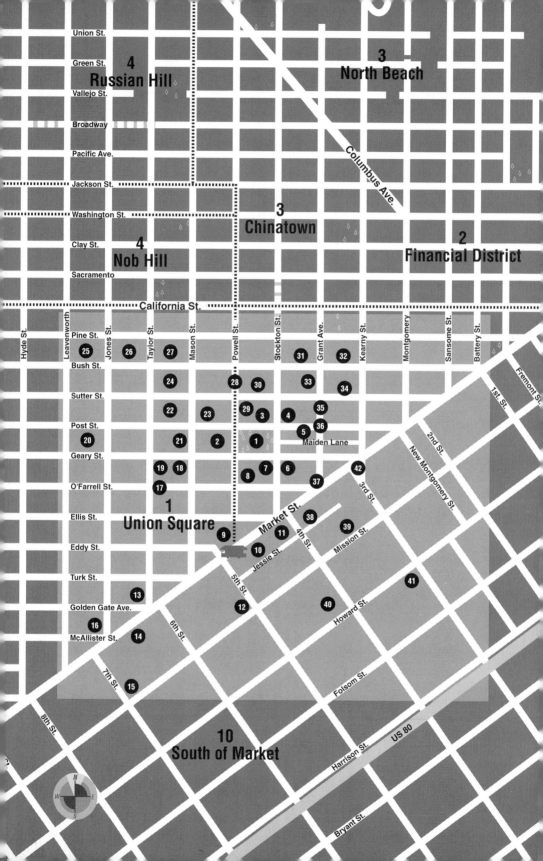

1. Union Square
2. St. Francis Hotel
3. E. side Union Square
   Qantas Building
   Bullock & Jones Store
   Hyatt on Union Square
4. Commercial building 278-
   99 Post St.
   Gump's
5. Circle Gallery
6. Neiman-Marcus
7. I. Magnin & Co.
   Macy's
8. Commercial building
   200-16 Powell St.
9. Market Street
   Hallidie Plaza
   Powell St. BART Station
   Bank of America
   James Flood Building
10. Hale Bros. Dept. Store
    Nordstrom/S.F.Shopping
    Center
    The Emporium
11. Commercial building 825-
    33 Market St.
    Pacific Building
    Apparel Mart
12. Old U.S. Mint
13. Fox Warfield Theatre
    Golden Gate Theatre
    Apts. 50 Golden Gate Ave.
14. Eastern Outfitting Co.
15. U.S. Post Office & District
    Court of Appeals Building
16. Old Hibernia Bank Building
17. San Francisco Hilton
    Nikko Hotel
    Downtown Center Garage
18. Geary Theatre
    Curran Theatre
19. Clift Hotel
    Bellevue Hotel
20. Alcazar Theatre
21. Native Sons Building
    S.F. Water Department
22. Bohemian Club
    Olympic Club
    Pan-Pacific Hotel

23. First Congregational
    Church
    Medico-Dental Building
    Elks Club
    Chamberlain Building
24. Metropolitan Club
    YWCA
25. Apts. 1086, 1060 Bush St.
26. Apts. 972-80 Bush St.
    Galleria
27. Dennis T. Sullivan
    Memorial Home
28. Family Club
    Town house 535 Powell
    Chesterfield Apartments
    Academy of Art College
29. Sir Francis Drake Hotel
30. Medical-Dental Office
    Building
31. Notre Dame des Victoires
    S.F. Environmental Center
32. S.F. Fire Station No. 2
33. Pacific Telephone &
    Telegraph
34. W. & J. Sloane Building
    Goldberg Bowen Bldg.
    Bemiss Building
35. White House
    Hammersmith Building
36. Shreve Building
    Hastings Building
    Phoenix Building
    Head Building
    Rochat Cordes Building
37. Wells Fargo Bank
    Cable Car Clothiers
    Phelan Building
    Humboldt Bank Building
38. Marriott Hotel
    Jessie St. Substation
    St. Patrick's Church
39. Aronson Building
    Yerba Buena Center/
    Gardens
    Moscone Center
40. Yerba Buena West Bldg.
    Woolf House
41. Mendelsohn House
    Museum Parc Condos
    St. Francis Square
42. First Nationwide Bank
    Lotta's Fountain
    Hearst Building
    Central Tower

Union Square (**1**) has been the heart of San Francisco's shopping and hotel district since well before the 1906 earthquake leveled its first commercial buildings. Laid out in 1850 during the mayoralty of John W. Geary, the informal grassy plot, then the heart of a residential district, acquired its name in the 1860s when pro-Union rallies were held there. Its civic status was further assured by the erection of the monument to Admiral Dewey's 1898 victory over the Spanish at Manila Bay. The 95-foot high column was designed in 1901 by Robert Aitken, sculptor, and Newton Tharp, architect. The monument survived both the 1906 disaster and the 1942 transformation of the square into the first-ever, under-a-park garage, designed by Timothy Pflueger in cooperation with the city park department. Built in wartime, the concrete structure was meant to double as a bomb shelter. Its covering has minimal but effective landscaping and room for people and for seasonal floral displays that contribute to the square's festiveness.

Around the square and on the adjacent blocks is one of the most compact and varied retail cores in the country, remarkably unaffected by the post-World War II flight of shopping to the suburbs. The buildings on the square are a generally undistinguished but agreeable hodgepodge covering the period from 1906 to the 1980s. What unity the square's buildings once had in terms of height and scale has not survived recent development.

The St. Francis Hotel, the square's oldest building, claims its west side. Even though somewhat overshadowed by a tower addition, the hotel confronts the square with great dignity. The square's north side has changed the most. Until 1980, a fitting mate for the St. Francis, the Fitzhugh Building, stood at the northwest corner. The planning policy of the times viewed its 140-foot height as a reasonable one for future buildings on the square.

The 1972 building for Qantas next door to the Fitzhugh adhered to the limit, but the same architects were unable to persuade the Hyatt Hotel to build a 140-foot pavilion on the square in front of their tower. Instead, they settled for a triangle of commercial space on Post Street that matched the lower height of Bullock and Jones. Just short of a decade later a long battle to save the Fitzhugh Building was lost; the Saks Building that replaced it did not match either height. All of this suggests that the framing of an urban square in the manner of Paris' Place Vendome is still best done the way it was done there: by building all the facades first.

Bisecting the east side of the square is a narrow pedestrian street that was once a notorius alley lined with prostitutes' cribs, but is now a decorous shopping mall euphemistically called Maiden Lane.

The heavily remodeled south side retains a relatively uniform height. I. Magnin and Company, the most architecturally distinguished building, anchors the southwest corner along with Johnson/Burgee's Neiman-Marcus store on the site of the old City of Paris. Powell Street, where the cable car reigns, is introduced by two worthy buildings, if you disregard the ground floors. The more commanding one is G.A. Lansburgh's 1908 Elkan Gunst Building at 301 Geary.

This brief review of Union Square's development suggests that commercial vitality, not architecture, is its most significant aspect. Indeed, the economic advantage of being "on the Square" has furnished the impetus to change its character over the years, even in the face of considerable opposition.

1. Union Square
1850
Geary to Post, Powell to Stockton Sts.

2. St. Francis Hotel
1904-07, 1913, Bliss & Faville
Hotel Tower, 1972, William Pereira
301-45 Powell St.
Gutted in the 1906 fire, the hotel was restored and en-larged by the first architects. In 1913 an addition on the Post Street end altered its symmetrical E shape. Typical of the Renaissance Revival style then in vogue, the building is treated like a stretched Italian palazzo with an ornate cornice and a ground floor arcade. Wide, rusticated bands running up the mid-section tie the top and bottom togeth-er. The ground floor arcade extends its influence across the sidewalk to include the light standards, presumably designed by Bliss & Faville, and the boxed trees.

2. St. Francis Hotel

3. Saks Fifth Avenue
1981, Hellmuth, Obata & Kassabaum
364-85 Post St.
Qantas Building
1972, Skidmore Owings & Merrill
350 Post St.
Designed to be a background building between two ornate Classical neighbors, Qantas now looms blandly over the stripped palazzo that is Saks.
Bullock & Jones Store
1923, Reid Bros.
370 Post St.
Hyatt on Union Square
1972, Skidmore Owings & Merrill
345 Stockton St.
A well-mannered design with commercial space on the square and a mostly unshaded plaza. A special delight is the drought restricted fountain set into the plaza steps. Designed by Ruth Asawa, the bronze reliefs on the drum were cast from "bakers' clay," a flour, salt, and water dough modeled by family members, neighbors, and scores of school children into scenes of San Francisco.

3. E. side of Union Square

4. Commercial building
1910, D. H. Burnham & Co., Willis Polk, designer
278-99 Post St.
A good example of a Neoclassical commercial building in which the "architecture" was designed to ride above the changing shop fronts.

Gump's
1861; rem. 1908, Clinton Day
246-68 Post St.
Originally built in 1861 but remodeled extensively after the fire, Gump's Gallery is the oldest continuously operating gallery in northern California. The department store actually evolved from the family's gallery and has continued to present the region's major trends in art and home furnishings.

5. Circle Gallery (former V. C. Morris Store)
1949, Frank Lloyd Wright; rest., 1983, Michele Marx
140 Maiden Lane
Although this design anticipated the Guggenheim Museum's celebrated spiral, it was actually a remodeling of an old building into a retail space for the Morrises, purveyors of fine crystal and other interior appointments. Greatly to their credit the gallery owners restored the neglected interior and reinstated Wright's furnishings.

5. Circle Gallery

6. Neiman-Marcus
1982, Johnson/Burgee
S.E. corner Stockton and Geary Sts.
Replacing a revered landmark, the 1896-1908 City of Paris store by Clinton Day and Bakewell & Brown, this design preserves the latter's great stained glass rotunda but not in its original central location.

7. I. Magnin & Co.
1946, Timothy Pflueger
233 Geary St.
This elegant skin, hung on a 1905 office building frame, was made flush to keep off the pigeons who, as Union Square's most numerous residents, should, after all, influence its architecture. The design was so successful with shoppers and so discouraging to pigeons that the same design was used in Seattle.

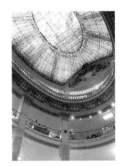
6. Neiman-Marcus

Macy's
1928, Lewis P. Hobart
101 Stockton St.
Rising above a marble-clad base, the conventionally composed pier-and-spandrel walls that retain their windows have the kind of eye appeal that is sadly lacking in the blank modern additions to the store on Union Square.

8. Commercial building
1933
200-16 Powell St.
A Moderne jewel box that awaits restoration.

7. I. Magnin & Co.

9. Market Street

Our first look at Market Street takes in the retail area, which, having risen with confidence after 1906, declined in the Depression and post-World War II suburbanization of living and shopping. Generous injections of cash have periodically raised the tone of the street, giving the blocks between 4th and 5th and Stockton and Powell streets the kind of authority a great street deserves.

Hallidie Plaza
Lawrence Halprin & Assoc.
Powell St. BART Station
1973, Skidmore Owings & Merrill

9. Powell St.BART Station

One of the city's oldest transportation modes, the cable car, meets the newest one, the Bay Area Rapid Transit, at this historic transportation node of Powell, 5th, and Market streets. From 1903-49 the San Francisco-San Mateo Interurban line ended near 5th and Market; the network of the Market Street Railway Company's lines served the area from all over, at one time requiring four tracks on the street. In the 1970s the city took advantage of the construction of BART to change the street pattern by extending 5th across Market to connect with the north grid and by closing the end of Eddy to vehicles. A sunken plaza, named for cable car inventor Andrew S. Hallidie, was created to give access to the station. The idea was to woo a sophisticated public to Market Street by creating two pleasant, protected outdoor rooms clad in costly and durable materials, where civic entertainment would take place. For the most part fine and civil buildings strengthen the space; however, its social use does not yet conform to the visions of planners, architects, and merchants.

9. Bank of America

Tourists wait in line for the cable cars, evangelists harangue the bystanders, and street musicians play while people sleep on the benches. Distressing as this situation is to those who had hoped to gain a safe precinct for people of means, this is a place where center-city public life is revealed in all its complexity.

Bank of America
1920, Bliss & Faville
1 Powell St. at Hallidie Plaza

9. James Flood Building

A handsome Renaissance Revival palace designed fittingly for the Bank of Italy, now the Bank of America. Bliss & Faville's competition-winning design reveals their admiration for McKim, Mead & White's University Club in New York. The architects economized by cladding the building's base in granite and the rest in less expensive terra cotta. The sculpture above the entrance is by John Portonavo; the interior is worth seeing.

James Flood Building
1904, Albert Pissis
870-98 Market St.
Virtually complete in 1906, the Flood building was mostly rebuilt after the earthquake and fire. The rounded corner element is boldly articulated; the engaged colonnade is a *leitmotif* echoed in the Emporium and the former Hale Bros. store across the street. The dull ground floor mask will be removed in the projected restoration, which will also reduce the size of what is now the largest Woolworth's in the country. The architect intended to "give a touch of grandeur to Market Street." In front of 856 Market Street is the Albert S. Samuels Clock that Samuels and Joseph Mayer created in 1910 to stand across the street in front of the Samuels Jewelry shop.

10. The Emporium

10. Former Hale Bros. Department Store
1912, Reid Bros.; rem. 1989, Whisler-Patri
901-19 Market St.
A commercial palace in the Renaissance-Baroque tradition, this building has a new version of the glass and metal canopy that was removed in a previous modernization.

Nordstrom/San Francisco Shopping Center
1989, Whisler-Patri
5th and Market Sts.
A successful contextual design that has raised the tone of this important intersection. The rotunda with its double escalators makes the movement of shoppers appear almost choreographic.

10. Hale Bros. Department Store

The Emporium
1896, Joseph Moore; 1908, Albert Pissis
835-65 Market St.
Only the facade survives from Moore's original pre-fire building, which housed stores, offices, and the California Supreme Court. Using a strategy we now associate with historic preservation, Pissis kept the existing facade and designed the department store behind it with a skylit rotunda that was a standard component of late 19th-century department stores. The sandstone facade may always have been painted.

10. Nordstrom / San Francisco Shopping Center

11. Commercial building
1908, Lewis Hobart
825-33 Market St.
A respectable companion to its neighbors, Hobart's design observes their cornice line with a row of projecting balconies. As usual, ground floor remodelings have left the older architecture above with nothing to stand on.

The Pacific Building
1907, C. F. Whittlesey; 1981, Whisler-Patri
801-23 Market St.

In form and decorative detail the building recalls Louis Sullivan's Carson Pirie Scott Store in Chicago. Restoration efforts improved the ground floor, but the cornice is sadly missing. Worth noticing is the color scheme of green tile and cream terra cotta over a red tile base. Whittlesey, who worked for Sullivan before coming west, said that he chose the colors "because the climate of our city is decidedly gray."

The Apparel Mart
1981, Whisler-Patri
22 4th St.

A good example of a large building discreetly inserted into a mid-block site with minimal impact on the old Pacific Building next door on Market, to which it connects.

12. The Old U.S. Mint
1869-74, Alfred B. Mullet; 1976, Walter Sondheimer
5th and Mission Sts.

Compared to the architect's Second Empire style buildings in Washington and St. Louis, this Tuscan-Doric temple was unfashionable when it was built. Still, it was considered to be one of the best appointed mints in the country. Following a lengthy restoration, the mint opened as a museum in 1976 and is well worth a visit.

13. Fox Warfield Theatre
1921, G. A. Lansburgh
982-98 Market St.

Golden Gate Theatre
1922, G. A. Lansburgh
42 Golden Gate Ave.

Apartments
50 Golden Gate Ave.

Two combination theater-office buildings designed by the prominent local theater architect, who also designed the hall of the Opera House. The Market Street theater district, formerly in these blocks from 5th to 8th streets, started a comeback with the restoration of the Golden Gate Theatre in 1980. At No. 50 Golden Gate Ave., next to the theater, is an apartment house with grotesque heads on its facade.

14. Eastern Outfitting Co. Building
1909, George A. Applegarth
1019 Market St.

A remarkable bay window wall set in one section of a monumental Classical colonnade–too bad it's not a series.

13. Golden Gate Theatre

13. Apts. 50 Golden Gate Ave.

14. Eastern Outfitting Co.

15. U.S. Post Office & District Court of Appeals Building
1902-05, John Knox Taylor; 1931, George Kelham
7th and Mission Sts.
A powerful expression of the Federal authority in Neo-Baroque. Grand interiors, too.

16. Former Hibernia Bank Building
1892, 1905, 1907, Albert Pissis
1 Jones St.
The city's oldest Classic Revival style bank had a colonnade splayed to fit the triangular site and articulated like a folded-out Roman temple. The domed rotunda recalls parts of the Paris Opera House, which Pissis surely saw during his student days at the Ecole des Beaux Arts in Paris. The interior is also notable.

15. U.S. Post Office

17. San Francisco Hilton Hotel
1964, William Tabler; 1971, 1989, John Carl Warnecke
201 Mason St.
A succession of modish designs, the latest decidedly Postmodern. The 1971 aluminum-clad tower still holds its own, dominating the skyline in this part of town.

Nikko Hotel
1988, Whisler-Patri/Takenaka Komuten
222 Mason St.

Downtown Center Garage
1954, George A. Applegarth
325 Mason St.
A straightforward, uncluttered structure with a double spiral ramp at the corner, one of the last works of a well known Beaux-Artsian architect.

16. Former Hibernia Bank

18. Geary Theatre
1909, Bliss & Faville
415 Geary St.

Curran Theatre
1922, Alfred H. Jacobs
445 Geary St.
The facades of the city's two major theaters reveal the versatility of the academic Classical style. The facades have the same format, but the proportions and ornamental detail are sufficiently different to make each one a very distinctive composition.

17. Downtown Center Garage

18. Geary Theatre & Curran Theatre

20. Alcazar Theatre

21. Native Sons Building

22. Bohemian Club

19. Clift Hotel
1913, MacDonald & Applegarth;
1926, Schultze & Weaver
491-99 Geary St.
One of the most lavish of the area's many hotels, the Clift Hotel was built in anticipation of the incoming crowds for the 1915 Panama Pacific International Exposition. The client was a lawyer, Frederick Clift, for whom a "stone bungalow" suite was designed on an upper floor. (Photographs of the original interiors are in a case on the mezzanine.) In 1926 Schultze & Weaver, architects of the Waldorf Astoria and Sherry Netherlands hotels in New York, and the Biltmore in Los Angeles, designed a 240-room addition using the same exterior design--the heavy cornice is now gone. G. A. Lansburgh designed the Parisian Room and the Redwood Room. Anthony Heinsbergen, another eminent theater designer, was his collaborator for the Redwood Room, one of downtown's most elegant public rooms in the Moderne style.

Bellevue Hotel
1908, S.H. Woodruff; 1992, Roma Design Group
Geary and Taylor Sts.
A richly decorated Neo-Baroque essay now in restoration.

20. Alcazar Theatre
1917, T. Patterson Ross
650 Geary St.
Convincingly Islamic, and a great surprise on the street.

21. Native Sons Building
1911, Righetti & Headman/E.H. Hildebrand
414-30 Mason St.
Yet another Renaissance-Baroque commercial palace, this one is worth scrutinizing for its finely textured brick walls, graceful top floor loggia, and decorative detail, including panels by artist Jo Moro on the mezzanine.

San Francisco Water Department
1922, Willis Polk & Co.
425 Mason St.
A similar composition to the Native Sons Building, but with a more restrained use of materials and decorative detail. But observe that the ground floor drips with stony water which even runs over the keystone above the entrance arch. Inside on the north wall over the elevator is a mural by Maynard Dixon of the Sunol Water Temple built by the Spring Valley Water Company, the original clients for this building. The owner, William Bourn, was Willis Polk's patron. Polk designed his house at 2550 Webster Street and Filoli, his estate in Woodside.

22. Bohemian Club
1934, Lewis P. Hobart
625 Taylor St.
Olympic Club
1912, Paff & Baur
524 Post St.
Two distinguished club buildings. Although the latter is
firmly in the Ecole des Beaux Arts academic Classical
tradition, the former conveys the same exclusiveness with
a touch of the Moderne. The bronze and terra-cotta
plaques are by Carlo Taliabua, Haig Patigian, and Jo Moro,
prominent local artist-members of this colorful institution.
Pan-Pacific Hotel
1990, Portman Assocs.
Post and Mason Sts.

22. Olympic Club

23. First Congregational Church
1913, Reid Bros.
491 Post St.
Medico-Dental Building
1925, George Kelham/William G. Merchant
490 Post St.
Elks Club
1924, Meyer & Johnson
450-60 Post St.
Chamberlain Building
1925, Arthur Brown, Jr.
442-44 Post St.
This group of four buildings was designed by some of San
Francisco's best known practitioners of the first quarter of
the 20th century. Their range of size and type makes them
interesting to compare with each other and with other
examples of these architects' work.

22. Pan-Pacific Hotel

24. Metropolitan Club
1916, 1922, Bliss & Faville
640 Sutter St.
Originally the Women's Athletic Club, the design invites
comparison with Hobart's later Bohemian Club.
YWCA
1918, Lewis Hobart
620 Sutter St.

23. 1st Congregational Church

25. Apartments
1914, 1912
1086, 1060 Bush St.
Two that stand out from the rest in the block, but form
part of the great collection of post-fire apartment buildings
that were built in a hurry on the south slopes of Nob Hill
after the 1906 earthquake and fire.

26. 972-980 Bush St. Apts.

27. Dennis T. Sullivan Memorial Home

26. Apartments
1909, Frederick H. Meyer
980 Bush St.
Apartments
1914, Grace Jewett
972 Bush St.
Two substantial Renaissance Revival apartment buildings, the latter by Jewett, one of the few women architects in practice during this time.

The Galleria
1981, Kaplan, McLaughlin, Diaz
N.W. corner Taylor and Bush Sts.
A contemporary building that does not overwhelm its neighbors; beside the building at 828 Taylor you can glimpse a garden retreat tucked away inside the block.

27. Dennis T. Sullivan Memorial Home
1922
870 Bush St.
This building commemorates a tragedy of the 1906 earthquake that took the life of Fire Chief Dennis T. Sullivan, who was killed when the firehouse in which he lived shook apart. The memorial fund was used to build a new Fire Chief's home designed to resemble a firehouse.

28. The Family Club
1909, C.A. Meussdorffer
545 Powell St.
Town house
1911, C.A. Meussdorffer
535 Powell St.
Chesterfield Apartments
1911
560 Powell St.
Academy of Art College (Former Elks Building)
1909, A.A. Cantin
540 Powell St.
Built within two years of each other, these four buildings exhibit a wild variety of styles. The two by Meussdorffer illustrate his skill and confidence in rendering two period styles; the town house is a rare survivor in downtown. Both buildings have outstanding ornamental detail. Cantin's Elks Building improbably combines Classic and Mission Revival styles.

29. Sir Francis Drake Hotel
1928, Weeks & Day
432-62 Powell St.
Gothic motifs are freely used here to accentuate the hotel's stepped form, made fashionable by New York's 1918 zoning law for skyscrapers. The glazed void below the crown marks the Starlight Roof bar with a great city view.

30. Medical-Dental Office Building
1929, Miller & Pflueger
450 Sutter St.
One of the city's most admired office towers; its undulating wall inspired that of the former Bank of America Building at 555 California St. The skyscraper's low budget dictated the use of terra cotta instead of stone, and the minimal lobby. Although the smooth, continuous piers give the structure a vertical emphasis, the woven bevelled spandrels and corners create the appearance of a skin or wrapper that was prophetic of today's approach to cladding tall buildings.

30. Medical-Dental Office Bldg.

31. Notre Dame des Victoires
1913, Louis Brouchoud
564 Bush St.
This church occupies the site of the city's first French church; it is more significant as an historic center of San Francisco's influential French colony than as architecture.

San Francisco Environmental Center
1916, W. Garden Mitchell; 1982, Storek & Storek
530 Bush St.
A project that involved both historic preservation, in the conversion of a 1916 steam generating plant into office and retail space, and energy-conscious design in a ten-story office building that was the first to use both active and passive solar energy systems. Solar collectors are integrated with the building envelope on the upper floors.

31. Notre Dame des Victoires

32. S. F. Fire Station No. 2
1909, Newton J. Tharp
466 Bush St.
Appropriately, the city's first fireproof structure erected after the 1906 disaster, this work of civic monumentality expresses its dual function to house motorized equipment downstairs and people upstairs. A formal gateway to Chinatown was created here at Grant Avenue in 1976.

33. Pacific Telephone & Telegraph
1908, Ernest Coxhead
333 Grant Ave.
A facade composed of boldly scaled Classical elements in projected and recessed forms. Coxhead's skill at manipulating the Classical vocabulary is nowhere better shown than in the entrance composition, where an elegant portal with a swan-necked pediment is fused with an arch tied at the top by an outsized keystone to the belt cornice above. Don't miss the giant columns' capitals.

33. Pacific Telephone & Telegraph

34. Goldberg Bowen Bldg.

35. White House

35. Hammersmith Building

34. W. & J. Sloane Building
1908, Reid Bros.
220 Sutter St.

Goldberg Bowen Building
1909, Meyers & Ward
250-54 Sutter St.

Bemiss Building
1908
266-70 Sutter St.

Three handsome commercial buildings worthy of notice in an area that retains its post-1906 appearance. The W. & J. Sloane Building is the most conventional of the three, housing several art galleries. Bemiss's elegant, almost Miesian steel frame capped by a fringed metal valance accommodates what may have been the largest sheets of glass then available. The Goldberg Bowen Building's architects chose to decorate the frame with piers that erupt in floral bouquets at the cornice.

35. The White House
1908, Albert Pissis
255 Sutter St.

In 1968 an unusual preservation strategy converted what was once one of the city's two major French department stores, the Raphael Weill Company, into a parking garage with shops on the ground floor.

Hammersmith Building
1907, G. A. Lansburgh
301-03 Sutter St.

An improbable relic from the post-1906 earthquake downtown that makes much of its small scale, like a music box with a fancy lid.

36. Shreve Building
1905, William Curlett
201 Grant Ave.

Hastings Building
1908, Meyer & O'Brien
180 Post St.

Phoenix Building
1908, George A. Applegarth
220-28 Grant Ave.

Head Building
1909, William Curlett & Sons
201-09 Post St.

Rochat Cordes Building
1909, Albert Pissis
126-30 Post St.
Five solidly respectable buildings, the first four of which
compose a gateway to the heart of the shopping district to
the west. The Shreve Building is both the most intact and
the most luxurious in terms of materials.

37. Wells Fargo Bank
1910, Clinton Day
744 Market St.
Cable Car Clothiers
1919, Bliss & Faville
1 Grant Ave.

*37. Wells Fargo Bank &
Cable Car Clothiers*

Phelan Building
1908, William Curlett
760-84 Market St.
Humboldt Bank Building
1906, Meyer & O'Brien
783-85 Market St.
A vintage Market Street intersection framed by buildings
erected within four years of each other. The two smaller
buildings illustrate the versatility of Beaux-Arts Classicism
as well as the enduring power of the Pantheon as a
prototype for religious and financial temples. Across the
street the Phelan Building, built by a famous mayor and
U.S. senator, is a fine traditional rendering of a steel-
framed flatiron structure sheathed in terra cotta.

38. Marriott Hotel
1989, Anthony Lumsden (DMJM)
777 Market St. at 4th St.

37. Phelan Building

This building rivals the Transamerica pyramid as a city
emblem and has succeeded it as the building people most
love to hate. The tower's form was shaped by the codes;
the mirror glass looks suspiciously like contact paper but
glows dramatically at sunset. Across the street at 54 4th
St., the Victorian Hotel, c.1915 by William Curlett, recalls
an earlier era of hotel building for the 1915 PPI Exposition,
now the Marina district. Conveniently located near major
interurban and city transportation lines, the hotel plan
featured suites on the front for families and rooms on the
back for servants. Many hotels like this one once occupied
the south-of-Market blocks and served those who arrived
at the now demolished Southern Pacific Railroad station,
which stood at 3rd and Townsend streets.

38. Marriott Hotel

Jessie Street Substation
1905, 1907, 1909, Willis Polk
222-26 Jessie St.
St. Patrick's Church
1872; int. rem., 1907, Shea & Lofquist
756 Mission St.

39. Aronson Building
1903, Hemenway & Miller
700 Mission St.
Yerba Buena Center/Gardens
George R. Moscone Convention Center
1981, Add. 1991, Hellmuth, Obata & Kassabaum;
T.Y. Lin, structural engineer
Howard St. to Folsom St., 3rd St. to 4th St.

The first of three blocks that comprise the last of the major redevelopment areas cleared in the 1960s and left vacant until the building of Moscone Center in 1981 in spite of several attempts to put together a workable development plan for them. The middle block promises to be the most architecturally rewarding. An extension of the Moscone Center lies underground; above ground the Center for the Arts by Fumihiko Maki/Robinson Mills & Williams; the Center for the Arts Theater by James Polshek; and the Esplanade Gardens by Mitchell/Giurgola will be constructed in the next three years. The new S.F. Museum of Modern Art, designed by Mario Botta, is scheduled to be built on a mid-block site on 3rd St. between Mission and Howard sts. When finished, the city will have its long-promised new downtown cultural center.

40. Yerba Buena West Building
1982, Herztka & Knowles
4th St. bet. Mission and Howard Sts.
Woolf House
1979, Robert Herman & Assoc.
S.W. corner Howard and 4th Sts.

41. Mendelsohn House
1990, Robert Herman & Assoc./ Tito Patri, land. arch.
Museum Parc Condominiums
1989, J. Stavi Architects
300 Folsom St.

38. St. Patrick's Church

39. Moscone Center Addition

39. Downtown from Moscone Center

St. Francis Square
1983, Kaplan, McLaughlin, Diaz
3rd and Folsom Sts.
While the center blocks lay fallow, development proceeded around the edges, as these buildings attest. Of particular interest are the two subsidized housing projects by Robert Herman built by the Tenants and Owners Development Corporation. These are the fruits of the battle with the Redevelopment Agency over the lack of replacement housing for the occupants of the hotels that were demolished for the cultural center. The two buildings are named for heroes of this historic battle. Mendelsohn House, in particular, belies the belief that low-cost housing has to look it; behind it in the center of the block are wonderful allotment gardens for the residents of the neighboring buildings, who also have roof gardens.

41. St. Francis Square

42. First Nationwide Bank
1902, 1906, William Curlett; Add. 1964, Clark & Beuttler
700 Market St.
Charles W. Moore was a principal designer of the corner addition, which echoes the form of the older building in a way that is clearly contemporary. The structure turns the corner by making a major element of the stair tower.

Lotta's Fountain
1875, Wyneken & Townsend
Kearny and Geary Sts. at Market St.
Lotta Crabtree, the most highly paid American actress of her day, retired from touring in 1891 to San Francisco. Her $4 million fortune went to charity; the best known gift is this fountain. The shaft was lengthened in 1915 by eight feet to better match the Market Street light standards. In 1916 the merchants paid for their bas-reliefs, created by noted sculptor Arthur Putnam.

42. 1st Nationwide Bank

Hearst Building
1909, Kirby, Petit & Green
691-99 Market St.
Of the three newspaper buildings that once stood on this intersection, this is the only one that still is identifiable. The entrance is a showpiece of terra-cotta ornament.

Central Tower (former S.F. Call Building)
1938, Albert Roller; rem. 1989, Kotas/Pantaleoni
703 Market St.

42. Hearst Building

A remodeling in so-so Moderne of a fine Neo-Baroque design by the Reid Bros. The recent ground-floor remodeling has restored some of its elegance.

3
Telegraph Hill

Union St.

Green St.

3
North Beach

Vallejo St.

Broadway

Pacific Ave.

Jackson St.

San Francisco Bay

Washington St.

Clay St.

Sacramento

2
Financial District

California St.

Pine St.

Bush St.

Sutter St.

Post St.

Market St.

10
South of Market

Columbus Ave.

Stockton St.

Grant Ave.

Kearny St.

Montgomery

Sansome St.

Battery St.

Front St.

Davis St.

Drumm St.

Embarcadero

Steuart St.

Spear St.

Mission St.

Main St.

Beale St.

Fremont St.

1st St.

Ecker

Jessie

New Montgomery St.

2nd St.

3rd St.

4th St.

Howard St.

Folsom St.

Harrison St.

Bryant St.

Brannan St.

US 80

1. Monadnock Building
   Sheraton Palace Hotel
2. New Montgomery St.
   Buildings
   Sharon Building
   Call Building
   Rialto Building
3. Pacific Telephone &
   Telegraph Co.
4. Crocker Bank Hdq.
   Mechanics' Institute
5. Hobart Building
6. Hunter-Dulin Building
   French Bank Building
   Hallidie Building
7. Russ Building
   Mills Building
   Mills Tower
8. California Commercial
   Union
9. Bank of America World
   Headquarters
   588 California St. Bldg.
10. Security Pacific Bank
    Merchants Exchange
    Building
    Insurance Exchange
    Building
11. Kohl Building
    456 Montgomery Building
12. Bank of Italy/Bank of
    America
13. Transamerica Building
    Washington Montgomery
    Tower
14. 343 Sansome St.
15. Embarcadero W./Former
    Federal Reserve Bank
16. Bank of California
    Bank of California Tower
17. Bank building

18. J. Harold Dollar Building
    California Center
    Robert Dollar Building
19. Royal Globe Insurance Co.
20. Pacific Coast Stock
    Exchange
    Trading room
    Office tower
21. Adam Grant Building
    Standard Oil Buildings
22. Crown Zellerbach Building
23. Citicorp Center
24. Standard Oil of California
25. Shell Building
    Flatiron Building
    Heineman Building
    Mechanic's Monument
26. 100 First St. Building
27. Transbay Transit Terminal
28. Shaklee Terraces
29. Industrial Indemnity
    Building
30. Tadich Grill
31. Embarcadero Center
    Hyatt Regency Hotel
32. Alcoa Building
33. Home Savings of America
    Building
34. 100 California St.
    Security Pacific Bank
    Building
35. 101 California St. Building
36. 388 Market St. Building
37. Pacific Gas & Electric Co.
    Matson Building
38. S.F. Federal Reserve Bank
39. 135 Main St. Building
40. Rincon Center
    Rincon Towers
41. YMCA
    Bayside Plaza
42. Jewish Community Centers
43. Audiffred Building
44. Southern Pacific Building
45. M. Justin Herman Plaza
46. Ferry Building
    Embarcadero Promenade

2

Financial District

Most of what is now the densest part of the city was once water. The shoreline was roughly at Montgomery Street; the east-west streets ended in wharves. To the south the great diagonal of Market Street was laid out parallel to the road from the bay to Mission Dolores, and to the north was the original settlement of Yerba Buena around Portsmouth Square, a collection of humble buildings that achieved city status overnight with the discovery of gold in the Sierra foothills. By 1850 a financial district fed by the Gold Rush had grown up around Montgomery and Washington streets. The location was convenient both to the Customs House and the gambling houses around Portsmouth Square and to the commercial wharves that extended out into the bay. These became streets lined with buildings set on the hulks of abandoned ships. During 1850 two devasting fires drove the bankers to remove themselves from crime-infested Sidneytown at the base of Telegraph Hill, whose denizens had set the fires, and to shift from wooden to more fireproof brick buildings. The more permanent structures were built on choice sites to the south that the fire had cleared. The Customs House also moved to a brick building at Montgomery and California streets. Other factors contributing to the move south were the improvement of the central wharves of Clay and Sacramento and the cutting through of Commercial Street from the Long Wharf to Kearny Street. When income from the city's booming service industries surpassed that from gold in 1850, the ties to Portsmouth Square were loosened.

From 1850 to 1875 banks set the trend for the southward shift along Montgomery toward Market, influencing the relocation of legal services, real estate interests, and stock and insurance brokers. After 1888 the district began to expand vertically, encouraged by the advent of the earthquake-resistant steel frame. Buildings over ten stories rose on the fringes of the district and on California Street. Even the 1906 disaster did not dislodge the banks from Montgomery and California streets; the intersection is still the district's heart.

Until recently the triangle these two streets make with Market Street defined one of the country's most compact clusters of skyscrapers. The forest of towers was dense but not overwhelming. A boom in office building that began in the late 1970s brought "Manhattanization" and public reaction in the form of anti-highrise initiatives of inspired futility. In 1985 the Downtown Plan revised height and bulk limits, created more restricted height zones, and instigated a yearly cap on development and a stringent project-by-project review. But by then the old scale was gone and the district's boundaries had pushed out, jostling Chinatown and Jackson Square and creating a larger and duller forest of towers on the much larger blocks south of Market. Still, the district is more dramatic than most of its kind, thanks mostly to the surrounding water which, since the removal in 1991 of the Embarcadero Freeway, damaged in the 1989 earthquake, is once more visually accessible. Unforgettable contrasts still exist at the district's edges, as when Montgomery Street bursts through its canyon into pre-fire Jackson Square and up Telegraph Hill, or when the cable cars climb California Street to Nob Hill.

1. Monadnock Building
685 Market St.
1906-07, Meyer & O'Brien

Interrupted by the earthquake and rebuilt afterward, the building was renovated in 1986-88. The entrance lobby has outstanding *trompe l'oeil* murals by the Evans & Brown Co. featuring famous people from the city's past who are identified on a handout available at the security desk. Do visit the sculpture garden in the interior court.

Sheraton Palace Hotel
1909, Trowbridge & Livingston; rem., 1991, Skidmore Owings & Merrill/Page & Turnbull
633-65 Market St.

The airy opulence of the newly restored Garden Court in this block-size hotel captures the spirit of William Ralston's first Palace Hotel of 1873, long the west coast's finest. The warm brick exterior, stitched like a tapestry with terra-cotta ornament and crowned with a fancy cornice, dignifies the whole block. The recent remodeling added a new section to the hotel and, best of all, restored the original ceiling heights and the grand public rooms.

1. Monadnock Building and Sheraton Palace Hotel

1. Sheraton Palace Hotel

2. New Montgomery Street buildings

Now that the South of Market is being developed with the office and mixed-use buildings that the north-of-Market area can no longer accommodate, the story of this short street is worth recalling. In the late 19th century a similar condition inspired capitalists William Ralston and Ashbury Harpending to set up the New Montgomery Real Estate Company to launch a drive to the profitable south waterfront area. Rincon Hill, where the city's first millionaires had lived, was in the way; two stubborn residents, John Parrott and Milton Catham, stopped the street's progress at Howard by refusing to sell their property. Attempts to make the spur street the equal of its namesake faltered in bad times. The expensively improved lots did not sell when offered in 1869. Ralston then upped the ante by announcing the construction of the world's finest hotel, the Palace, at the head of the street—to no avail. Ralston's empire collapsed with the closing of the Bank of California on August 26, 1875; Ralston drowned mysteriously that afternoon while taking his usual bay swim. The street lived on, never attaining the status its founders wanted, but boasting some substantial buildings long before the adjoining steets did. Some of these are:

Sharon Building
1912, George Kelham
39-63 New Montgomery St.
A right-angle building that is not much more than a facade
on the main street; the ground floor has a colorful old
restaurant, the House of Shields.

Call Building
1914, Reid Bros.
74 New Montgomery St.
Originally built for the newspaper industry, the building is
anchored at each end by a well-composed and richly
detailed Classical pavilion.

Rialto Building
1902, Meyer & O'Brien; 1910, Bliss & Faville
116 New Montgomery St.

3. Pacific Telephone & Telegraph Co.
1925, Miller & Pflueger/A. A. Cantin; rest. 1990
134-40 New Montgomery St.
Eliel Saarinen's second-prize design for the Chicago
Tribune Tower competition was the main inspiration for
this influential skyscraper. Though the building appears as
a stepped block from New Montgomery Street, it is a
notched L from the southwest, contributing a welcome
variety to the skyline. The eclectic but original ornament is
well integrated into the building's form. The recent
restoration included the recreation by sculptor Manuel
Palos of the original 13-foot terra-cotta eagles that were
removed from the top parapet in the 1950s. The black
marble Moderne lobby is embellished with a stenciled
ceiling *a la Chinois* and elaborate elevator doors.

*3. Pacific Telephone &
Telegraph Co.*

4. Former Crocker Bank Headquarters
1983, Skidmore Owings & Merrill
1 Montgomery St.
A distinguished design, commendable for its sensitivity to
both urban planning and preservation issues.The subtle
play of light on the plaid pattern of polished and thermal-
finished granite and the reflective, colored-glass windows
change the tower's visual image during the course of the
day. Next to the tower the pedestrian corridor through the
barrel-vaulted Crocker Galleria is unfortunately interrupted
by unsightly escalators. The roof garden created on the
top of the old bank building's 1908 banking hall, designed
by Willis Polk, is accessible from the upper level of the
Galleria. It is a welcome, outdoor city room. Across the
street on the corner is sculptor Douglas Tilden's Admis-
sion Day monument of 1897.

*4. Former Crocker Bank
Headquarters*

Mechanics' Institute
1909, Albert Pissis
57-65 Post St.
One of the state's first educational institutions with a fine library on the arcaded floor. A mural by Arthur Mathews is in the marble elevator lobby.

5. Hobart Building
1914, Willis Polk
582-92 Market St.
An idiosyncratic design rumored to be a favorite of its designer. The Hobart's eccentricity has become increasingly apparent with age, particularly when compared with its immediate neightbors. Shaped to address its polygonal site, the building had its bare flank exposed when a neighboring structure was torn down; the tower now seems to be peering over its shoulder in embarrassment. The ground floor remodeling is sad. Down the block at 562 and 567 Market are two more Willis Polk buildings.

5. Hobart Building

6. Hunter-Dulin Building
1926, Schultze & Weaver
111 Sutter St.
A combination of the Romanesque and Chateauesque Revival styles with the building's shaft a clear expression of the structural frame and the chateau on top more staid than picturesque. The array of decorative motifs ranges from medallions with wistful young women shouldering garlands, a belt cornice with squat eagles and ox heads, to the Neo-Norman arched entrance and the pseudo-Medieval lobby. This free-wheeling approach to historicism typified this New York firm's work.

French Bank Building
1902, Hemenway & Miller; rem. 1907-13, E. A. Bozio
108-10 Sutter St.
An exposed-frame, Chicago School building that was gussied up after the fire. The ground floor columns display a handsome scrolled shield with a caduceus, the symbol of Mercury, the god of commerce.

6. Hallidie Building

Hallidie Building
1917, Willis Polk
130-50 Sutter St.
Credited as the first use of the glass-curtain-wall, the facade of this building is more curtainlike than almost anything since. The elaborate cast-iron cornice, which resembles a Victorian window valance, contributes to the impression that the glass grid is a curtain. The fire escapes recall pull cords.

7. Russ Building
1927, George Kelham
235 Montgomery St.

For many years the city's largest and tallest office building, its Gothicized tower marked the center of the financial district until the 1970s, when it was dwarfed by a forest of new towers. The Gothic ornament is more perfunctory than inventive; the lobby is worth a visit.

Mills Building
1891, Burnham & Root; 1908, 1914, 1918,
D. H. Burnham & Co./Willis Polk
Mills Tower
1931, Lewis P. Hobart
220 Montgomery St.

7. Mills Building

The only surviving pre-fire skyscraper that clearly reflects the great Chicago School tradition from which it sprang; the wall composition recalls Adler & Sullivan's Auditorium Building of 1888. Damaged but structurally intact after the 1906 earthquake and fire, the building was restored and twice enlarged by Willis Polk, who headed the local D. H. Burnham & Co. office. Lewis Hobart's tower respects the original design. The arched entrance with its fine detail leads to a restrained lobby with a graceful branching stair and unusual foliated balusters.

8. California Commercial Union
1923, George Kelham/Kenneth MacDonald
315 Montgomery St.

A Renaissance Revival design with a touch of local color in the medallions on either side of the entrance; one shows a California bear shambling over the skyline.

9. Former Bank of America World Headquarters
1969, Wurster, Bernardi & Emmons/Skidmore Owings &
Merrill/Pietro Belluschi, consultant
555 California St.

9. Former Bank of America Headquarters

The city's most important office building but no longer owned by the world's largest bank. The tower's faceted form was partly inspired by Pflueger's 450 Sutter building. The height and dark red color insure its dominance of the skyline, but at sunset it becomes eerily transparent. The shaded, windswept north plaza has a polished black granite sculpture by Masayuki Nagare dubbed "the Banker's Heart" by an irate citizen. An opulent three-level banking hall fronts on Montgomery St.

7. Russ Building

9. 588 California St.

11. Kohl Building

11. 456 Montgomery Building

588 California St. Building
1987, Johnson/Burgee
The spooks on the roof are the talking points of this graceless try at reviving the 1920's skyscraper.

10. Security Pacific Bank
1922, George Kelham; rem. 1941, The Capitol Co.
300 Montgomery St.
A building remodeled to conform to the tasteful modern Classicism of the 1940s with great success. The ground floor remained intact, contributing an impressive colonnade to the street. The banking hall, refurbished by Baldwin-Clarke in 1978, is worth seeing as is the lobby inside the 300 Montgomery St. entrance with its fine marble walls and Moderne lighting fixtures.

Merchants Exchange Building
1903, D. H. Burnham & Co./Willis Polk
465 California St.

Insurance Exchange Building
1913, Willis Polk
433 California St.
Two buildings with similar wall compositions and surface treatment. The Merchants Exchange (rebuilt after the fire) served as a local model for later buildings in the financial district: the Matson and PG&E buildings on Market Street. An interior, skylit arcade leads to the old Merchants exchange hall, attributed to Julia Morgan. Mimicking a Roman basilica, the hall is lavishly detailed and bathed in a natural light. The seascape paintings are by William Coulter. In the old days, merchants assembled in this hall where news about the ships coming into the harbor was transmitted to them from the lookout tower on the roof.

11. Kohl Building
1904, Percy & Polk; 1907, Willis Polk
400 Montgomery St.
Restored by Polk after the fire, the ground floor has suffered the usual depredations. The entrance portico is still a fine composition; the marble lobby is mostly original. The best part of the building is its ornate top.

456 Montgomery Building
1983, Roger Owen Boyer Assoc./MLT Assoc.
A highrise tower set back from the street to incorporate the temple-form facades of Albert Pissis's 1908 Anton Borel & Co. bank and Howard & Galloway's 1908 Sutro & Co. The latter is the more carefully detailed and costly design. In 1841 when the Hudson's Bay Company was located near here, this was the waterfront. Commercial Street, from Montgomery down to the bay, was the Central or Long Wharf, begun in 1848 and extended in 1850 when it was the city's major pier. The first U.S. branch mint in

California was located at 608-10 Commercial; in 1875 the U.S. Subtreasury Building replaced it, was gutted by the 1906 fire and rebuilt as the one-story structure now tucked under the Bank of Canton, at 558 Montgomery, SOM, 1989. The old building now houses the Chinese National Historical Society.

12. Former Bank of Italy/Bank of America
1908, Shea & Lofquist
552 Montgomery St.
A rich facade that, like some other buildings in the district, economizes by using expensive granite cladding on the ground floor and inexpensive terra cotta that mimics granite on the upper floors. The white marble interior is a real jewel box. Historic views of the city are on display.

13. Transamerica Building
1971, William Pereira & Assoc.
600 Montgomery St.
The butt of many jokes when it first appeared, this pyramid tower has settled into the affections of many people; its pointed top is now a valuable anchor for the eye amidst all those unmemorable others. Still, the way the building rests spiderlike on the ground, ignoring its context, is hard for many to forgive. Next door is Redwood Park, completed in 1971 by Tom Galli.

13. Transamerica Building

Washington Montgomery Tower
1984, Kaplan, McLaughlin, Diaz
695 Montgomery St.
One of the first mixed office-and-residential-use buildings.

14. 343 Sansome St.
c.1930, Hyman & Appleton; 1990, Johnson/Burgee
A 1908 building restyled in Moderne recently joined by a restrained Postmodern design with Sullivanesque detail.

15. Embarcadero West/Former Federal Reserve Bank
1924, George Kelham; 1991, Studios Architecture/ Kaplan, McLaughlin, Diaz
400 Sansome St.
A design in transition from the academic Beaux-Arts tradition on the ground level to *Le Style Moderne* on the upper part, as you can see by comparing the Ionic capitals of the free-standing columns with those of the giant pilasters above. The lobby, with murals by Jules Guerin, and the former banking hall are worth a visit.

15. Embarcadero West/Former Federal Reserve Bank Building

16-17. Bank of California and Bank building

18. California Center

16. Bank of California
1907, Bliss & Faville
Bank of California Tower
1967, Anshen & Allen
400 California St.

The banking temple at its best, with a beautifully detailed Corinthian order for the colonnade. Inside, the banking hall is a great cage with a coffered ceiling. Next door, the 1967 tower's fretted floor spandrels pick up the rhythm of the fluted columns. The ground floor cornice of copper stamped with a curvilinear pattern holds its own against the Classical riches of its neighbor.

17. Bank building
1977, Skidmore Owings & Merrill
350 California St.

A sculptural, contemporary version of the Classical skyscraper with the corners visually strengthened by paired columns. Panels of precast bosses attempt to overcome the blankness of the typical office tower; expanses of glass permit a view into the banking hall. At the top of the wall at the back of the property walrus heads wreathed in rope peer over tiny icebergs. Forlorn relics, they solemnly represent the Alaska Commercial Building that once occupied the site.

18. J. Harold Dollar Building
1920, George Kelham
341 California St.
California Center
1986, Skidmore Owings & Merrill
345 California St.
Robert Dollar Building
1919, Charles McCall
301-33 California St.

In order to get the prestigious California Street address and preserve two landmark buildings that were headquarters for the Robert Dollar Steamship Lines, this office building/hotel was driven into the middle of the block and provided with shopping arcades that permit circulation through it. The top with its twin masts is a handsome addition to the skyline.

19. Royal Globe Insurance Company
1907, Howells & Stokes
201 Sansome St.

An exemplary Edwardian building. The entrance composition and ornamental detail of the base and attic sections provide a visual feast. The company had a similar building in the east with the same cladding.

20. Pacific Coast Stock Exchange
1915, J. Milton Dyer; 1930, Miller & Pflueger
Trading room
301 Pine St.
Office tower
155 Sansome St.

This mausoleum-like block is a 1930 remodeling of a temple-front structure that had housed the U.S. Treasury. The monumental pylons in front have cast-stone sculptures by Ralph Stackpole. The trading hall interior has a curvilinear grill made of thin metal strips laid endwise on a frame to form a lightweight ceiling beneath the air plenum, an ingenious way of creating an apparently changing depth of field that the same architects used in Oakland's famous Paramount Theater. The tower next door has a restrained Moderne entranceway and a notable lobby. The City Club now occupies the upper floors that originally housed the Stock Exchange Club. Tours of this exceptionally fine interior with a mural by Diego Rivera and numerous artworks by local artists can be arranged through the Mexican Museum at Fort Mason.

20. Pacific Coast Stock Exchange

21. Adam Grant Building
1908, c.1910, Howard & Galloway
114 Sansome St.
Former Standard Oil Building
1912, 1916, Benjamin C. McDougall
200 Bush St.
Former Standard Oil Building
1922, George Kelham
225 Bush St.

22. Crown Zellerbach Building

Three buildings with richly detailed exteriors. The last named has a Mediterranean crown—-a loggia capped with a red tile roof supported by a heavy, corbeled cornice.

22. Crown Zellerbach Building
1959, Hertzka & Knowles/Skidmore Owings & Merrill
1 Bush St.

The first of the city's glass-curtain-walled towers in the first and best of the tower-plaza settings. Expensive walls like those of the tower, where the air-conditioning console is set in to permit the glass to extend unbroken from the floor to above the ceiling, will never be done again. The same goes for the elegant but extravagant placement of the elevators and stairs in their own mosaic-clad tower outside the office block. The playful round building, originally a bank, is an integral part of the gently sinking plaza with a fountain by David Tolerton.

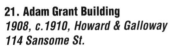

23. Citicorp Center
1910, Albert Pissis; 1921, George Kelham
1984, Pereira & Assoc.
1 Sansome St.

Originally the London Paris National Bank. The erection of the Citicorp tower turned it into the most atmospheric atrium in town.

24. Standard Oil of California
1964, 1975, Hertzka & Knowles
555-75 Market St.

The plaza with its lush garden by Osmundson & Staley steals the show here. The intersection offers a chance to compare changing fashions in corporate plazas. Ecker and Jessie are two mid-block streets that reveal the possibilities for creating lively pedestrian passageways in the large South of Market blocks.

25. Shell Building

25. Shell Building
1929, George Kelham
100 Bush St.

A slender, stepped tower clad in rusticated beige terra cotta. Shell forms are well integrated into the design even when nearly out of sight—the projecting shells near the top conceal lighting that occasionally turns the crown to gold. The entrance lobby carries out the general theme.

Flatiron Building
1913, Havens & Toepke
540-48 Market St.

Heineman Building
1910, MacDonald & Applegarth
130 Bush St.

Mechanic's Monument
1894-95, Douglas Tilden, sculpt.; Willis Polk, arch.
Mechanic's Plaza

Polk designed the base of this heroic sculpture by Tilden, a deaf mute who was an internationally known artist. James Donahue gave the monument in memory of his father, Peter, who in 1850 started the state's first iron-works and machine shop, established the first gas company for street lighting in the city in 1852, and later initiated the first streetcar line. Bronze sidewalk plaques note the original shoreline of Yerba Buena Cove.

26. 100 First Street Building

26. 100 First Street Building
1989, Skidmore Owings & Merrill/Heller & Leake

A schematic design with assorted elements of different scales that don't do much for this very prominent tower.

27. Transbay Transit Terminal
1939, Timothy Pflueger/Arthur Brown, Jr.,
and John J. Donovan, consulting arch.
425 Mission St.
Designed to handle the Key System trains that ran across the Bay Bridge from 1939 until 1958, this is now a bus terminal. The functionalist Moderne box encloses a well-designed circulation system. The construction of this terminal signaled the demise of the Ferry Building as the prime gateway to the city.

28. Shaklee Terraces
1982, Skidmore Owings & Merrill
444 Market St.
The rolled-back Market Street facade and finely scaled flush aluminum skin make this one of the more ingratiating of this generation of towers. It is connected by a hyphen to the 1908 Postal Telegraph Building by Lewis Hobart at 22 Battery Street.

28. Shaklee Terraces

29. Industrial Indemnity Building
1959, Skidmore Owings & Merrill
255 California St.
Once a giant, now a moderate-sized tower, but still remarkable for its deference in scale and wall composition to its neighbors, particularly Lewis Hobart's 1910-17 Newhall Building at 260 California Street. The executive offices are on the second floor under the arched vaults, facing a garden terrace designed by Lawrence Halprin.

30. Tadich Grill
1909, Crim & Scott
240-42 California St.
The restaurant started up in 1865 on the site of the Transamerica pyramid and moved here later.The interior is a fine period piece, but the facade also deserves notice for the simple elegance of its terra-cotta frame.

29. Industrial Indemnity Building

31. Embarcadero Center
1967-81, John C. Portman, Jr.
Bounded by Clay, Battery, Sacramento, Drumm,
California, and Market Sts. and M. Justin Herman Plaza
Hyatt Regency Hotel
1989, John C. Portman, Jr.
333 Battery St.
An 8 1/2-acre portion of the 51-acre Golden Gateway Redevelopment Center fostered by M. Justin Herman, San Francisco's entrepreneurial Redevelopment Agency director from 1959 until his death in 1971. Called a city-within-a-city, the project was built incrementally over 14 years in tandem with the growth of the financial district. Often scorned in its early stages as a merely formal

gesture at multilevel urbanity, its present daytime population now fills its many levels. The complex of four towers
linked by footbridges plus the Hyatt Regency Hotel is
exceptional for its successful integration of shopping–on
the first three levels of each block-sized podium–and
office towers, whose coverage is limited to one-third of
the site. The towers, clad in rough-finished, precast concrete, are composed of slablike elements stepped to create
10 to 14 corner offices per floor instead of the usual four.
Their slender profiles are a welcome departure from the
heavier towers on the skyline. The city's requirement that
one percent of development money be spent for art has
endowed the Center with a number of works of art, including sculptures by Willi Gutman, Michael Biggers, Nicholas
Schoffer, Anne Van Kleeck, Louise Nevelson, Barbara
Showcroft, and Robert Russin; and tapestries by Fran-
coise Grossen, Lia Cook, and Olga de Amaral. Circulation
is baffling, but directories in each building give the loca-
tions of shops, restaurants, and works of art.

31. Embarcadero Center

The Center is introduced on Market Street by the Hyatt
Regency Hotel, completed in 1973 and one of Portman's
most successful atrium hotels. The great interior space
has a monumental spherical sculpture of aluminum tubing
by Charles Perry titled *Eclipse*. Seen from the Embarcadero, the staggered floors of the hotel recall an old-
fashioned typewriter keyboard. A dreadfully dull main entrance addresses the automobile rather than acknow-
ledging its important gateway corner to pedestrians.

32. Alcoa Building
1964, Skidmore Owings & Merrill; Sasaki Walker Assoc., land. arch.
1 Maritime Plaza

32. Alcoa Building

The major office tower in the Golden Gateway Redevelopment Project. Alcoa was the first design to use the seismic
X-bracing as part of its structural aesthetic. The idea was
used again in Chicago's Hancock Building, designed in the
firm's Chicago office. The formal plan for the garden
squares on top of the garages was intended to create the
effect of an outdoor sculpture museum. Major pieces are
by Marino Marini, Henry Moore, Charles Perry, and Jan
Peter Stern; the fountain is by Robert Woodward. Although the rooftop plazas are convincing pedestrian
precincts in the sky, the street level is a grim reminder of
what happens when an area is abandoned to auto traffic.

33. Home Savings of America Building
1990, Kohn Pederson Fox
200 California St.

A relatively modest tower that calls for attention through
an overly rich palette of materials.

34. 100 California St.
1959, Welton Becket & Assoc.
One of the early postwar office towers. The metal bolts on the piers were added later for seismic safety.

Security Pacific Bank Building
1972, Welton Becket & Assoc.
50 California St.
A later, less interesting building by the same firm. The Security Pacific Art Gallery, designed by Frederick Fisher in collaboration with artist David Ireland, is located on the first floor. Completed in 1990, the space is detailed in subtle and interesting ways; the window walls on the street are also used to showcase art.

35. 101 California Street Building
1982, Johnson/Burgee
An elegant silo that adds grace to the skyline; the sloping glazed atrium at street level is less elegant but the plaza is a welcome open space even if it does face north.

35. 101 California Street Building

36. 388 Market Street Building
1987, Skidmore Owings & Merrill
The most successful design to date for a Market Street triangle, this teardrop shaped tower is a mix of offices below and six residential floors at the top.

37. Pacific Gas & Electric Company
1925, Bakewell & Brown
245 Market St.
An engaged colonnade with a giant order topped by freestanding urns is the climax of this imposing facade. Clad in terra cotta cast to mimic granite, the decorative detail is exceptional. The sculptural group by Edgar Walter over the entrance is particularly fine.

36. 388 Market Street Building

Matson Building
1921, Bliss & Faville
215 Market St.
Now occupied by PG & E, the Matson was once the mainland headquarters for Hawaii's Big Five corporations. Like its neighbors, the building was designed to evoke the princely age of commerce embodied in the Renaissance palace. Nowadays these mercantile palaces recall the time when large office buildings lined the streets at uniform heights and spoke the same civilized language.

38. San Francisco Federal Reserve Bank Building
1982, Skidmore Owings & Merrill
100 block Market St.
A monumental loggia along Market and a reticent but granite-clad stepped facade distinguish this complicated building, which has everything from executive offices to warehousing operations.

38. Federal Reserve Bank Building

39. 135 Main Street Building
1989, Robinson Mills & Williams

A disconcerting attempt at monumentality on the ground floor but very discreet above. Behind the building is a network of alleyways, some landscaped, that offer the pedestrian shortcuts and relief from the streets.

39. 135 Main Street Building

40. Rincon Center (former post office)
1939-40, Gilbert Stanley Underwood
99 Mission St.
Rincon Towers
1989, Pereira & Assoc.
88 Howard and 101 Spear Sts.

Often called PWA Moderne, the minimalist Classicism employed by the Public Works Department is well represented here in symmetrical massing and a colonnade reduced to barely projecting piers capped by a narrow lintel. The WPA murals inside are notable. In 1989 the post office building became the frontispiece for a mixed use development that features a large, midblock atrium with a fountain that rains from the ceiling. The residential towers that front on Howard Street are handsome additions to the dull assortment of towers in SOMA.

40. Rincon Center (former post office)

41. YMCA
1924, Carl Werner
166 The Embarcadero

A handsome facade long obscured by the only recently demolished Embarcadero Freeway decks.

Bayside Plaza
1986, Tower Architects
188 The Embarcadero

Designed to reflect its waterside location with a sculpture by Ruth Asawa in front.

42. Jewish Community Centers
1986, Skidmore Owings & Merrill
121 Steuart St.

A restrained design that complements the older buildings that are found on the street.

43. Audiffred Building
1889; 1980-81, William E. Cullen
1-21 Mission St.

Built by Hippolyte Audiffred to recall his native France, the building survived the 1906 fire but was gutted by another fire in 1980. It has since been rehabilitated. The nautical ornament on the ground floor cornice is a delightful reminder that the building was once right on the water.

43. Audiffred Building

44. Southern Pacific Building
1916, Bliss & Faville
1 Market St.
A vast Renaissance palace built to house one of the city's first major corporate headquarters.

45. M. Justin Herman Plaza
1971, Mario Ciampi/Lawrence Halprin &
Assoc./John Bolles
Foot of Market St.
Part of the Market Street Beautification Project, the plaza suffers some from its north orientation. Since the completion of the Embarcadero Center, the daytime crowd enlivens the space as do frequent craft markets and entertainment. The fountain by Armand Vaillancourt used to have the double-decker freeway as a backdrop. Now that the freeway is gone, the array of angular concrete forms can no longer be joked about as a stockpile of spare freeway parts. For the moment it seems overexposed. The plaza's other sculptures are an equestrian statue of Juan Bautista de Anza by Julian Martinez, a gift from the governor of Sonora, Mexico and a 1986 painted and welded steel monument to the International Longshoremen's and Warehousemen's Union that commemorates the 1934 Maritime Strike. Ten local artists collaborated on the sculpture calling themselves *METAL*.

45. M. Justin Herman Plaza

46. Ferry Building
1895-1903, A. Page Brown/Edward R.A. Pyle, State
Dept. of Engineering
Foot of Market St.
Before the bridges and the recently demolished freeway were built, this was the city's transportation hub. Some 170 ferries docked every day disgorging their passengers for an easy walk to downtown offices or to the trolley line up Market. The completion of the bay bridges, the Key System, and the Transbay Terminal diverted much of the traffic to rail, bus and auto. When the ferries stopped in 1958, the building was converted into offices. A mezzanine floor intercepts the great skylit galleries that ran the length of the building. Plans have been made to renovate the building and create a multi-purpose complex on the site, but so far none of them has been implemented. The Agriculture Building that stands south of the Ferry Building is a richly ornamented relic of the 1915 Panama Pacific International Exposition.

46. Ferry Building

1992 demolition of Embarcadero Freeway damaged in 1989 earthquake

Embarcadero Promenade
1982, MLTW/Turnbull Assoc./Donlyn Lyndon
A nice beginning to a promenade that may one day stretch along the waterfront to Folsom Street.

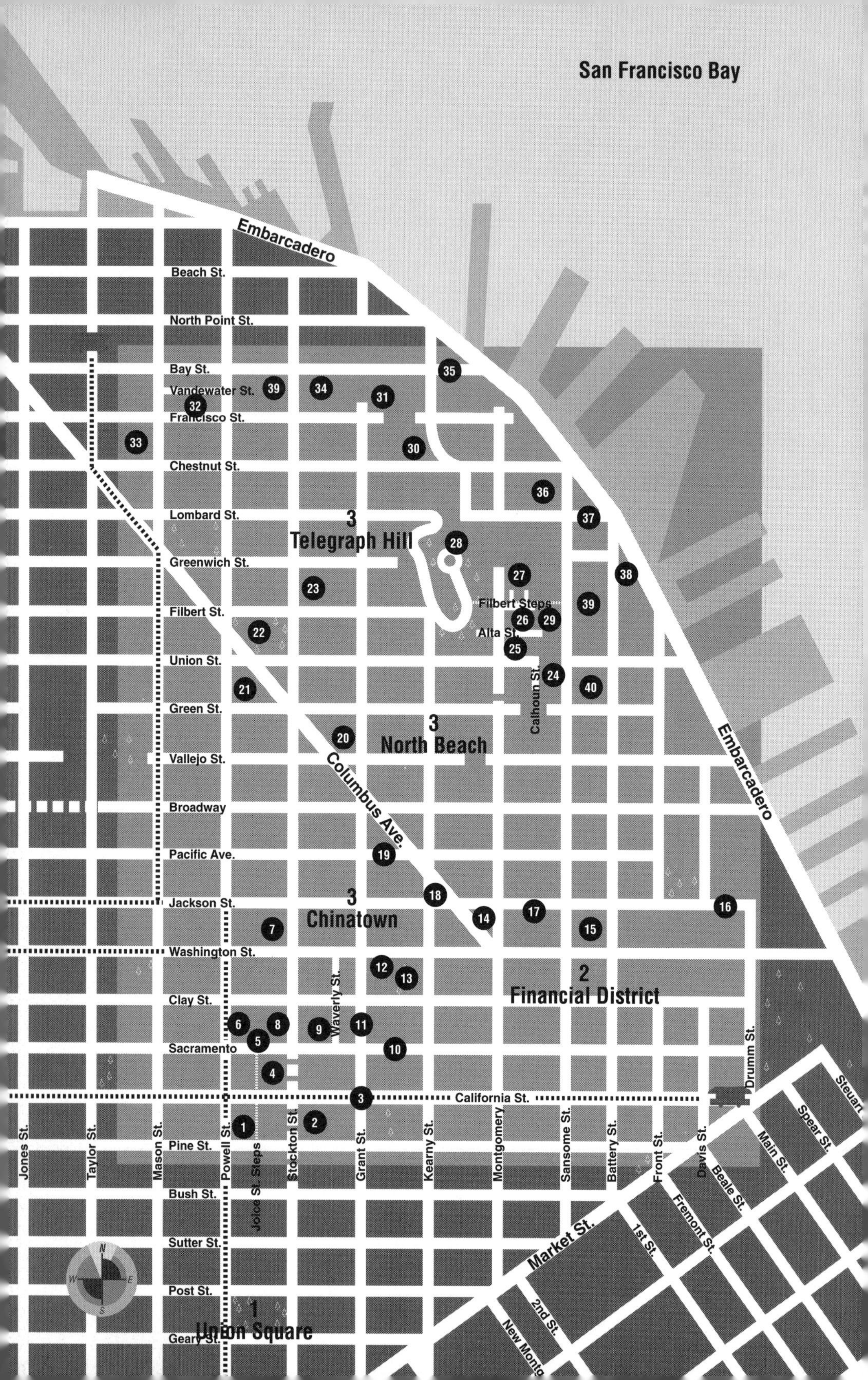

San Francisco Bay

Embarcadero

Beach St.
North Point St.
Bay St.
Vandewater St.
Francisco St.
Chestnut St.
Lombard St.
Greenwich St.
Filbert St.
Union St.
Green St.
Vallejo St.
Broadway
Pacific Ave.
Jackson St.
Washington St.
Clay St.
Sacramento
California St.
Pine St.
Bush St.
Sutter St.
Post St.
Geary St.

3 Telegraph Hill

3 North Beach

3 Chinatown

2 Financial District

1 Union Square

Filbert Steps
Alta St.

Columbus Ave.
Embarcadero

Jones St.
Taylor St.
Mason St.
Powell St.
Joice St. Steps
Stockton St.
Grant St.
Waverly St.
Kearny St.
Montgomery
Sansome St.
Battery St.
Front St.
Davis St.
Drumm St.

Market St.
1st St.
Fremont St.
Beale St.
Main St.
Spear St.
Steuart

New Mont
2nd St.

Calhoun St.

N
W E
S

Since 1880 the boundaries of Chinatown have been California to Broadway and Kearny to Stockton Street. Grant Avenue, named for the general, was first called the *Calle de la Fundacion;* it connected the Mission Dolores to the Presidio. In 1835 the Englishman William Richardson drew a map showing his tent store at the intersection of the Calle and Clay Street, which ran downhill to the edge of the bay, then marked by Montgomery Street. By 1837 Richardson had built an adobe house called La Casa Grande; its location is marked by a plaque at 823 Grant. A sprinkling of other buildings soon followed that comprised the tiny port city called Yerba Buena.

The first Chinese, most of whom were from Canton (Kwangtung), came for the Gold Rush. Their numbers were sufficient to establish the *hui-kuan,* or district associations, whose memberships were based on common origin of place or family. Hui-kuan headquarters are Chinatown's most distinctive building type. Their mainland prototype consisted of a series of structures separated by courtyards. The most important component, the temple, stood at the end of the complex. Because this horizontal form was impossible in a dense urban location, the typical 19th-century commercial building was adapted for the purpose by stacking the components vertically. In this arrangement the temple occupied the top floor and became the most important part of the facade. These buildings are easily identified by their top floors, which have curving roof eaves and balconies with ritual bells, lanterns, and other trappings that are displayed on holidays. They are also likely to have the colors red, yellow, and green as part of their fabric. All three colors mean health, wealth, and good luck, making Chinatown the only neighborhood to have a color scheme.

By 1852 the Chinese had settled around the intersection of Dupont, as the Calle was renamed that year, and Sacramento, replacing the original French residents. The combination of discrimination at the mines and the mines' diminishing returns brought the Chinese back to the city where by 1860 they formed five percent of the population. In the 1860s they took over the manufacturing of footwear, clothing, and cigars. Their frugality and dedication to work did not endear them to the predominantly white male population.

Despite the inhumane treatment resulting from the anti-Chinese movement and the Chinese Exclusion Act of 1882, the Chinese persevered. When the 1906 fire razed Chinatown along with the rest of downtown, a group of merchants saw an opportunity to revamp the squalid, vice-ridden image caused by the district's gambling, opium, and prostitution dens; the alleys notorious for such pursuits, Waverly, Ross, and Spofford, were linked to the infamous Barbary Coast nearby. Whereas the pre-fire Chinatown was built mainly with undistinguished prefabricated wooden buildings, the post-fire "city-within-a-city" was reconstructed of durable brick. To lure tourists to this Oriental bazaar, the buildings were done up with architectural *chinoiserie.*

The gateway buildings, the Sing Chong and Sing Fat, at the intersection of Grant and California marked the beginning of the bazaar. At Jackson Street the market section began, and still does, except that its bustle spills over onto the neighboring streets. Much of the new building is out of scale with the old and sadly lacking in its naive theatricality. The vitality of the district was never really expressed in its architecture although that is often colorful. The street life and festivals remain exotic.

1. Joice Street Steps
One of the charming byways that contributes to San Francisco's Old World charm.

2. Ritz Carlton Hotel
1909, LeBrun & Sons; 1913, Miller & Colmesnil/ Miller & Pflueger; 1991, Whisler-Patri Assoc.
600 Stockton St.
Monumental Roman-Renaissance grandeur in gleaming terra cotta. Originally built for an insurance company, the building has been successfully converted into a hotel.

3. Sing Chong Building
1908, T. Patterson Ross and A. W. Burgren
601-15 Grant Ave.
Sing Fat Building
1908, T. Patterson Ross and A. W. Burgren
717-19 California St.
Old St. Mary's Church
1853-54; 1907-09, Craine & England; 1969, Welsh & Carey
Grant Ave. at California St.
Paulist Center of the West
1964, Skidmore Owings & Merrill
600 California St.
St. Mary's Square
1960, Eckbo, Royston & Williams
Statue of Sun Yat-Sen by Beniamino Bufano
The pagodalike towers of the two gateway buildings to the post-fire Oriental bazaar signal the shopping, originally much more exotic, to come along Grant Avenue. The colorful street lights topped with lanterns are a relic of the 1915 Panama Pacific Exposition. Old St. Mary's preceded this post-fire Chinatown by half a century. Although it too burned in 1906, the granite foundations from China and the brick and iron walls imported from the eastern U.S. survived. The church was soon restored, was remodeled and enlarged in the 1920s, burned again in 1969, and was again restored. St. Mary's academic Gothic Revival form was complemented in 1964 by the addition of a respectful but clearly contemporary brick rectory.

4. Mei Lun Yuen Chinatown Housing
1982, Architects Associated
Stockton and Sacramento Sts.
A well-planned, mixed-use development with 185 units of public housing. Years in the making, the project is the result of much community participation and patient effort on the part of the architects to make the most of a low budget and a difficult site.

1. Joice Street Steps

2. Ritz Carlton Hotel

3. Old St. Mary's Church

5. Donaldina Cameron House
1908, Julia Morgan; rem. 1940s; add. 1972, E. Sue
920 Sacramento St.
In 1873 the Presbyterian Church set up a foreign mission to serve San Francisco's Chinese. After the original hall burned in 1906, a new one was built on the present site and officially named for its famous director in 1942. The architect was rightly favored by many eleemosynary institutions; she knew how to design practical buildings that had dignity and presence.

6. Former Chinatown Women's YWCA Residence Hall
1932, Julia Morgan
940-50 Powell St.
YWCA Clay Street Center
1931, Julia Morgan
965 Clay St.
Two facilities designed concurrently by Morgan, for some years the official YWCA architect for the western region. The first, a severe, elongated Tuscan villa, is now for senior citizens; the latter, an active social center, is more stylistically adventuresome and has an urbane yet residential scale and plan.

7. Commodore Stockton School Annex
1924, Angus McSweeney; rem. 1974-75, Bruce, Wendell & Beebe
Washington St. at Stone St.
A handsome blend of Mediterranean and Oriental imagery.
Gum Moon Residence
1912, Julia Morgan
940 Washington St.
Methodist Church
1911, Clarence Ward
Grant Ave. at Washington St.
The Protestant missions in Chinatown were largely devoted to rescuing Chinese girls from prostitution. They were run by dedicated women of enormous energy. Their favorite architect, Julia Morgan, was of the same stripe. This understated Florentine villa was the residence for the original Methodist Church next door, also designed by Morgan, which burned in 1906, and was replaced by the present building, designed in 1911 by Clarence Ward.

4. Mei Lun Yuen Chinatown Housing

5. Donaldina Cameron House

6. Commodore Stockton School Annex

7. Gum Moon Residence

7. Methodist Church

8. St. Mary's Chinese Mission

8. Chinese Consolidated Benevolent Association of the United States (Six Companies)
1908
843 Stockton St.
This building for the six *hui-kuan*, which banded together in the 1860s to battle legal and extra-legal actions against their members, is a strong expression of the association type commonly found in Chinatown.

St. Mary's Chinese Mission
c.1906
902 Stockton St.

Waverly Place, Spofford, and Ross
The blocks between Stockton and Grant and Sacramento and Jackson are laced with alleys once notorious for gambling and other vices that contributed to Chinatown's lurid past. Today they are less colorful. At 36 Spofford is a modest building designed by Charles M. Rousseau and built in 1907 for the Chee Kung Tong, the Chinese Freemasons. For six years it was a major center of Sun Yat Sen's revolutionary movement. After 1906 Waverly Place was lined with three- and four-story association buildings. Two architecturally interesting ones that remain are at the Washington Street end; another particularly colorful example is the 1911 Sue Hing Benevolent Association at nearby 125-29 Waverly Place.

9. Chinese Baptist Church
1887, G.H. Moore; rebuilt 1908, G. E. Burlingame
15 Waverly Pl. at Sacramento St.

10. Nam Kue School
1925, Charles E. Rogers
765 Sacramento St.
A more traditional Chinese institutional building with a forecourt. The school was established to instruct Chinatown youth in Chinese culture.

Chinese Chamber of Commerce
1912
728-30 Sacramento St.

11. Building
c.1915
745 Grant Ave.
A fancy rendition of the association building type. Across the street at 736-38 Grant is the *Chinese World* (newspaper) building of 1907.

Soo Yuen Benevolent Association Building
1907-19, Salfield & Kohlberg
801-07 Grant Ave.
An unusual interpretation of the association building type that wraps around the corner lot in an imaginative way with a tripartite facade and a graceful balcony.

12. Bank of Canton (former Chinese Telephone Exchange)
1909
743 Washington St.
The site of San Francisco's first newspaper, the *California Star,* later became the home of the country's only Chinese telephone exchange. Outmoded by the 1950s, the exchange closed and the building interior was remodeled for its new occupant, the Bank of Canton.

10. Nam Kue School

13. Portsmouth Square/Chinese Cultural and Trade Center with Holiday Inn
1971, Clement Chen/John Carl Warnecke & Assoc.
750 Kearny St.
Once the plaza of the Spanish colonial port town of Yerba Buena, renamed San Francisco in 1847. By 1844 the first official building, a customs house, was built at the northwest corner of the plaza. In 1846 Captain Montgomery raised the American flag here and named the plaza Portsmouth Square after his U.S. Navy sloop. At the time of the Gold Rush the square acquired the set of hotels and gambling houses that, along with the customs house, were vital to the town's economy. As the city center moved southward and the mining industry ceased to be the city's economic base, the square declined in civic importance and finally became a city park. In 1963 a split-level park with garage below, designed by Royston, Hanamoto & Mays, reshaped the square. Various monuments, including one to Robert Louis Stevenson designed by Bruce Porter and Willis Polk in 1897, were reinstalled. A plaque giving the history of the square is by the stair from the upper to the lower level. The brutally scaled Holiday Inn building gets its name from a token level of community space beneath the high-rise motel.

13. Portsmouth Sq./Chinese Cultural & Trade Center with Holiday Inn

14. Old Transamerica Building
1911, Salfield & Kohlberg
4 Columbus Ave. at Montgomery St.
A wedding cake building that reveals terra cotta's ability to rival stone in the rendering of decorative detail. Originally two stories high, the top story was added later. First called the Fugazi Banca Popolare, the company began in 1859 as John Fugazi's travel agency with banking on the side.

14. Old Transamerica Building

16. Golden Gateway Redevelopment Project, Phase 1 residential development

16. Golden Gateway Redevelopment Project, Phase 2 residential development

15. U.S. Customs House
1906-11, Eames & Young
555 Battery St.
Although most of the post-fire buildings downtown used stone sparingly, usually in combination with less expensive terra cotta, the federal government built for the ages, as in this Customs House building. Handsome decorative detail using patriotic symbols of authority enriches the exterior. The interior has generous public spaces, a handsome stairway and other fine details.

16. Golden Gateway Redevelopment Project
Battery St. to the Embarcadero; Broadway to Clay St.
Urban renewal plan
1957, Skidmore Owings & Merrill
Phase 1 residential development
1961-63, garages, point towers & town houses
Wurster Bernardi & Emmons/DeMars & Reay
Jackson St.
Phase 1 town houses
1961-63, Anshen & Allen; Sasaki Walker Assoc.,
land. arch.
Washington St.
Phase 2 residential development
1981-82, condominiums, Fisher-Friedman
Davis St. to Broadway
This first major downtown housing development, a Redevelopment Agency project, replaced the city's produce market with slab towers and a neat, suburban village of town houses. In 1981-82 Fisher-Friedman designed the final residential increments of the project, which has pleasant interior courts, commercial space on the ground floors and parking below grade. By now both blocks of housing have become period-pieces, but their existence has contributed greatly to the urbanity of this part of town.

17. Jackson Square
Jackson St. bet. Montgomery and Sansome Sts.,
Hotaling Pl., and Montgomery to Washington St.
The city's first official Historic District and the only group of downtown business buildings to survive the 1906 earthquake and fire. Except for the elaborate, prefabricated cast-iron and cast-stone facades of the Hotaling buildings, which housed a wholesale liquor business, the buildings are relatively simple; the sharp change in scale from the adjacent financial district buildings heightens the 19th-century character of the historic district.

Building
400-01 Jackson St.
A post-1906 rebuilding of a c.1882 office structure.

Ghirardelli Building
1853
415-31 Jackson St.

Tobacco and coffee warehouse
1861
435-41 Jackson St.

Jackson Hotaling Annex East
c.1860
443-45 Jackson St.

Hotaling Building
1866
451-61 Jackson St.

17. Hotaling Building and Hotaling Annex West

Hotaling Annex West
c.1860
463-73 Jackson St.

Building
432 Jackson St.
Rebuilt after 1906 from rubble of other buildings.

Solari Building, East-Larco's Building
1866
470 Jackson St.

Bank of Lucas Turner & Co.
1853, Keyser & Brown after a design by Reuben Clark
498 Jackson St. to 804 Montgomery St.
Now the home of the west coast's premier architectural
bookstore, William Stout's Architectural Books.

17. Golden Era Building

Golden Era Building
1852
732 Montgomery St.
Mark Twain and Bret Harte were among the contributors to
The Golden Era, an early literary magazine.

Genella Building/Belli Annex
1851
728-30 Montgomery St.

Belli Building-Langerman's Building
1851
722-24 Montgomery St.

17. Bank of Lucas Turner & Co.

Burr Building
1859-60
530 Washington St.

Nearby on the corresponding blocks of Pacific Avenue was the Barbary Coast, once the city's major vice center. After many ups and downs it vanished in the post-World War II era. The buildings were rebuilt after 1906 to their pre-fire scale. The area has some sensitive rehabilitations of old buildings for new uses. One Jackson Place, remodeled by Lloyd Flood in 1964, was downtown's first conversion of warehouses into an interior shopping mall.

18. Columbus Tower

The term **North Beach** refers to the area west of Telegraph Hill that once was a sand beach. The shoreline has been extended about four blocks by fill and bounded by a sea wall constructed between 1881 and 1913. At the foot of Powell was Harry Meigg's 2,000-foot wharf and amusement park, the location of Abe Warner's famous Spider Palace where the cobwebs were so thick that they were said to support human weight. Besides bath-houses and other facilities for swimming and healthful recreation, the area was also home to a number of prominent citizens before the 1860s when Rincon Hill replaced it as the zone of "better residence." A number of industries took advantage of the waterside location. Of the ten breweries located there by 1876, only the old Malting House on Francisco between Mason and Powell streets survives. North Beach was long the local equivalent of New York's Greenwich Village. Over the years its ethnic complexion has changed from Italian to mostly Chinese.

Varennes St. in North Beach

18. Columbus Tower
1905, Salfield & Kohlberg; rem. 1959, Henrik Bull
Columbus Ave. and Kearny St.
An eye-catching landmark for those coming downtown, the building is owned by Frances Ford Coppola.

19. City Lights Books Store and Vesuvio's
1913, rem. 1918, Italo Sanolini
235-53 Columbus Ave.
Two social landmarks of the Beat Generation era, the first was the country's first all-paperback bookstore, as well as a principal hangout for the literati, including Allen Ginsberg, Jack Kerouac, Kenneth Rexroth, Lawrence Ferlinghetti, the owner, and many other notable beatniks. Across the alley, Vesuvio's was an extension of this memorable scene. Though most of the other gathering places have passed on, a few, such as the Cafe Trieste, survive along upper Grant Avenue.

20. St. Francis of Assisi Church
1860, rem. 1913, C. J. I. Devlin
610 Vallejo St.
The exterior of this church, including the towers, survived the 1906 fire and was incorporated into the present structure. This was the city's first parish church after the Mission Dolores; it was founded by the French community. Stylistically, it is related to Old St. Mary's.

21. Fugazi Hall
1912, Italo Sanolini
678 Green St.
John Fugazi, donor of Fugazi Hall, was also the founder of the Transamerica Company. He competed with two other Italian bankers, A. P. Giannini and Andrea Sbarbaro, but eventually all three combined to create the giant Bank of America. Fugazi gave this cultural and community center in perpetuity to the Italian community.

20. St. Francis of Assisi Church

22. Washington Square
Columbus Ave. to Stockton St., Union to Filbert St.
Blighted by unkempt cemeteries in its first decade, this early rectangular plot was leveled in the 1860s and became a favorite place to promenade after Montgomery Avenue, renamed Columbus in 1909, was cut across one corner of it in the 1870s. Lillie Coit's monument to the Volunteer Fire Department, sculpted by Haig Patigian and installed in 1933, and the 1879 statue of Ben Franklin are in the Square. In 1958 Lawrence Halprin & Associates and Douglas Baylis designed the present landscape, which is so sympathetic to its surroundings and to the activities of the square that it seems as though it had always existed.

SS Peter and Paul Church
1922-24, Charles Fantoni; 1939, John A. Poporato
666 Filbert St.

22. SS Peter and Paul Church

This Italianesque Gothic Revival church anchors the square claiming it as the traditional center of the Italian community. The original design, perhaps derived from Orvieto cathedral, called for a large mosaic for the central facade. This scheme was abandoned in 1939 when Poporato was commissioned to finish the church. One of its high moments came when Cecil B. DeMille featured it in his 1923 silent film, *The Ten Commandments*.

23. Former Telegraph Hill Neighborhood Association

24. Kahn house

26. 1360 Montgomery St.

23. Former Telegraph Hill Neighborhood Association
1908-09, Bernard Maybeck; add. 1913, 1928; rem.
1940s, John Kelly; add. 1980s, AGORA
1736 Stockton St.
An historic neighborhood center founded by Alice Griffith, a pioneering social worker, the building's alpine chalet style was often used by Maybeck. The many alterations of form and use have preserved the attractive courtyard.

24. Kahn house
1939, Richard Neutra
66 Calhoun Terrace
A rare northern California example of the European International style by its southern California master.

25. Houses
1309, 1315 Montgomery St.
1860s
25, 29 Alta St.
c.1870
31 Alta St.
1852
287-89 Union St.
1850s
293 Union St.
1860s
Although most of Telegraph Hill's buildings are post-1906, two clusters of houses on the eastern flank of the hill reveal what it looked like in its early period. The simple wood-frame buildings of almost miniature scale resemble the prefabs shipped from New England to this Yankee outpost. Few have escaped alterations, but they have a time-bound quality that matches their setting.

26. Apartment house
1937, J. S. Malloch, builder
1360 Montgomery St.
One of the city's best examples of the Style Moderne, this was the luxurious apartment building featured in the 1946 Humphrey Bogart, Lauren Bacall movie *Dark Passage.*

Julius's Castle
1922, Louis Mastropasqua
End of Montgomery St.
One of the hill's most colorful landmarks.

27. Filbert Steps, Darrell Place, Napier Lane Residence
1942, Gardner Dailey
351 Filbert St.
Below Pioneer Park, where Coit Tower stands, Filbert becomes a flight of steps. No. 351 is a building that exemplifies early Bay Area Modernism in its cubistic form.

The Montgomery Street landscaping was for many years the personal effort of Grace Marchant, whose contribution is commemorated by a plaque. A cluster of houses from the 1860s and 1870s is at 228 and 224 Filbert and across the way on the two pedestrian lanes, Darrell Place and Napier Lane. As of this writing the dates of the Napier Lane houses are: No. 10, 1875; No.15, 1884; No. 16, 1872; No. 21, 1885; No. 22, 1876, and No. 32-34, 1890, but remodeled. No. 36 Darrell Place is a condominium building by Ace Architects intended as an homage to Bay Regional architecture. A flight of wooden steps leads down the precipitous hillside. The hill's scarred flanks bear witness to the quarrying operations that chipped away at its base for years until stopped in 1903. Among other uses the quarried rock became fill for the Embarcadero.

27. Residence, 351 Filbert

28. Coit Tower
1934, Arthur Brown, Jr.
End of Telegraph Hill Blvd.

This emblematic landmark occupies the site of the first west coast telegraph, a semaphore, which in 1849 connected Point Lobos with Point Loma, as the hill was then called. By 1853 an electromagnetic line took its place. The next landmark, a castlelike observatory built in 1882, burned in 1903. In 1929 Lillie Coit, a local heroine with a penchant for firefighting, died, leaving the city a bequest for beautification. A monument was commissioned from Arthur Brown, Jr., principal architect of the San Francisco Civic Center. The result, popularly decoded as a stylized hose nozzle, may also be seen as a declassified column because of its fluted shaft and missing capital. The recently restored interior features WPA murals by several artists; it is well worth a visit.

28. Coit Tower

29. Garfield School
1981, Esherick Homsey Dodge & Davis
420 Filbert St.

A successful redesign of a previous school. Through its informal massing, plan, choice of color and materials, this building escapes being an institutional blockbuster.

28-29. Garfield School and Coit Tower

31. Telegraph Terrace

32. Vandewater St. buildings

36. Telegraph Landing

30. House
1929
298 Chestnut St.

The Mediterranean imagery used in this villa is more typical of 1920s mansions in other areas of the city such as Pacific Heights and St. Francis Wood.

31. Telegraph Terrace
1984, Backen Arrigoni & Ross
Grant and Francisco Sts.

Contemporary eclectic Mediterranean styling picturesquely composed and well sited—it fits right in even though it is the newest and largest project on the hillside.

32. Vandewater Street/Buildings
No. 15
1974, Jerry Weisbach
No. 33
1981, Donald MacDonald
No. 55
1981, Daniel Solomon & Assoc.

A North Beach alleyway with several recent buildings which give it a past-to-present character.

33. San Remo Hotel and Restaurant
c.1915; rem. 1978, Monte Bell
2237 Mason St.

A pleasant and understated remodeling that enhances the old North Beach character of this building.

34. Trinity Properties
1979, Esherick Homsey Dodge & Davis
333 Bay St.

Headquarters for a major local real estate developer designed in the contemporary shingle style of the 1970s.

35. Municipal buildings
c.1925
111 Bay St.

Handsome proto-modern, background buildings.

36. Telegraph Landing
1979, Bull, Field, Volkmann & Stockwell
1 Chestnut St.

The first condominium project at this end of the Embarcadero, the units are carefully oriented to give privacy and select views of the bay or the interior court.

37. Warehouse
c.1900; rem. 1980, Hellmuth, Obata & Kassabaum
1 Lombard St.
An extensive interior remodeling of one of the fine warehouse buildings in the north Embarcadero district.

38. Former Beltline Roundhouse
1914; rem. 1985, Tower Architects
1500 Sansome St.
A pleasant conversion into offices of the only railway roundhouse that ever stood on the Embarcadero.

Fog City Diner
1987, Pat Kuleto
1300 Battery St.
A smart design that recalls an older diner in the area, and a good restaurant—at this writing.

39. Levi's Plaza
1982, Helmuth, Obata & Kassabaum/Howard Friedman/Gensler & Assoc.; Lawrence Halprin, land. arch.
Battery St. to Sansome St., Union St. to Greenwich St.
A benchmark in corporate headquarters design, this lowrise complex of brick buildings is scenographically composed to enhance the view of Telegraph Hill and even incorporate it as borrowed scenery. The well-orchestrated site plan integrates the buildings with the landscaped plaza and provides a sweeping suburban park across Battery that is the most luxuriously appointed corporate front yard in town. The fountains are the latest in Lawrence Halprin's line of Sierra mountainscape tour de forces. Also commendable is the rehabilitation of two older warehouse buildings, the Italian Swiss Colony Building (1903, Hemenway & Miller) and the 1879 Cargo West Building at Battery and Union.

39. Levi's Plaza

40. The Ice Houses

40. The Ice Houses No. 1 & No. 2
1914; rem. 1970, Wurster Bernardi & Emmons
1265 Battery St., 151 Union St.
The first of many conversions of old warehouses to new uses that have enlivened the area with often inventive designs melding the old and the new. A pleasant walk down Battery Street, the verge of the original waterfront, will reveal many more.

San Francisco Bay

Aquatic Park

52

Jefferson St.

50

53

Fisherman's Wharf

Beach St.

51

North Point St.

Vandewater St.

Bay St.

48 **49** **47** **54**

46

Columbus Ave.

Francisco St.

Water St.

45

42 Culebra

43 **49** **44**

Chestnut St.

39

41

Lombard St.

40

Greenwich St.

38

Southard

Filbert St.

4
Russian Hill

Van Ness Ave.

Union St.

36

37

Macondray Lane

32 **33**

35

Green St.

34

30

Vallejo St.

Glover St.

28

31

29

Broadway

27

Pacific Ave.

26

Jackson St.

24 **25**

Washington St.

4
Nob Hill

21 **23**

Clay St.

22

20 **17** **16** **15**

18

Sacramento

19

8 **12** **14**

5 **6**

California St.

Octavia St.

Gough St.

Franklin St.

Pine St.

4

Polk St.

Larkin St.

Hyde St.

3

Leavenworth St.

7

Jones St.

2

Taylor St.

9

10

1

Mason St.

11

13

Powell St.

Joice St.

Stockton St.

Bush St.

N
W E
S

Post St.

1
Union Square

Geary St.

4

1. Apts. 900 block Pine St.
2. Apts. 1100 block Pine St.
3. Marie Antoinette Apts.
4. Trinity Church
5. First Church of Christ, Scientist
6. Royal Theatre
7. Cathedral Apartments
8. Grace Cathedral
   Cathedral House
   Diocesan House
   Cathedral School
9. Masonic Memorial Temple
10. Huntington Hotel
    Nob Hill Center Garage
    Town house 1021 California St.
    Morsehead Apartments
11. Town houses 831-49 Mason St.
12. Pacific Union Club
13. Mark Hopkins Hotel
14. Stanford Court Hotel
    Fairmont Hotel
15. Brocklebank Apartments
16. Nob Hill Apartments
17. Apts. 1230, 1242 Sacramento St.
    Chambord Apartments
18. Apts. 1200 block Leavenworth St.
19. Coronado Apartments
    Apts. 1590 Sacramento St.
    Apts. 1601 Sacramento St.
    Apts. 1451 Larkin St.
    Apts. 1560 Larkin St.
20. Apts. 1400 block Clay St.
21. Clayerest Apartments
    House 1329 Clay St.
    Clay-Jones Apartments
    Comstock Apartments
    Apts. 1300 block Jones St.
22. Apts. 1135-41 Taylor St.
23. Apts. 1200 block Taylor St.
    Apts. 1200 block Washington St.
24. Flats 1314-30 Taylor St.
    Hillgate Manor
25. Cable Car Barn & Museum
26. Apts. 1425 Taylor St.

27. Talbot-Dutton house
28. Houses 2200 block Van Ness Ave.
29. Nuestra Señora de Guadalupe
30. 1000 block Vallejo St.
    Russian Hill Place
    Florence St.
    Ina Coolbrith Park
31. Condominiums 15-17 Glover St.
32. Holy Trinity Russian Orthodox Cathedral
33. Alhambra Theatre
34. Apts. 1101 Green St.
35. Houses 1000 block Green St.
36. Macondray Lane
37. Houses 800-900 block Union St.
    1800 block Mason St.
38. Southard Place
39. Fannie Osborne Stevenson house
    Lombard St. wiggle
40. House 65 Montclair Ter.
41. Wright house
42. Houses 100 block Culebra Ter.
43. House 998 Chestnut St.
44. S.F. Art Institute
    House 805-07 Chestnut St.
45. Walters house
46. Houses & Apts. 800 block Francisco St.
47. Houses 2423, 2455 Leavenworth St.
    Studio 2508 Leavenworth
48. Cottages 2540-50 Hyde St.
49. Terraced houses 757-65 Bay St.
    House 737 Bay St.
50. National Maritime Museum
51. Ghirardelli Square
    Tower Building
52. Hyde St. Pier
53. Haslett Warehouse Bldg.
    Cannery
54. North Point public housing

Nob Hill / Russian Hill

4

Nob Hill / Russian Hill

Only a few people ventured to live on the knoblike hill that rose up sharply behind the burgeoning city of the 1850s and 1860s. Rincon Hill was the prime residential neighborhood and remained so until Andrew Hallidie invented the cable car, which ran first up Clay Street in 1873 and then up California Street in 1878. Thereafter the hill was called Nob, perhaps because of its shape, but also, allegedly, because the first hill climbers were called "nabobs" (a word that once applied to Europeans who got rich in India). The Big Four, who controlled the all-powerful railroads, the Comstock Bonanza kings, and other assorted millionaires built a stand of mansions redolent of instant wealth that were all leveled in the fire that followed the 1906 earthquake except the brownstone mansion (**12**) that belonged to James C. Flood, and the Fairmont Hotel (**14**) still under construction when the disaster struck. The hill's first owners have been perpetuated in the hotel names (the Mark Hopkins, the Fairmont, and the Stanford Court) and various relics of the pre-fire scene. One such remnant is the impressive Sierra granite wall, contributed by the engineers of the Central Pacific Railroad in the mid-1870s, that surrounds the block on which the mansions of Mark Hopkins and Leland Stanford stood. Elegance did not depart the hilltop with the nabobs after the fire. The hotels, town houses, and Grace Cathedral preside over one of the city's truly urbane areas. Still, the hill is much larger than its illustrious center; the overall population is mixed both ethnically and economically, as the reader who follows this tour will see.

One of the city's most homogeneous stands of apartment houses occupies the downtown slopes of Nob Hill. Since most of them were built within a few years after the 1906 fire, they convey the fashionable streetscape of that time. Although their names may be unfamiliar today, the architects of these buildings were among the post-fire decades' most active practitioners. The viewer will note thematic variations on styles that are difficult to classify. The basic vocabulary of decorative detail is Classical, but there is also a sprinkling of the curvaceous floriate forms associated with Art Nouveau. A few contemporary designs have been pieced into the old fabric. A walk up and down Pine, Bush, and the cross streets in this district will be particularly rewarding to those for whom architectural sightseeing is a typological game.

Russian Hill was so named because some graves allegedly containing the bones of Russian sailors were discovered there. Whether or not any Russians ever set foot on the hill is still in doubt, but the name is secure. Both historically and architecturally this is one of the city's richest areas, worth exploring at leisure. The 1000 block of Vallejo marks the hill's 360-foot summit and a high point of architecture as well. While those who wished to lord it over downtown lived on Nob Hill, a bohemian aristocracy inhabited the more rustic slopes of Russian Hill, where the Livermore family had a farm and orchard and where lived such writers as Ina Coolbrith, Bret Harte, and Charles Warren Stoddard, known collectively as the Golden Gate Trinity. Coolbrith, state poet laureate, lived at Taylor and Vallejo, where there is now a tiny park named for her. Helen Hunt Jackson also lived and died on the hill's eastern brow. Perhaps because it was so sparsely built and because there were wells, a few enclaves escaped the 1906 fire. The largest of these is a woodsy block bounded by Green, Taylor, Broadway, and Jones. Tucked in here and there on its slopes are some very early, nearly invisible houses. Out of respect for the occupants' privacy we list only the visible ones, a considerable treasure trove.

1. 901-23 Pine St.

1. Apartment houses
900-08 Pine St.
1915, Rousseau & Rousseau
901-23 Pine St.
1911, Sitler Bros., builders
930 Pine St.
1911, Rousseau & Rousseau
950 Pine St.
1912, Joseph Cahen
955, Nob Hill Ct.
1974, Beverly Willis & Assoc.
961 Pine St.
1912, James F. Dunn
972-76 Pine St.
1910, John A. Poporato
985-95 Pine St.
1909-11, Cunningham & Politeo

2. Apartment houses
1111 Pine St.
1909, C. O. Smith
1144 Pine St.
1968, Whisler-Patri
1145 Pine St.
1912, Charles J. Rousseau
1155 Pine St.
1913, F. S. Holland
1163 Pine St.
1913, Rousseau & Rousseau

3. Marie Antoinette
Apartments

3. Marie Antoinette Apartments
1909
1201 Pine St.
French flats
1919, James F. Dunn
1250 Pine St.
The entrance composition of the first building is truly eye-catching; the second is one of the half dozen or so often-flamboyant exercises in French Art Nouveau that Dunn built in various parts of the city.

3. French flats

4. Trinity Church
1893, A. Page Brown
1666 Bush St. at Gough St.
A massive fortresslike street; the large square tower is open to the interior.

5. First Church of Christ, Scientist
1915, Edgar Mathews
1700 Franklin St.
Polychromed terra cotta and varicolored brickwork enrich this otherwise staid Lombard-Gothic Revival church. The interior is worth seeing.

6. Royal Theatre
1925, Miller & Pflueger
1529 Polk St.
One of several exotic theaters designed by this firm in the '20s and '30s, but not so exotic as the nearby Alhambra.

7. Cathedral Apartments
1930, Weeks & Day
1201 California St.
This firm designed two of the largest apartment buildings on the top of Nob Hill, as well as two of the major hotels. Although the work is more competent than exciting, its consistency and restraint help knit this otherwise not very coherent assemblage of buildings together.

8. Grace Cathedral
1928-33, 1936-41, Lewis P. Hobart;
1961-1964, Weihe, Frick & Kruse
California St. bet. Taylor and Jones Sts.
Cathedral House
1911-12, Lewis P. Hobart
1055 Taylor St.
Diocesan House
c.1912. Austin Whittlesey
1051 Taylor St.
Cathedral School
1965, Rockrise & Watson
1275 Sacramento St.
This complex of buildings occupies the site of the Charles Crocker mansion. After the mansion was destroyed in 1906, the family gave the property to the Episcopal diocese, which commissioned the English architect George Bodley for a design that was set aside for lack of funds. Lewis P. Hobart's design for the church was constructed in two phases; construction stopped again in

4. Trinity Church

8. Grace Catherral

1941, and the building was finally completed in 1964. Constructed of reinforced concrete for seismic reasons, the exterior surface was bush-hammered to give it a more stonelike quality and is now much admired. On its completion in 1964, replicas of Ghiberti's bronze doors from the Cathedral Baptistry in Florence, Italy, were installed at the new east end. The stained glass in the west end is by the Charles Connick Studios in Boston, while that in the east end is by Gabriel Loire of France and the Willet Studios in Philadelphia. Tours of the interior are given several times a week. Cathedral House was originally designed as the Church Divinity School of the Pacific, but is now used for offices, as is the Diocesan House next door. Both buildings are well scaled to buffer the street edge and help define an entrance court. The new Cathedral School is neatly shoehorned into its restricted site and its rooftop playground is an architectural feature.

10. Morsehead Apartments

9. Masonic Memorial Temple
1958, Albert Roller
1111 California St.
A gleaming white monumental mass that, if it does nothing else, firmly anchors one corner of the hilltop.

10. Huntington Hotel
1924, Weeks & Day
1075 California St.
Nob Hill Center Garage
1956, Anshen & Allen
1045 California St.
Town house
1911, George Schasty
1021 California St.
Morsehead Apartments
1915, Houghton Sawyer
1001 California St.
Though quite different in style and scale, these four buildings go together very well. The hotel epitomizes discretion and taste, and the garage is, for the times, remarkably deferential to its old neighbors. Schasty's town house is a welcome transplant from New York, while Sawyer's apartment house, also reminiscent of Paris, turns the corner gracefully by means of its baroque cornice and balconies.

11. Town houses
1917, Willis Polk
831-49 Mason St.
An urbane row that continues the spirit of good taste and deference to its neighbor buildings.

12. Pacific Union Club (orig. James Flood mansion)
1886, Augustus Laver; 1908-12, Willis Polk/D. H.
Burnham & Co.; 1934, George Kelham
1000 California St.
Huntington Park

12. Pacific Union Club

Because it was built of Connecticut brownstone and not wood, Flood's mansion survived the 1906 fire that devastated the more ostentatious homes of his neighbors. When the gutted shell was to be restored as the new home of the Pacific Union Club, William Bourn, Willis Polk's great patron who was on the building committee, got him the commission. Polk's sensitive remodeling, which consisted of adding wings and altering the top floor, improved the proportions and changed the architectural character from that of a dry, tightly drawn 19th-century town house to a more free and gracious Neoclassical 20th-century manor house. The interiors, accessible only to members, are the quintessential image of a gentleman's club. The bronze fence surrounding the property is the city's finest; Flood allegedly employed one man just to polish it. West of the club is Huntington Park, where stood the David Colton house later purchased by Collis P. Huntington, who gave the land to the city after 1906. This oasis features a replica of the Tartarughe Fountain in Rome minus the tortoises. To sit in the park on a sunny day is to feel on top of the world.

12. Huntington Park

13. Mark Hopkins Hotel
1925, Weeks & Day
999 California St.
The city's most flamboyant Stick Style palace occupied this site before the fire. Built by Mark Hopkins, the most aesthetic of the Big Four, the pinnacled pile was really for his wife, who inherited it when Hopkins died in 1878. In 1893, she gave it to the San Francisco Art Association (now the Art Institute), which occupied it until it burned in 1906 and subsequently sold it to purchase the Institute's present site on Russian Hill. The hotel is in the simplified Gothic Revival style of the 1920s and is notable for its site plan, which incorporates a drive-in entrance court, and for the 1936 rooftop lounge designed by Timothy Pflueger, the Top of the Mark, long the most famous cocktail lounge in town and ancestor of many hoteltop restaurants.

13. Mark Hopkins Hotel

Stanford Court
1911, Creighton Withers; rem. 1972, Curtis & Davis
905 California St.
The California Street Cable Car line was started by Leland Stanford as a tidy investment that could also, if he wished, transport him to his door. After 1906 a luxury apartment house with an inner court replaced his palace. It was converted at great expense to a luxury hotel, but somehow the low-ceilinged court does not convey a sense of the grandeur one anticipates.

14. Fairmont Hotel
1906, Reid Bros.; rest. 1907, Julia Morgan;
tower add. 1962, Mario Gaidano
950 Mason St.

14. Fairmont Hotel

James G. Fair, a Comstock silver king, owned the property, but his daughter, Tessie Fair Oelrichs, built the hotel, which was on the verge of opening when the 1906 disaster struck. Julia Morgan restored and completed the interior, but Dorothy Draper is rumored to have designed the lobby appointments, including the wonderful carpet. The Fairmont and the Pacific Union Club are the two most complementary structures on the hill, the one huge and light, the other compact and dark. Despite the much larger size and Neo-Baroque grandeur of the hotel, its scale does not diminish the importance of the former mansion. Inquire at the hotel desk for the location of the Reid Brothers rendering of the hotel with terraced gardens that were never built. Ride the elevator in Gaidano's 1962 tower for an unforgettable view of the city.

15. Park Lane Apartments

15. Brocklebank Apartments
1926, Weeks & Day
1000 Mason St.
Park Lane Apartments
1924, Edward E. Young
1100 Sacramento St.
The drive-in court of the Brocklebank echoes that of the Mark Hopkins on the other side of the Fairmont and provides a protected circulation zone along this side of the hill. The Moderne-style Park Lane Apartments provide a counterbalancing mass for the Brocklebank.

15. Brocklebank Apts.

16. The Nob Hill
1958
1190 Sacramento St.
An unusually slender apartment tower that preserves the scale of the hilltop.

17. Apartments
1916, Arthur Laib
1230, 1242 Sacramento St.
Parisian influence is very strong in these two finely detailed apartment houses in a particularly choice block. The incongruous tiled roof on No. 1242 was probably a later remodeling.

The Chambord Apartments
1921, James F. Dunn; 1985, rest., Marquis & Assoc.
1298 Sacramento St.
Often remarked on for its kinship with the work of Antonio Gaudi, this apartment building owes its swelling forms to an unusual floor plan in which oval living rooms are stacked in the corners of the building and expressed in the bowed-out balconies.

17. 1230, 1242 Scaramento St.

18. Apartments
1202-06 Leavenworth St.
c.1911, Charles McCall
1201-19 Leavenworth St.
1908-09, James F. Dunn
McCall's design for this brown-shingled apartment house was for years attributed to Julia Morgan because of its resemblance to Morgan's rural-suburban residential buildings in Berkeley. Across the street is an example of Dunn's pre-Francophile style in a Classic Revival apartment house that rambles on and on up the block.

17. Chambord Apts.

19. Coronado Apartments
1911
1590 Sacramento St.
Apartments
1601 Sacramento St.
c.1910
1451 Larkin St.
c.1910

18. 1202-06 Leavenworth St.

20. 1425-29 Clay St.

21. 1329 Clay St.

22. 1135-41 Taylor St.

1560 Larkin St.
1907

Apartment houses listed here and in the following entries were built, with a few exceptions, during the post-fire decade. They have an engaging diversity of style within the two broad and enduring categories of Classical and Medieval: some have a more or less symmetrical composition and use a Classical vocabulary of ornament, and others are composed asymmetrically or picturesquely and use decorative motifs associated with Gothic. Yet there are no hard and fast rules; some designs are a rich stew of both. The last two buildings listed above are good examples of the two stylistic types.

20. Apartments
1425-29 Clay St.
1907, G. H. Osterbeck, builder
1417-27 Clay St.
1909

21. Clayerest Apartments
1912-13, E. L. Marlsbury
1357 Clay St.
House
1908, McCall & Wythe
1329 Clay St.
Clay-Jones Apartments
1929, Albert H. Larsen
1250 Jones St.
Comstock Apartments
1960, Hammarberg & Herman
1333 Jones St.
Apartments
1913, Henry C. Smith
1342 Jones St.
Apartments
1908, W. G. Hind
1350 Jones St.

A diverse group. The first listing, the Clayerest, exemplifies a building type that is found throughout the older neighborhoods and is sometimes called Edwardian to distinguish it from Victorian styles. Its characteristics are rounded bays—-although slanted bays are sometimes used for variety—Classical porticos, and substantial cornices with dentil courses and modillions. The house at 1329 Clay is a good example of Elizabethan Revival style, one of a variety of medieval styles that became popular in the late 19th century and crossed over into the 20th. The thirty years that separate the Clay-Jones from the Comstock reveal significant changes in scale and massing. Though the Comstock is a relatively thin slab, its dehumanized base with auto access and two levels of parking breaks the continuity of the street in ways that the previous generation of giants such as the Clay-Jones did not.

22. Apartments
1908, Bakewell & Brown
1135-41 Taylor St. at Pleasant St.

A restrained shingled block designed as a home and studio for the artist Emil Pissis. Oddly enough, the most formal elevation is up the hill on the side street.

23. 1224-32 Taylor St.

23. Apartments
1224-32 Taylor St.
1914, Austin Whittlesey
1250 Taylor St.
1911, U. E. Evans
1255-57 Taylor St.
1915, Falch & Knoll
Apartments
1230-38 Washington St.
1909, Charles Whittlesey
1240-54 Washington St. (1315 Taylor)
1910, Henry C. Smith

No. 1224-32 is strongly influenced by contemporary Parisian apartment design. Charles Whittlesey favored the Pueblo Revival style, as can be seen in 1240 Washington, which also fronts on Taylor. Next door at No. 1230 is a vigorous example of the Craftsman style.

23. 1255-57 Taylor St.

23. 1240 Washington St.

24. Row of flats
1910, Arthur J. Laib
1314-30 Taylor St.
Clearly a more modest budget dictated this row of Mission Revival flats than Laib's more Parisian apartments.

Hillgate Manor
1923, Henry Gutterson
1360-90 Taylor St.
An agreeable way of planning a moderate-sized apartment building that gives the occupants the amenity of a garden court and the passersby a visual treat. This type of building in the city appears to have been a rare commission for Gutterson—more's the pity.

24. 1314-30 Taylor St.

25. Cable Car Barn and Museum
c.1910
1200 Mason St.
This is the last cable car powerhouse in operation in the world and worth a visit both for the machinery and for the museum collection, which includes the original Clay Street cable car. Hallidie was an English-born inventor and engineer who came to San Francisco during the Gold Rush era and produced the west coast's first wire cable, the first step in the invention of the cable car. Both a building and a plaza are named for him.

27. Talbot-Dutton house

26. Apartments
1929, Albert H. Larsen
1425 Taylor St.
This Neo-Churrigueresque apartment house is almost interchangeable with some in the same style that were built by H. C. Baumann, a competitor in the business of apartment house design.

27. Talbot-Dutton house
1875; add. 1905
1782 Pacific Ave.
This elegant Italianate was a wedding present from a lumber tycoon to his daughter. In 1905, a matching wing was added that created the unusual double-bay facade.

29. Nuestra Señora de Guadalupe

28. Houses
2209 Van Ness Ave.
1901
2256 Van Ness Ave.
1908, Moses Lyon

29. Nuestra Señora de Guadalupe
1906,1912, Shea & Lofquist
908 Broadway
Once the parish church for the city's Latin quarter, this lovely landmark still evokes the Mediterranean world.

30. 1000 block Vallejo St., Russian Hill Pl.
Florence St. and Ina Coolbrith Park

Willis Polk designed the double access ramp in 1914 when the Livermore family commissioned him to design the houses at 1, 3, 5, and 7 Russian Hill Place, built in 1916. The plan of the block is scenographic, with the ramps converging on a central access to the heart of the block, while the flanking side streets, Russian Hill Place and Florence Street, are lined with houses that define a keyhole view and shield the block's interior. Polk's Russian Hill Place houses make two important contributions: on the Jones Street side they form a subtly articulated wall closing off the street and on the upper side they become cottages lining a brick-paved country lane. Polk's use of overscaled Classical detail is particularly effective here. No. 1085 Vallejo by Charles McCall and Nos. 35, 37, and 39 Florence Street by Charles Whittlesey (c.1920) depart from Polk's variations on the Spanish Mediterranean theme. Whittlesey's are Pueblo Revival, but they perform the same functions as Polk's designs in regard to their relationship to the street.

30. 1,3,5,7, Russian Hill Place

30. 35, 37, 39 Florence St.

Until very recently the interior of the block was quite open. The Hermitage condominiums by Esherick Homsey Dodge & Davis, designed with great respect for their famous setting, occupy the sites of two famous brown-shingle houses that were demolished for a fortunately never realized high-rise scheme. Still recalling the early context of the hill are the Marshall houses at 1034 and 1036, two of three gable-roofed, brown-shingled re-minders of New England farmhouses. They were built by a parishioner of Joseph Worcester, pastor of the Sweden-borgian Church, whose rustic cottage once stood at the end of the row. The Livermore house on the back of the lot at 1045 dates from 1865. Willis Polk remodeled it c.1891, and Robert A. M. Stern designed significant additions and alterations in 1990—the entrance is now on Florence. A landmark of the Second Bay Region Tradition is the Polk-Williams house at 1013-19. Willis Polk designed it for his family, which, at the time it was built in 1892, included his father, mother, brother, and wife. The client for this double house was a painter, Mrs. Virgil Williams, whose husband had founded the California Institute of Design. Polk apparently waived the commission in exchange for the eastern frontage of the lot. The shingled facade does not

30. Former Livermore house

30. Hermitage condominiums

30. Polk-Williams house

32. Holy Trinity Russian Orthodox
Cathedral

33. Alhambra Theatre

divide neatly in two parts, but rather suggests a street row in a medieval village. The old saw about the house with the Queen Anne front and the Mary Ann behind fits well here. The back tumbles down the hillside, taking advantage of the slope to add layers of space. Polk's studio was on a lower rear level. The interior of the house is a remarkable sequence of vertically organized spaces.

At the head of the Vallejo Street steps leading down to Mason is Ina Coolbrith Park.

31. Condominiums
1982, Daniel Solomon & Assoc.
15-17 Glover St.
An ingenious use of a narrow site.

32. Holy Trinity Russian Orthodox Cathedral
1909
1520 Green St.
One of the city's many notable wooden vernacular churches, this one replaces an earlier church destroyed in 1906.

33. Alhambra Theatre
1930, Miller & Pflueger
Polk St. bet. Union and Green Sts.
Moorish was but one of several exotic styles used for early movie palaces; this is San Francisco's only example.

34. Apartments
c.1925, H. C. Baumann
1101 Green St.
One of Baumann's several Neo-Churrigueresque apartment blocks with a well-detailed lobby. Fortunate are those who live on the upper floors!

35. Houses
1088 Green St. (former firehouse)
1907
1085 Green St.
1966, Joseph Esherick
1067 Green St. (Feusier Octagon)
1857; add. 1880s
1055 Green St.
1866; rem. 1916, Julia Morgan
1045 Green St.
1880s

1039-43 Green St.
1880s
Except for 1085 this is a rare group of survivors of the 1906 fire; the flats, No. 1039-43, were moved here after the fire. The Feusier Octagon, like the octagonal house occupied by the Colonial Dames, was inspired by Orson Fowler's tract on healthful living, A Home for All. The added Mansard roof made it fashionable in the 1880s.

35. 1067 Green St. (Feusier Otagon)

36. Macondray Lane
A walk down this two-block pedestrian street on the steep north face of Russian Hill should make you want to move right in—unless both your soul and your feet are flat. Macondray Terrace, the 1981 condominiums by Hood Miller Assoc. get high marks for sensitive siting, planning, use of materials, and compatibility with a difficult site.

37. Houses
858, 864, 873 Union St.
1910-12, John A. Poporato
811 Union St.
1912, Charles Fantoni
887 Union St.
1917, Paul DeMartini
901 Union St.
1907, Righetti & Kulh
919, 920 Union St.
1907,1917, John A. Poporato
927, 953, 988 Union St.
1909,1907, John A. Poporato
940 Union St.
1922, Louis Traverso
962 Union St.
1917, Rousseau & Rousseau
1800 block Mason St.
1909-11, Paul J. DeMartini and Louis Traverso
(except Nos. 1834-38, Biglietto & Trevia)

35. 1039-43 Green St.

Italian architect-builders had lucrative practices in this neighborhood after the 1906 fire. These blocks are representative of the kind of multi-unit buildings that were considered simply adequate for the neighborhood population of the time, but today represent priceless investments.

37. 900 block Union St.

38. Southard Place
1981, Daniel Solomon & Assoc.
Southard Pl. and Greenwich Ter.
Another well-designed condominium complex by a leading firm in the field.

39. Fannie Osborne Stevenson house
1900, Willis Polk; later add.
1100 Lombard St.
Additions have made a hodgepodge of this house, but the client, widow of Robert Louis Stevenson, and the architect, a staunch member of San Francisco's Bohemia, validate its claim to importance.

Lombard Street wiggle
Designed in the 1920s as an alternative to the scary grade that drivers encounter on Filbert Street two blocks away, this may be San Francisco's most famous street. On any given day photographers cluster at the top or bottom of the block and fashion models–both humans and automobiles–often appear. The gardens in the median strip are communally owned and cared for.

38. Southard Place

40. House
1938, Gardner Dailey
65 Montclair Ter.
An example of Gardner Dailey's personal adaptation of the European International style.

41. Wright house
1907, Willis Polk
950 Lombard St.

42. Houses
1963, Joseph Esherick & Assoc.
120-22, 126-28 Culebra Ter.
The architect's house plus rental units, neatly tucked into a tight site on a very steep hillside.

39. Fanny Osborne Stevenson house

43. House
1948, John Funk
998 Chestnut St.
The cubistic geometry of this California International Style shows off to advantage on this spectacular site.

44. San Francisco Art Institute
1926, Bakewell & Brown;
add. 1970, Paffard Keatinge Clay
800 Chestnut St.
Two versions of exposed concrete, each highly successful in its own way. The older building is a stripped-down but gracious Mediterranean Revival building cast as a monastery complete with cloister. The contemporary

40. House 65 Montclair Terrace

addition is in Le Corbusian *beton brut* with rooftop elements treated as sculpture and walls articulated with the master's work in mind. Don't miss the Diego Rivera mural.

House
1927, B. F. Wayne
805-07 Chestnut St.
A very sensitive site plan for this house, which combines traditional Mediterranean Revival elements with nontraditional materials such as industrial steel sash windows.

43. 988 Chestnut St.

45. Walters house
1951, Wurster, Bernardi & Emmons
2475 Larkin St.
This large town house is handled with a splendid disregard for formality. Its casual exterior covers an interior of great dignity and spatial interest, organized to take maximum advantage of the view.

46. Houses and apartments
800 Francisco St. (Moderne apartments)
c.1940, James Hjul, engineer
807 Francisco St.
1890s; rem., Joseph Esherick
825 Francisco St.
Before 1854, R. C. Ruskin; rem. several times
864 Francisco St.
1912, John Galen Howard and Mark H. White
888 Francisco St. (Knorr house)
1979, Don Knorr
898 Francisco St. (Patigian house)
1914, Ward & Blohme

44. San Francisco Art Institute

This block has a remarkably varied group of houses ranging from one of the city's oldest at 825, through almost every architectural period and style to Don Knorr's late 1970s contemporary.

47. Houses
c.1926, Winfield Scott Wellington
2423, 2455 Leavenworth St.
Were these houses stuccoed, their cubistic geometry would reveal their modernity. Shingled and weathered, they blend in perfectly with their context.

45. Walters house

Studio
1961, Clark & Beuttler, Charles W. Moore, designer
2508 Leavenworth St.
This studio addition to an older house is ingeniously angled to catch the view and define the entry.

46. 800 Francisco St.

46. 898 Francisco St.

47. Studio

48. Cottage row

49. Terraced houses

48. Cottage row
c.1900, Lucius Solomon, builder
2540-50 Hyde St.
An engaging gable-roofed row.

49. Terraced houses
1850s; rem. 1937, William W. Wurster
757-63, 765 Bay St.
House
1937, William W. Wurster
737 Bay St.
The first group is beautifully sited to step down the hill. All are deceptively simple early Wurster.

50. National Maritime Museum
1939, William Mooser, Sr. & Jr.
680 Beach St. at Polk St.
Looking appropriately like an oceanliner's superstructure, this streamlined Moderne landmark houses historical material on west coast shipping, including a fine collection of models and photographs. The murals are by Hilaire Hyler and Sargent Johnson. Originally designed to serve as a bath house, it was converted to a museum in 1951. A walk out to the end of the curving breakwater that protects Aquatic Park provides a great view back to San Francisco.

51. Ghirardelli Square
1860-1916
Tower Building
1915, William Mooser; rem. 1962-67, Wurster, Bernardi & Emmons
Polk St. to Larkin St., Beach St. to North Point St.
Deservedly one of the great tourist landmarks, this collection of old (and one new) brick buildings originally housed the Ghirardelli Chocolate Company. It was taken over and remodeled into restaurants and shops by developer William Matson Roth as an almost non-profit venture. The fountain is by Ruth Asawa, and the landscaping by Lawrence Halprin.

52. Hyde Street Pier (San Francisco Maritime Historical Monument)
End of Hyde St. at Jefferson St.
Administered by the state, the pier has a fascinating collection of old vessels open for visit.

53. Haslett Warehouse Building (Fromm & Sichel Headquarters)
c.1880; rem. 1973, Wong & Brocchini
N.E. and S.E. cor. Hyde and Beach Sts.
Old and new brickwork at one of the city's busiest corners, terminus of the Hyde Street cable car.

The Cannery
c.1909 ; rem. 1968, Joseph Esherick & Assoc.
2801 Leavenworth St.
An old warehouse was gutted and given a whole new interior structure to house shops and restaurants on three levels with an interior court.

54. North Point public housing
1950, Ernest Born and Henry Gutterson
Bay St. and Columbus Ave.
These now somewhat battered balcony-access apartments reflect International Style housing design of the post-World War II era. A block south and east on Water Street is a row of simple but charming shanties that were built to rehouse people after the 1906 fire.

50. National Maritime Museum

51. Ghirardelli Square

52. Hyde Street Pier

53. Haslett Warehouse

1. Apts. 1600, 1695 Beach
Double houses 1627-29,
1633-37 Beach St.
2. Apt. house 3650 Fillmore
3. Marina Middle School
4. S.F. Gas Light Company
5. Heritage Retirement
Community
6. Fort Mason
Brooks house
Moody house
Haskell house
7. Moderne shops 2240-68
Chestnut St.
8. Crocker Bank
9. Vedanta Society
10. House 2460 Union St.
11. St. Mary the Virgin
Episcopal Church
12. The Octagon
13. Houses 2421, 2423 Green
14. St. Vincent de Paul
15. Leander Sherman house
16. Flats 1950-80 Green St.
17. Golden Gate Valley
Branch Library
18. House 1641 Green St.
19. Apts. 2415 Franklin St.
20. Warren Perry house
21. Casebolt house
22. House 2440 Vallejo St.
23. Apts. 2255-63 Vallejo St.
24. Apts. 1737-57 Vallejo St
Burr house
25. Convent of the Sacred
Heart/Hammond Mansion
Flood Mansion (2nd)
Grant Mansion
26. Mansion 2201 Broadway
Italian Consulate
27. Flood Mansion (1st)
Sara Dix Hamlin School
28. Apts. 2000 Broadway
29. Apts. 1945, 1955
Broadway
30. House row 2414-24 Gough
House 2340 Gough St.
31. Bourn house

32. Apts. 2340 Pacific Ave.
33. Leale house
34. House 2698 Pacific Ave.
House 2600 Pacific Ave.
35. Music & Arts Institute
House 2600 Jackson St.
36. Houses 2415-21 Pierce
37. Calvary Presbyterian
Church
Christian Education
Building
38. Apts. 2411 Webster St.
39. Whittier house
40. Greenlee Terrace Apts.
41. Haas-Lilienthal house
42. Spreckels Mansion
43. Houses 2500 block
Washington St.
44. Houses 2637-73 Clay St.
45. Houses 2200-2300 blocks
Webster St.
46. Presbyterian Medical
Center
Professional Office
Building
47. House 2004 Gough St.
48. Barreda house
49. Georgian Revival house
House 2212 Sacramento
Mansion Hotel
50. House 2151 Sacramento
51. Houses 1911-21
Sacramento St.
52. Selfridge house
53. Houses 2100 block
California St.
54. Temple Sherith Israel
55. Houses 2018-26
California St.
56. Atherton house
House 1976 California
Tobin house
57. Wormser-Coleman house
Lilienthal-Pratt house
Coleman house
Bransten house
58. Mary Ann Crocker
Old Ladies' Home
59. St. Dominic's Church

Pacific Heights / Inner Marina

Pacific Heights / Inner Marina

*T*hough the city annexed Pacific Heights as part of the Western Addition in the early 1850s, it became a neighborhood in its own right by the turn of the century. Before that the hollow north of the ridge was called Golden Gate Valley, an appropriately pastoral name for the vegetable and dairy farms that dotted the landscape. The *Laguna Pequeña* by the bay shore drew the first settlers because of its fresh water supply from springs. Here laundries and dairy farms flourished, the latter so much so that by the 1870s the area was called, as it is today, Cow Hollow. By this time the heights above began to be built up with more pretentious homes whose owners, unable to find space in other fashionable areas of the city, were attracted by the splendid views. They were not pleased, however, by the barnyard aromas from Cow Hollow, so in 1891 the city shut down the dairy industry and assigned prisoners the task of filling the lagoon with sand from the nearby dunes. Even so, Cow Hollow remained a zone of modest residences compared to the more prestigious Pacific Heights.

During the fire that raged for days after the 1906 earthquake, the Army Corps of Engineers dynamited Van Ness Avenue (which runs north-south in a valley) to stop the blaze because it was the first natural break in the terrain. The resulting destruction of the mansions that lined the boulevard prepared the way for the street's transformation from a prime residential area to the commercial strip it has been ever since, for it was here that the retailers found space to relocate their businesses.

Today Pacific Heights is one of the city's most richly varied residential areas, with houses of every size and pretension, and a remarkable collection of churches and temples. Its chief commercial strip, along Union Street, has a variety of shops and restaurants catering largely to the upper-class neighborhood around it, as does the other shopping area along Chestnut in the Marina. Fillmore is the main north-south shopping artery spanning Pacific Heights and the Western Addition. Because of the steepness of the slope down to the north from the ridge, most of the great mansions have spectacular views of the Golden Gate and Marin County. It is wise to plan walking tours in an east-west direction (although there are some steep surprises even here) and to travel north and south in a car with good brakes.

1. 1695 Beach St.

1.Double house 1627-29 Beach St.

5. Heritage Retirement Community

1. Apartment houses
1600 Beach St.
1936, Richard R. Irvine
1695 Beach St.
1931, Richard R. Irvine
Double house
1627-29 Beach St.
1935, S.A. Colton
1633-37 Beach St.
1939, Oliver Rousseau

2. Apartment house
1933, Richard R. Irvine
3650 Fillmore St.

The characteristic building types in the Marina are apartment houses, double houses and flats, and single houses; the dominant styles are the range of Mediterranean Revival modes from Spanish to French, and the Modernistic or Moderne styles, which use the vocabulary of stylized ornament associated with Art Deco. In general, simplified planar forms with ornament restricted to openings and edges, a pastel palette, and a uniform height and scale contribute to the homogeneity of the district. Although the first impression may be one of sameness, there is considerable variation from the bay to Chestnut Street. The district is very walkable.

3. Marina Middle School
1936, George W. Kelham/William P. Day
3500 Fillmore St. at Bay St.

One of the few large-scale public schools built in the Depression; the stylized decorative detail reflects the influence of *Le Style Moderne.*

4. Former San Francisco Gas Light Company
1893
3640 Buchanan St.

This brick Richardsonian block is the lone survivor of a former gasworks. It has a walled garden and a handsome interior space.

5. Heritage Retirement Community
1924-25, Julia Morgan
3400 Laguna St.

Julia Morgan designed a number of buildings for benevolent organizations; they are notable for their logical plans and quiet dignity. The Heritage organization, originally a refuge for homeless Gold Rush children, has an L-plan with a pleasant and protected south-facing garden court.

6. Fort Mason

The Spanish armed Black Point, or *Punta Medanos*, as they called it, with a few guns in 1797. By 1822 only one was left. Although the point was declared a U.S. military reservation in 1850, the Army did not occupy it until the Civil War. In the meantime several houses were built by squatters, the most famous of whom was John C. Fremont, whose house was demolished in 1864 for a Civil War gun battery. Although they have since been altered, three other houses do remain from the pre-Army days. They form an irregular row north from the gate on Bay Street as follows:

8. Fort Mason

Quarters 2, Brooks house, 1855
Quarters 3, Moody house, 1855
Quarters 4, Haskell house, 1855

In 1877 the larger residence just south and east of these was built as the commanding general's house; it was later converted to an officers' mess. The other buildings on the upper level are mostly WPA Mission Revival structures. One of them houses a youth hostel. The fort was used for coast defense batteries until the turn of the century, but its most important function was as port of embarcation for overseas forces from 1912 through the Korean War.

Today the piers on the lower level that served this function have a new life as the Fort Mason Center, home to a variety of cultural activities, including: the Craft and Folk Art Museum, the Museo Italo Americano, the African American Historical and Cultural Society, the Children's Art Center, and the Mexican Museum; as well as the Life On The Water and the Magic Theatres; offices for non-profit organizations such as the Earth Island Institute and the Media Alliance; and the famous vegetarian restaurant, Greens. This portion of the site is accessible from Marina Boulevard. The entire site is now part of the Golden Gate National Seashore and is under the direction of the National Park Service.

7. Moderne commercial group
1933, Frederick Quandt
2240-68 Chestnut St. at Avila St.
A rare row of almost intact Moderne shop fronts.

8. Crocker Bank, Marina branch
1973, Wong & Brocchini
2055 Chestnut St.
A redwood pavilion with a metal tent roof at the east end of the Marina's bustling shopping strip that runs for several blocks along Chestnut Street.

9. Former Headquarters of the Vedanta Society
1905, Joseph A. Leonard
2963 Webster St. at Fillmore St.
The structure makes for a delightful meeting of the mysterious East and the uninhibited West.

9. Vedanta Society

10. House
c.1872; rem. 1892, Mooser & Cuthbertson
2460 Union St.
An Italianate house updated with a Mansard roof to produce an odd piece of eclecticism.

11. St. Mary the Virgin Episcopal Church
1891; rem. 1953, Warren Perry
2301 Union St.
The courtyard fountain is fed by one of the springs that nourished Cow Hollow's early dairies. The informal shingled church also reflects the area's pastoral past. Warren Perry's sympathetic remodeling shifted the entrance from Steiner to Union Street.

10. 2460 Union St.

12. The Octagon/National Society of Colonial Dames
1857; rem. 1953, Warren Perry
2645 Gough St.
Orson Fowler's best selling book, *A Home for All, or The Gravel Wall and Octagonal Mode of Building,* first published in 1849, was the inspiration for about seven octagonal houses in San Francisco. Only two remain, and of the two only this one preserves most of its original appearance despite being moved across the street and remodeled. Now a museum, it is open to the public.

12. The Octagon

13. Two houses
1893, 1895, Ernest Coxhead
2421, 2423 Green St.
The quiet exterior of Coxhead's own house at No. 2421 conceals an ingenious interior, with a long glazed entrance gallery on the west side running from a high-ceilinged

living room on the street to the dining room on the rear garden. The master bedroom on the upper floor has a select view through the corner bay window.

14. St. Vincent de Paul
1916, Shea & Lofquist
Green and Steiner Sts.
The exaggerated scale of the fake half-timbering, the gabled gambrel roofs, and the tower of this huge church make it unusual among the many Roman Catholic churches designed by this firm in the city. It is stylistically related to the smaller-scale San Anselm's in San Anselmo.

15. Leander Sherman house
1879
2156 Green St.
Built by the founder of the city's leading music store, this house with a Mansard roof has a three-story music room where Paderewski, Schumann-Heink, and Lotta Crabtree (a next-door neighbor), among others, performed.

14. St. Vincent de Paul

16. Flats
1875
1950-80 Green St.
This early row of apartments was moved here in 1891. The present front was originally the back.

17. Golden Gate Valley Branch Library
c.1910, Coxhead & Coxhead
Green and Octavia Sts.
This terra-cotta-clad branch library shows Ernest Coxhead in a less inventive format than his other, more free-wheeling works that draw on Classical sources.

18. 1641 Green St.

18. House
1940, William W. Wurster
1641 Green St.
A classic Wurster house that demonstrates that unpretentious design can be assertive.

19. Apartments
1915, James F. Dunn
2415 Franklin St.
One of the most elegant of Dunn's essays in this imported Belle Epoque style.

19. Apts. 2415 Franklin St.

20. Warren Perry house
1925, Warren Perry
2530 Vallejo St.
A quiet shingled house, more academically "eastern" than most local work.

21. Casebolt house
1865-66
2727 Pierce St.
Set back in the center of the block, this great Italianate was once the manor house of Cow Hollow. Henry Casebolt, a Virginia blacksmith who arrived and made his fortune during the Gold Rush era, used salvaged ship timbers for much of his mansion's structure. The white wood exterior was once speckled with dark tones to mimic stone, which, for eastern pioneers, was a classier material.

21. Casebolt house

22. House
1968, John L. Field
2440 Vallejo St.
This house is a contemporary version of the 19th-century slanted-bay town house.

23. Apartment group
1909, Stone & Smith
2255-63 Vallejo St.
The Craftsman style lent itself to picturesque massing and interesting off-street courts.

23. 2255-63 Vallejo St.

24. Apartment group
1920s
1737-57 Vallejo St.
The city's only version of the once-popular Norman farmhouse compound. The court spaces are similar to contemporary Craftsman apartment groups.

Burr house
1875, Edmund M. Wharff; rem. 1941,
William W. Wurster
1772 Vallejo St.

25. Convent of the Sacred Heart /Andrew Hammond Mansion
1905
2252 Broadway

(Second) James L. Flood Mansion
1912, Bliss & Faville
2222 Broadway

25. Flood Mansion (Second)

Joseph D. Grant Mansion
1910, Hiss & Weekes (N.Y.)
2200 Broadway
Over the years this school has acquired three of the city's most imposing houses, of which the Italian Renaissance palazzo by Bliss & Faville is the prize.

26. Mansion
1914, G. Albert Lansburgh
2201 Broadway
Italian Consulate
2151 Broadway
Two more handsome brick mansions. Lansburgh's design is notable for its restraint and its strong geometry.

27. Flood Mansion (First)

27. (First) James L. Flood Mansion
1900-01, Julius E. Krafft
2120 Broadway
Sara Dix Hamlin School
1965, Wurster, Bernardi & Emmons
2129 Vallejo St.
The imposing Mannerist mansion on Broadway is backed up by Wurster, Bernardi & Emmons's simple and straight-forward classroom building below.

28. Apartments
1973, Backen, Arrigoni & Ross
2000 Broadway
Luxury apartments in Brutalist-style concrete.

28. Apts. 2000 Broadway

29. Two apartment buildings
c.1925, H. C. Baumann
1945, 1955 Broadway
Baumann designed so many Churrigueresque apartment buildings all over the city that they have become a distinc-tive part of its architectural image. Two more are up the hill at 2070 and 2090 Pacific. (Note also the Classical details of the house at 1905 Broadway.)

30. House row
1895, George Hinkel
2414-24 Gough St.
House
1904, Howard & White
2340 Gough St.
A characteristic Queen Anne row by a member of a prolific family of late 19th-century builders, and an elegant Spanish Colonial style house show how tastes changed in the period around the turn of the century.

31. Bourn house
1896, Polk & Polk
2550 Webster St.

A compact clinker-brick block with Willis Polk's bold Classical detailing, this was designed for the president of the Spring Valley Water Company for whom Polk also designed two great estates: Filoli, near Woodside, a few miles from the city, and the so-called Empire Cottage at his Empire mine near Grass Valley.

31. Bourn house

32. Apartment building
c.1930
2340 Pacific Ave.

Another fine representative of Art Deco styling.

33. Leale house
c.1853
2475 Pacific Ave.

One of the few remaining early dairy farmhouses, this one had its facade modernized c.1875.

34. House
1904, Sidney B. Newsom & Noble Newsom
2698 Pacific Ave.

The sons and successors to the original Newsoms, who designed often flamboyant High Victorian houses, here follow the turn-of-the-century trend to Classicism.

House
1937, William W. Wurster
2600 Pacific Ave.

34. 2698 Pacific Ave.

35. Music & Arts Institute (former residence)
1894, Willis Polk
2622 Jackson St.

Probably Polk's first major independent commission, this sandstone house has his characteristic rather heavy, spare application of Classical detailing.

House
1897, Ernest Coxhead
2600 Jackson St.

36. Houses
c.1910, Edgar Mathews
2415-21 Pierce St.

35. 2600 Jackson St.

37. Calvary Presbyterian Church
c.1900
Christian Education Building
1979, Robinson, Mills & Williams
Fillmore and Jackson Sts.
Rebuilt using materials from the original church, which
stood on Union Square (demolished c.1898). The recent
school building provides continuity from past to present.

38. Apartment house
c.1915, James F. Dunn
2411 Webster St.
Dunn's Francophilia varied from the tasteful to the extravagant, as demonstrated here.

38. 2411 Webster St.

39. Whittier house
1894-96, E. R. Swain & Newton J. Tharp
2090 Jackson St.
Imported brownstone and a composition that recalls the
early work of McKim, Mead & White contribute to the
eastern look of this rather somber mansion.

40. Greenlee Terrace Apartments
1913, Arthur J. Laib
1925-55 Jackson St.
Laib created a densely packed complex in the picturesque
Mission Revival style.

39. Whittier house

41. Haas-Lilienthal house
1886, Peter R. Schmidt
2007 Franklin St.
One of the great monuments of the city's Victoriana, this
queen of Queen Anne villas is owned by the Foundation for
San Francisco's Architectural Heritage and is open for
tours. (Call 441-3000 for information.) These two families
were among the founders of the city's influential Jewish
community and were related to the owners of the cluster
of houses at California and Franklin streets.

42. Spreckels Mansion
1913, MacDonald & Applegarth
2080 Washington St.
A French palace for French Alma de Bretteville Spreckels,
for whom Applegarth also designed the Palace of the
Legion of Honor in Golden Gate Park.

41. Haas-Lilienthal house

42. Spreckels Mansion

46.Presbyterian Medical Center

47. 2004 Gough St.

43. Houses
Brown-shingled double house
c.1900
2576 Washington St.
Stick Style houses
1887
2527, 2531 Washington St.
Italianate house
1879
2560 Washington St.
This block has a good range of older houses, from the exuberantly painted Queen Anne house at No. 2527, to the handsome dark-shingled double house at No. 2576.

44. Victorian row houses
1875, The Real Estate Assoc., builders
2637-73 Clay St.
A vintage row of Italianate houses from this famous local design-build firm.

45. Italianate row houses
2209-35, 2239-53 Webster St.
1878-79, Henry Hinkel
2244-50, 2315-21 Webster St.
1878-79, The Real Estate Assoc.
This fine row by the oldest of this famous family of five brothers is part of a historic district that extends along Webster from Jackson to Clay. Of the 25 houses included in the district, 12 are by Henry Hinkel and five by the Real Estate Associates, his competitors. Other builders are also represented. Since all the houses were built between 1878 and 1880, the street has a rare period homogeneity.

46. Presbyterian Medical Center
Webster St. to Buchanan St. bet. Sacramento St. and Washington St.
An outgrowth of the old Stanford University Medical School, founded here in the 1880s, whose original buildings have been demolished. This is an example of the problems of scale and circulation brought on by large institutions with heavy parking requirements in a residential area. Skidmore Owings & Merrill did a master plan for the expansion of the hospital after Stanford moved to Palo Alto in the 1960s, and designed two buildings, the Dental School of the University of the Pacific at 2155 Webster Street (1965) and the Research Building at 22 Webster

Street (1963). Stone, Marraccini & Patterson then took over and did the massive new hospital in 1972. One of the most interesting buildings is the old Health Sciences Library at 2395 Sacramento, designed c.1905, which has murals by Arthur Mathews.

Professional Office Building
1986, Kaplan, McLaughlin, Diaz

47. House
1889, T. C. Matthews & Son
2004 Gough St.
A Queen Anne house with plaster reliefs affixed to the facade like patterns appliqued on a Victorian sampler.

48. Barreda house
1880; rem. 1904, Willis Polk
2139-41 Buchanan St.
Fernando Barreda was minister from both Spain and Peru to the Court of St. James and the U.S. This was remodeled by Polk when the architect married Barreda's daughter.

49. 2212 Sacramento St.

49. Georgian Revival house
1903
2245 Sacramento St.

House
1895, A. Page Brown
2212 Sacramento St.
A huge Colonial Revival box including the requisite Palladian window.

Mansion Hotel
1887
2220 Sacramento St.
A house in transition from Queen Anne to Colonial Revival that has suppressed its towers.

50. 2151 Sacramento St.

50. House
1881; rem. c.1910
2151 Sacramento St.
Willis Polk allegedly remodeled this house, which was briefly the home of Arthur Conan Doyle.

51. Five houses
c.1870-1895
1911-21 Sacramento St.
A widely varied group, ranging from Italianate to early Classic Revival, in an area otherwise largely consisting of apartment buildings.

51. 1911-21 Sacramento St.

53. 2129 California St.

54. Temple Sherith Israel

56. Atherton house

52. Selfridge house
c.1878; rem. 1930s, Julia Morgan
2615 California St.
Selfridge was the builder of 2603-13 California as well as this fine Stick Style manslon.

53. Houses
2129 California St.
1882, Samuel & Joseph Cather Newsom
2145-49 California St.
1882, Samuel & Joseph Cather Newsom
2151, 2159 California St.
1880s
2165 California St.
1882, McDougall & Sons
2175-87 California St.
1879
The first two houses by the Newsoms have distinctive decorative detail. Note the leatherlike strap work in the spandrel of No. 2129 and the flat-sawn, cut-out stenciled forms on No. 2145. Nos. 2151 and 2159 have the kind of elegance associated with the Hinkels, while No. 2165 has urns and garlands. An unusually cohesive row on a stretch of California Street rich in late 19th-century houses.

54. Temple Sherith Israel
1905 California and Webster Sts.

55. Houses
1880-90
2018-26 California St.
A striking series—no two alike. No. 2026 was updated after the 1906 fire with curved glass windows in the front bay and the addition of carved panels below the cornice.

56. Atherton house
1881-82, Moore Bros., Charles Tilden, builders
1990 California St.
House
1883, Schmidt & Havens
1976 California St.
Two of California Street's most exuberant Victorians, showing the transitions from Italianate to Stick-Eastlake and Queen Anne. The Atherton house was enlarged and re-styled a decade after it was built (the date 1881 appears over a pair of upper-story windows). The California Street

addition completely changed the orginal house and gave it the scale of a rural Queen Anne villa that appears to be almost bursting out ot its site. In 1923 Charles J. Rousseau, member of an important family of architects, bought the house, which served as home to his heirs for more than 50 years.

Tobin house
1913, Willis Polk
1969 California St.
Half of a Gothic double house Polk designed for the de Young sisters, one of whom moved away from the city and never built her half.

57. Wormser-Coleman house
1876; rem. 1895, Percy & Hamilton
1834 California St.
Lilienthal-Pratt house
1876
1818-20 California St.
Coleman house
1895, W.H. Lillie
1701 Franklin St.
Bransten house
1904, Herman Barth
1735 Franklin St.
This corner announces Pacific Heights as an area of stately mansions as you come from downtown. The families were related, which permitted the last house to be oriented toward a communal south garden. The styles range from full-blown Queen Anne on the corner to Georgian Revival at 1735.

58. Mary Ann Crocker Old Ladies' Home
1890, A. Page Brown
Pine and Pierce Sts.
A Queen Anne/Shingle style building that recalls early McKim, Mead & White, whose office the architect worked in before coming to the west. Originally there were two stories to the structure.

59. St. Dominic's Church
1927, Arnold S. Constable; rest. 1992,
Esherick Homsey Dodge & Davis
Bush and Steiner Sts.
Dry-but-scholarly Gothic, lavishly executed throughout.

57. Wormser-Coleman house

58. Mary Ann Crocker Old Ladies' Home

59. St. Dominic's Church

San Francisco's drive to rise phoenix-like from the ashes coincided happily with the completion of the Panama Canal. The dual triumph was celebrated in 1915 with the splendiferous Panama Pacific International Exposition. The site, located between Black Point and the Presidio, was created by a massive tidal land fill project carried out by the Army Corps of Engineers. The Exposition was the last of the great fairs to be planned and designed in the Beaux-Arts Classical style initiated by the 1893 Columbian Exposition in Chicago.

According to Louis Christian Mullgardt, who wrote the introduction to *The Architecture and Landscape Gardening of the Exposition*, "The arrangement of this Exposition is distinctive because of its Court Composition. Eight Palaces seemingly constitute a single structure, containing five distinct courts or places for large public gatherings, which are open to the sky." The Expo's Architectural Commission was composed of Willis Polk, chairman; Clarence Ward; W.B. Faville; George W. Kelham; Louis C. Mullgardt of San Francisco; McKim, Mead & White; Carrere & Hastings; and Henry Bacon of New York. John McLaren was in charge of landscaping, Karl Bitter and A. Stirling Calder of sculpture, Jules Guerin of color and decoration. There was also a Department of Travertine Texture to supervise the composition of colored surface materials in order to unify the buildings and sculpture. The most spectacular structure was Mullgardt's glittering Tower of Jewels, but the entire complex celebrated the consumption of energy through spectacular night illumination and fireworks displays. The only structure to survive on the site was the beloved Palace of Fine Arts. The Marina—as the greensward bordered by walks and roadways that skirted the bay was called—remains; its name was given to the district as a whole following the demolition of the fairgrounds. What replaced the great stucco palaces of the Expo was a small scale stuccoed Mediterranean village with scenographic charm but no great architectural distinction. The neighborhood was first populated by Italian families.

Although the character of the neighborhood does not change, the area west of Presidio Avenue and north of California Street is known as Presidio Heights, mainly because its northern edge extends along the ridge above the Presidio grounds. Those residents who enjoy the Presidio forest as "borrowed scenery" are fortunate indeed.

1. Palace of Fine Arts
1915 Panama Pacific International Exposition,
Bernard Maybeck
Baker St. at Beach St.

1. Palace of Fine Arts

In 1915 Louis C. Mullgardt, who designed the other showpiece of the PPIE, the Tower of Jewels, described the Palace's design as "a free interpretation of Roman forms and a purely romantic conception, entirely free from obedience to scholastic precedent. Its greatest charm has been established through successful composition; the architectural elements have been arranged into a colossal theme...into which the interwoven planting and the mirror lake have been incorporated in a masterful way." Until 1962 the crumbling stucco original of this beloved relic of the Exposition survived in the melancholy state Maybeck said was the right mood for the fine arts. Then, thanks largely to the generosity and persistence of Walter Johnson, who matched the funds raised by the city, it was restored in concrete. The exhibition building behind the rotunda was given a new life as a home for the Exploratorium, an auditorium, and other cultural activities.

2. St. Francis Yacht Club
1928 Willis Polk; rem. 1978, Marquis Assoc.
The Marina

After this venerable San Francisco institution suffered fire damage in 1976, the interior was redone by Marquis.

3. Double house (Dr. William Schiff house)
1937, Richard Neutra & Otto Winkler
2056-58 Jefferson St.

4. Rosstown town houses

A steel and glass facade with standard industrial window sash. Like the Kahn house on Telegraph Hill, it had almost no influence in the Bay Area.

4. Rosstown town houses
1967, John L. Field
2600 block Union St. near Divisadero St.

A mannered row designed to relate to its older neighbors.

5. House
1890, A.C. Schweinfurth; rem. 1955, John Funk
2516 Union St.

A simplified Colonial Revival house of quiet distinction by an architect who belonged to the group of architects who forged the Bay Area's first regional approach to design.

6. Houses
2517-25 Lyon St.
c.1920

2535-37 Lyon St.
1912, S. G. Holden
2545-47 Lyon St.
1915, William F. Knowles
2601 Lyon St.
c.1920
A Spanish-Mediterranean enclave perched on the Presidio wall. No. 2601 is a handsome terminus for Green Street.

6. 2601 Lyon St.

7. House
1939, William W. Wurster
2633 Green St.
One of Wurster's few overt nods toward what was then the new International style.

8. House
1901, Edgar Mathews
2508 Green St.
A half-timbered Craftsman house, whose mate to the left is almost certainly also by Mathews, a prolific designer of shingled houses and apartments in Pacific Heights.

9. House
1950, Joseph Esherick
2960 Vallejo St.
This shingled house carries on the Cow Hollow tradition of *rus in urbe*. The south court below street level creates an inviting entrance for visitors.

8. 2508 Green St.

10. Houses
c.1905
2727, 2737 Vallejo St.
House
1938 Wurster, Bernardi & Emmons
2795 Vallejo St.
A pair of dark-shingled houses of the First Bay Tradition, and what was originally a dark Wurster, Bernardi & Emmons box. The stairway is indicated to the outside world by a diagonal across the hall window.

11. House
1938, John E. Dinwiddie
2660 Divisadero St.
A lone example in San Francisco of the residential work of this prominent local 1930s Modernist. The canted, boxed window was later imitated by tract builders so often that it became a cliche.

10. Houses 2700 block Vallejo St.

11. 2660 Divisadero St.

12. 2330 Lyon St.

16. 2550 Divisadero St.

12. House
c.1920
2330 Lyon St.
A rambling Mediterranean style house with an arcaded entrance court on the uphill side. In plan, if not in style, this is kin to the post-World War II ranch house.

13. Napthaly house
1913, Willis Polk
2960 Broadway
A delightful pink Mediterranean villa.

14. House
1926, Henry Smith
2901 Broadway
An example of determined Neoclassicism prevailing over almost all odds. Perched on a cliff, this Renaissance palace is approached by a complicated ramp from below.

15. House
1900, Willis Polk
2880 Broadway
A Neoclassical manor house that recalls the London work of the English architect John Nash.

House
1913, Walter Bliss
2898 Broadway
An elaborate Dutch-Colonial manor house that contrasts wonderfully with Polk's pastel palace next door.

16. House
1939, William W. Wurster
2560 Divisadero St.
A simplified Regency-Revival house with well-proportioned massing. Wurster appears to have favored brick for his more traditional designs and wood for the more informal and more personal houses he designed.

House
1990, Esherick Homsey Dodge & Davis
2550 Divisadero St.
House
1966, John L. Field
2512 Broadway
House
c.1930, Paul Williams
2555 Divisadero St.

A rare northern California work by Williams, one of the country's first prominent black architects, who practiced in Los Angeles and exported this narrow bit of Hollywood Regency style to San Francisco.

17. Houses
2 Laurel St.
c.1945; rem. Clark & Beuttler
3377 Pacific Ave.
1908, Julia Morgan
3355 Pacific Ave.
1925, Louis M. Upton
3343 Pacific Ave.
1903, Albert Farr
3333 Pacific Ave.
1903, Albert Farr
3323 Pacific Ave.
1963, Joseph Esherick

18. 3232 Pacific Ave.

Though not a showcase for idiosyncratic design like the next block, the houses in this block quietly affirm the strength of the tradition. No. 2 Laurel and No. 3323 Pacific are respectful modern additions.

18. Houses
3200 Pacific Ave.
1918
3203 Pacific Ave.
c.1890; rem. c.1904, Willis Polk
3232 Pacific Ave.
1902, Ernest Coxhead; rem. 1959, John Funk
3233 Pacific Ave.
1909, Bernard Maybeck

18. 3200 block Pacific Ave.

3234 Pacific Ave.
1902, Ernest Coxhead
3235 Pacific Ave.
c.1910, William F. Knowles
3236-40 Pacific Ave.
c.1910, William F. Knowles
3255 Pacific Ave.
c .1910, Ernest Coxhead; rem. Willis Polk

This steep block is an architectural treasure trove. Nowhere else in the city is there such a harmonious stand of houses from what has been termed the First Bay Tradition, a west coast "Shingle style" that mixes elegance of detail with informality in materials and form—don't miss the back side for real vernacular informality. The designers' names are a roster of the turn-of-the-century group of eastern immigrants who brought forth a first flowering of regional design.

19. 3198 Pacific Ave.

19. House
1912, Ernest Coxhead
3151 Pacific Ave.

The exigencies of hillside sites encouraged a remarkable freedom in plan and massing that, when combined with fine traditional detail as in Coxhead's work, produced houses that were truly original without self-consciously making a great point of it.

House
1892, Samuel Newsom
3198 Pacific Ave.

An outstanding example of the plasticity often achieved by wrapping with shingles the curved and angled forms of houses that mixed various Queen Anne and Colonial Revival style elements.

20. 3095 Pacific Ave.

20. House
1959, Wurster, Bernardi & Emmons
3095 Pacific Ave.

A late Wurster, Bernardi & Emmons boxy design, more mannered than the 1930s work.

House
1953, Joseph Esherick
3074 Pacific Ave.

In his third San Francisco town house Esherick spaced four-by-fours across the facade to express the structural module of the frame. Compare this very restrained structural decoration with the 19th-century designers' elaboration of structural members as surface ornament in the so-called Stick Style houses.

21. 1 Raycliff Terrace

21. Houses
1 Raycliff Ter.
1951, Gardner Dailey
25 Raycliff Ter.
1959, Wurster, Bernardi & Emmons
55 Raycliff Ter.
1957, rem. Germono Milono

75 Raycliff Ter.
1951, Joseph Esherick
2889 Pacific Ave.
1890, Arthur Brown, Jr.
2870 Pacific Ave.
1937, Wurster, Bernardi & Emmons
2830 Pacific Ave.
1910, Albert Farr
2820 Pacific Ave.
1912, Willis Polk & Co.
2810 Pacific Ave.
1910, Albert Farr
2800 Pacific Ave.

21. 2800 Pacific Ave.

1899, Ernest Coxhead
A catalog of two generations of local domestic architecture, Raycliff Terrace is a rare collection of Bay Region Modernism that reveals its evolution over two decades. The other houses provide the traditional context against which Modernism took its stand.

22. House
1940, Michael Goodman
3550 Jackson St.
A self-conscious expression of the International style, which later softened into a more regional interpretation.

22. 3550 Jackson St.

23. Roos house
1909, 1925, Bernard Maybeck
3500 Jackson St.
Maybeck's most lavish city residence, for which he designed all the interior appointments including furniture. The half-timbered English Tudor mode is enlivened by Maybeck's personalized Gothic details in the roof brackets and balcony railing.

24. Frank King house
1917, Bliss & Faville
50 Laurel St.
A huge Georgian Revival mansion fit into a small site.

23. Roos house

25. Double house
c.1900; rem. 1915, Bruce and Robert Porter
21-23 Presidio Ave.

A talented amateur, Bruce Porter, contributed to the First Bay Tradition in architecture, stained glass, and landscape design. His own house, designed for him by his friend Ernest Coxhead, is around the corner at 3234 Pacific Ave.

26. Howard house
1939, Henry T. Howard
2944 Jackson St.
One of the best of the city's few examples of streamlined Moderne from the 1930s.

27. Batten house
1892, Willis Polk
116 Cherry St.
A study in the subtle manipulation of facade elements to create balanced asymmetry.

25. 21-23 Presidio Ave.

28. Koshland Mansion
1902, Frank Van Trees
3800 Washington St.
The *Petit Trianon* transplanted. A comparison with Mendelsohn's Russell house across the street reveals how much the image of the mansion changed in 50 years.

29. Russell house
1952, Eric Mendelsohn
3778 Washington St.
Except for the trace of early Mendelsohn streamlining in the rounded corner bay and porthole windows, this house, well sited in its parklike setting, is a perfect example of the second wave of Bay Area regionalism.

26. Howard house

30. Goldman house
1951, Joseph Esherick
3700 Washington St.
A straightforward wooden box that balances the barnlike informality of vertical siding and double-hung windows with delicate railings and concrete sonotube columns. The L-plan creates an elegant side garden court and processional entranceway that is sheltered from the street.

31. House
1928, Arthur Brown, Jr.
3690 Washington St.

32. House
c.1900, Bliss & Faville
3638 Washington St.

28. Koshland Mansion

Two houses that draw on the Classical vocabulary of forms in different ways. The latter has particularly delicate ornamental detail. Note the variety of stair windows on the side elevation of this house.

33. House
1929, Willis Polk
3450 Washington St.

34. House
1912, Oliver Everett
3340 Washington St.
A lavishly detailed town house in a version of the French Second Empire style that seems *retarditaire* for the date.

30. Goldman house

35. Swedenborgian Church
1894, A. Page Brown
2107 Lyon St.
A beloved landmark of the early Craftsman era, this church brought together the talents of Brown; Bruce Porter, who sketched the original design and did the stained glass; Bernard Maybeck; and A.C. Schweinfurth, who did the drawings in Brown's office.The prime mover behind it all was the Rev. Joseph Worcester, pastor of the church, and friend and patron of the artists and architects who fostered the Bay Area branch of the California Arts and Crafts Movement.The garden provides an appropriate introduction to the church interior, a living room with a roof supported by untrimmed madrone tree trunks and a great brick fireplace. The stained-glass windows by Porter are complemented by landscape paintings by William Keith. The pegged wooden chairs with seats and backs of woven rushes that Maybeck may have designed were credited by Gustav Stickley as the inspiration for Mission furniture. Rarely have nature and architecture been so well married.

31. 3690 Washington St.

Flats
c.1905, Edgar Mathews
2106-10 Lyon St.
An appropriately Craftsman group of flats across from the Swedenborgian Church.

35. Swedenborgian Church

36. Engine Co. 23 Firehouse

37. Shingle apartments

38. 30 Presidio Terrace

36. Engine Company 23 Firehouse (now residence)
1893
3022 Washington St.

This churchlike Victorian firehouse with its hose-tower steeple has become a studio-residence.

37. Shingle apartments
c.1905, Edgar Mathews
2874-76 Washington St.

The multi-dormered roofscape of this shingled apartment helps make this group outstanding.

38. Presidio Terrace
1905, Fernando Nelson, developer

This exclusive development with houses by many prominent architects was the crowning achievement of Nelson's prolific building career. No. 30, which was his own home, occupies the most important site on the left just past the entrance; it was designed by W. R. Yelland in 1930.

9 Presidio Ter.
c.1910, Albert Farr
10 Presidio Ter.
c.1910, Charles Whittlesey
16 Presidio Ter.
1905, Bakewell & Brown
19 Presidio Ter.
c.1910, Charles Whittlesey
20 Presidio Ter.
1910, Lewis P. Hobart
23 Presidio Ter.
c.1910, Julius E. Krafft & Sons
28 Presidio Ter.
1908-09, A. F. Whittlesey
30 Presidio Ter.
1930, W. R. Yelland
32 Presidio Ter.
c.1910, Charles Whittlesey
34 Presidio Ter.
c.1910, George Applegarth
36 Presidio Ter.
1911, Julia Morgan

39. House
c.1903, Sidney B. Newsom & Noble Newsom
166 Arguello Blvd.

The younger Newsoms designed this high, narrow, vaguely Elizabethan house.

40. Houses
250 Locust St.
1945, Wurster, Bernardi & Emmons

301 Locust St.
1954, Wurster, Bernardi & Emmons

41. House
1895, Coxhead & Coxhead
3362 Clay St.

42. House
1897, McDougall & Son
3100 Clay St.
An elaborate towered Queen Anne house in transition to
the Colonial Revival style. Across the street at 3101 Clay is
an apartment house with an amazing cornice.

43. Apartment house
c.1900
2971-73 Clay St.
This Queen Anne apartment house displays some very
impressive Classical ornament.

40. 250 Locust St.

44. Temple Emanu-El
1924-26, Arthur Brown, Jr., John Bakewell, Jr.,
Sylvan Schaittacher; Bruce Porter, int. dec.;
Bernard Maybeck, G. Albert Lansburgh,
Edgar Walter, consultants
N.W. cor. Arguello Blvd. and Lake St.
A monumental Neo-Byzantine Roman temple with a
handsome forecourt. The interior is richly appointed and
well worth visiting. The stained-glass windows, *Fire* and
Water, installed in 1972-73, are by Mark Adams.

44. Temple Emanu-El

45. House
1907, Stone & Smith
3779 Clay St.
A quirky corner-lot house that combines elements of the
Craftsman and the Mission Revival styles.

46. Houses
1942, Wurster, Bernardi & Emmons
250 Locust, 301 Locust, 3655 Clay St.
Three houses that show a range of expressionism from
Modernistic formality at 250 Locust to Bay Region Modern
informality at 301 Locust and 3655 Clay Street.

47. House
1909, Bliss & Faville
3581 Clay St.

48. Pacific Heights town houses
1979, Daniel Solomon & Assoc.
1900 block Lyon St.
Contemporary Shingle style condominiums that fit very well into the old neighborhood.

49. Five cottages
c.1890
1805-17 Baker St.
The small scale streetscape was handled with real grace by Victorian builders.

50. St. John's Presbyterian Church
1905
S.W. corner Arguello Blvd. and Lake St.
A fine brown-shingled church with a country parish look that reflects the Richmond district's state of development in the early 1900s. The building incorporates pews, pulpit furnishings, and the rose window from the original church of c.1870. Other fine stained-glass windows come from a second church of 1888.

50. St. John's Presbyterian Church

51. Jewish Community Center of San Francisco
1932, Arthur Brown Jr./Hyman & Appleton
3200 California St.
Menorah Park Housing for the Elderly
1979, Stoller & Friedman/Segar/McCarthy & Miller
Sacramento and Walnut Sts.
The housing for this well-known cultural institution is linked to the older building through a series of sheltered courtyards that have turned the interior of the block into a well-orchestrated set of protected and inviting spaces.

52. Cottage row

52. Cottage row
1989, Kotas/Pantaleoni
2910 California St.
Fine condominiums imaginatively designed to look like cottages marching up a side street.

53. Jordan Park
1900-1920s, Joseph Leonard, Urban Realty Co.
California St. to Commonwealth Ave., Arguello Blvd. to Geary Blvd.
Leonard, the developer, was also responsible for Ingleside Terrace. The uniformly set-back detached houses compose a suburban streetscape with landscape amenities such as the palm trees on Palm Avenue. The individual houses listed here were chosen both for architectural interest and to present the range of styles in Jordan Park.

53. 12 Jordan Ave.

12 Jordan Ave.
55 Jordan Ave.
57 Jordan Ave.
71 Jordan Ave.
85 Jordan Ave.
20 Palm Ave.
104 Palm Ave.
129 Palm Ave.
30 Euclid Ave.
620 Euclid Ave.

54. Ortman-Schumate house
1870
1901 Scott St.
A great San Francisco Italianate landmark, this freestanding house with elaborate gardens gives a hint of what this part of the city looked like in the 1870s.

54. Ortman-Schumate house

55. Camp Fire Girls Golden Gateway Council
1929, Henry Gutterson
325 Arguello Blvd.
A residentially scaled complex with an inviting forecourt and a rich combination of Arts and Crafts materials.

56. Houses
1883, Charles Hinkel, builder
1703-19 Broderick St.
Although they show a transition from Italianate to Stick style, these seven houses were built at the same time by the ubiquitous Hinkel family.

55. 325 Arguello Blvd.

57. Roosevelt Middle School
1934, Miller & Pflueger
460 Arguello Blvd.
Fine constructivist brickwork reminiscent of Dutch Expressionist buildings of the late 'teens and 1920s. This happens to be one of the city's most distinguished works of public school architecture.

57. Roosevelt Middle School

1. Houses 2200 block Pine
2. Berge house
3. Taylor house
4. Houses 1800 block Pine
   Houses 1700 block Gough
5. Houses 2100 block Bush
   1-6 Cottage Row
6. Stanyan house
7. Houses Laguna St.
8. Pacific Hall
   Green's Eye Hospital
9. Morning Star Church
10. Houses 1700-1800
    block Webster St.
11. Red Cross Building
    Queen Anne Apts.
12. Thomas Payne house
13. 1335, 1337 Sutter St.
14. Regency Theatre
    Galaxy Theatre
15. Nihonmachi Mall
    Kokusai Theatre
    Soko Hardware Co.
16. Century Club
17. Daniel Burnham Court
18. Japanese Cultural and
    Trade Center
19. First Unitarian Church
20. Castle Apts.
    Alhambra Apts.
21. St. Francis Square
22. Laguna Heights
    Laguna-O'Farrell Apts.
23. St. Mary's Cathedral
24. St. Mark's Lutheran Church
25. Apts. 1050 Franklin St.
26. Cadillac Showroom
27. Former Packard Showroom
28. Fillmore Center

29. Family Service Agency
30. St. Paul's Lutheran
    Church and Rectory
    Apts. 951 Eddy St.
31. Stadtmuller house
32. House 807 Franklin St.
33. German Association
34. Opera Plaza
35. McDonald's
36. Federal Office Building
37. Motion picture studio
38. Hastings College of Law
    Law Center
39. William Taylor Hotel and
    Methodist Church
40. Friendship Village
    Former Holy Virgin Russian
    Orthodox Cathedral
41. State Bar Association
    555 Franklin St.
    S.F. Ballet Center
42. The Civic Center
    a. City Hall
    b. Opera House and add.
    c. Veterans Bldg./SFMOMA
    d. State Office Building
    e. S.F. Public Library
    f. Civic Center Auditorium
43. Federal Building
44. U.N. Plaza Building
    U.N. Plaza & fountain
45. New S.F. Public Library
46. Orpheum Theatre
    One Trinity Center
47. Davies Symphony Hall
48. New College of CA
49. High School of Commerce
50. Former Masonic Temple

7

Civic Center / Western Addition I

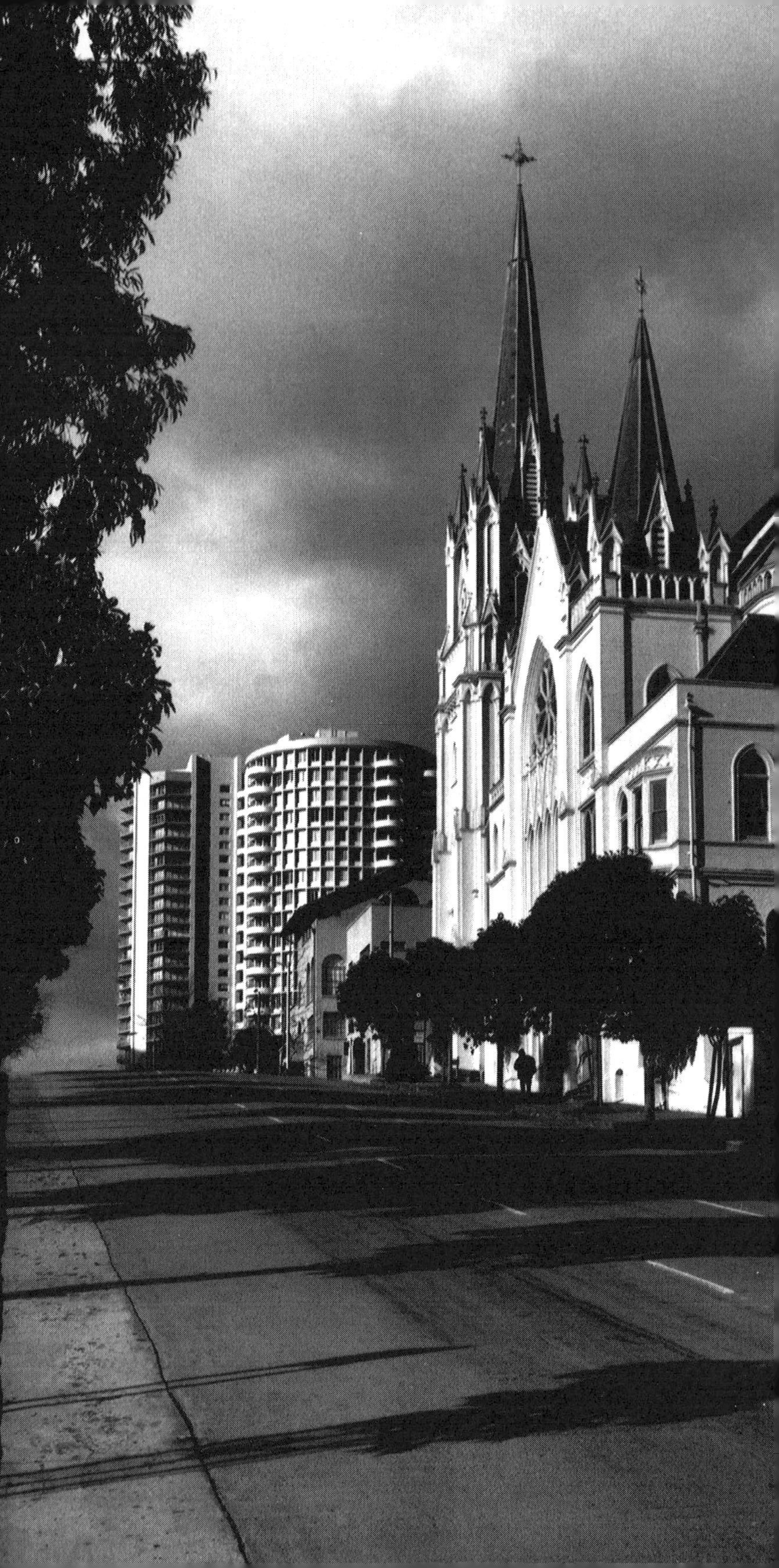

This area of the city has almost more than its share of architectural, social, and historical contrasts. The San Francisco Civic Center, one of the noblest monuments of the turn-of-the-century City Beautiful Movement is, for example, right next to the Tenderloin which, socially speaking, has had its ups and downs and currently is a damper to civic pride. North and west of the Civic Center is the Western Addition, which was one of the early 19th-century streetcar suburbs of the city and also the location of the city's first redevelopment area in which 28 blocks of residential architecture were completely razed in the "urban renewal" of the 1950s.

The Western Addition was the result of the Van Ness Ordinance, ratified in 1858, which extended the city's grid pattern of streets westward and designated the public squares of Jefferson, Alamo, Hamilton, and the so-called Hospital Lot, now part of Duboce Park. Hayes Valley, a 160-acre tract owned by Mayor Tom Hayes, lay between Alamo and Duboce parks on the western edge. Hayes' estate, which burned in 1872, included a pleasure garden with an art gallery and a concert hall; it was a kind of forerunner to the Civic Center.

The great surge of residential development in the Western Addition that accompanied the laying of streetcar lines in the mid-19th century created a homogeneous middle-class suburb that was disrupted after the 1906 earthquake and fire when dislocated downtown populations moved to the area in droves. Jews moved from the South of Market to the Fillmore area, and a smaller number of Japanese established "Little Osaka" nearby between Post and Sutter streets. In the 1960s the Japan Cultural Trade Center was built as the core of the first redevelopment area to make amends for the relocation of the Japanese residents of the area to detention camps. Largely because of protests from preservationists and residents, subsequent redevelopment efforts stressed rehabilitation rather than removal so that the edges of the redevelopment area have merged with the rest of the district.

Known for decades as the Tenderloin, the area east of Van Ness Avenue was rapidly rebuilt after the 1906 fire with hotels and apartment blocks to re-house those who had been burned out and to accommodate the anticipated flood of visitors to the 1915 Panama-Pacific International Exposition, the PPIE. For a while after the expo closed this was a close-to-downtown, medium-to-high density residential area—and like all such districts, it was increasingly vulnerable to decline when the housing stock aged and automobile use increased the attractiveness of the outer suburbs. In the 1980s a number of the small hotels near Union Square were renovated.

Pine Street is the northern boundary of the Western Addition. The Bush-Pine corridor was developed in the 1870s and 1880s when the cable and streetcar lines were extended westward. The small tracts on typically long narrow lots, 25 by 100 feet, were financed by the enterprising building societies of the building and loan associations. Some of the lots were even sold by lottery. When the automobile replaced rail transit to the western neighborhoods, the inner suburbs declined. As the demolition for the Redevelopment Area proceeded in the late 1950s, community protest increased and halted the destruction near Bush, giving a reprieve to buildings in the blocks listed below.

2. Berge house

4. 1800 block Pine St.

5. 2100 block Bush St.

1. Houses
2208, 2210, 2212, 2231 Pine St.
1877, 1875, 1877, 1872
2255 Pine St.
1880, Samuel & Joseph Cather Newsom
2256-58 Pine St.
1880

No. 2231 has a New England farmhouse look that suggests an earlier date than 1872, but the owners may just have wanted a simple house. No. 2255 by the Newsoms resembles their own house at 2129 California Street.

2. Berge house
1884, B.E. Henrickson
1900 Webster St.

An unusual blind-window treatment, doubtless designed to enliven the side elevation while maintaining privacy, distinguishes the side of this elegant town house.

3. Taylor house
1880, Wolfe & Son
1911 Pine St.

4. Houses
1837 Pine St.
1890
1843 Pine St.
1873
1855 Pine St.
1876
1703 Gough St.
1875
1705 Gough St.
1875
1707 Gough St.
1885
1709 Gough St.
1875

5. Houses
2115-25 Bush St.
1874, The Real Estate Assoc., builder
2103-07 Bush St.
1874
2100-02 Bush St.
1883, Samuel & Joseph Cather Newsom
2104 Bush St.
1884, Wolf & Son

1-6 Cottage Row
1882, John Nash, builder

The south side has one of the best flat-front Italianate rows in the city. The whole block gives a good idea of the scale and character of tract development in this streetcar suburb by some of the most active real estate developers and builders of the last quarter of the 19th century.

5. Cottage row

6. Stanyan house
1852
2006 Bush St.

Though it is well known that many prefabricated houses were shipped to San Francisco from New England during the Gold Rush era, this house is one of the very few that has been so identified. The interior has typical mid-century detail but is scaled down, as are the room sizes, to New England proportions. The exterior and interior detail was prefabricated in New England and sent around the Horn. The Stanyans, who owned the house from 1854 to 1974, replaced their large garden with the flats built on speculation in 1892. Then as now open space was vulnerable to real estate pressures.

6. Stanyan house

7. Houses
Odd side, Laguna St.
1889, William Hinkel
Even side, Laguna St.
1877, The Real Estate Assoc.

Two of the most entrepreneurial of the19th-century builder-developers created this harmonious street. The Real Estate Associates's simple Italianate houses give way to fancier variations on the theme a decade or so later, as taste demanded more complicated frills.

8. Pacific Hall (Congregation Ohabai Shalome)
1895, Moses J. Lyon
1881 Bush St.

Hebraic-Victorian-Byzantine. Nearby at 1828-28 Pine Street is a fine row of 1870s houses.

8. Pacific Hall

Green's Eye Hospital
1915, Frederick Meyer
1801 Bush St.

The gigantic eucalyptus trees in front of this reticent Classical building are said to have been planted by Mary Ellen "Mammy" Pleasant, San Francisco's mysterious and sinister madam, and housekeeper to Thomas Bell, whose mansion stood on this site.

8. Green's Eye Hospital

10. 1737 Webster St.

9. Morning Star Church

11. Red Cross Building

9. Morning Star Church
c.1910
1715 Octavia St.

A tasteful design in the Japanese manner with fine terra-cotta tiles and decorative detail.

10. Houses
1717 Webster St.
1875
1737 Webster St.
1885, Samuel & Joseph Cather Newsom

One of the Newsoms's minor masterpieces designed in the 1880s rectilinear style called Stick. The interlocking of ornament with form is particularly masterful. This is one of the houses restored under the auspices of the San Francisco Redevelopment Agency and the Foundation for San Francisco's Architectural Heritage. It was moved here from 773 Turk Street in 1975.

1771 Webster St.
1881
1781-87 Webster St.
1885
1809-11 Webster St.
1880

11. Red Cross Building
1950, Gardner Dailey
1550 Sutter St.

The Americanized International style enlivened by board-form concrete texture and some Bay Region touches such as small-paned windows. There is a pleasant court and an elegant stairway in the lobby.

Queen Anne Apartments
c.1900
1590 Sutter St.

A fine example of its namesake period.

12. Thomas Payne house
c.1880, William Curlett
1409 Sutter St.

A candle-snuffer corner tower distinguishes this Stick Style house from those around it.

13. Commercial buildings
c.1900
1335, 1337 Sutter St.

A couple of quirky Classic Revival facades.

14. Regency Theatre
1911, O'Brien & Werner
1320 Van Ness Ave.

This former Scottish Rite Temple is one of several designed by this firm. The Masons seem to have favored Florentine palaces around the turn of the century. The opulent auditorium is now the movie theater.

Galaxy Theatre
1986, Kaplan, McLaughlin, Diaz
Van Ness Ave. at Sutter St.

15. Nihonmachi Mall
1976, Okamoto & Murata/Van Bourg Nakamura
Buchanan St. bet. Post and Sutter Sts.

Kokusai Theatre
1971, Okamoto & Murata/Van Bourg Nakamura
Post and Buchanan Sts.

Soko Hardware Co.
1980, Van Bourg Nakamura
1698 Post St.

14. Galaxy Theatre

Before renewal Japantown was commercially vital but structurally decrepit. Now it is less interesting but more sound, and is still well worth visiting for food and shops. The mall is well scaled and has fountain sculpture and street furniture designed by Ruth Asawa. The Soko Hardware Company still has an amazing variety of wares, and the architecture of the area succeeds in expressing ethnicity while blending in with the restored 19th-century neighborhood around it.

16. Century Club of California
1905; rem. 1914, Julia Morgan
1335 Franklin St.

18. Japanese Cultural and Trade Center

A chaste Classic Revival facade, originally a private home that for two years after 1906 housed the State Supreme Court of California.

17. Daniel Burnham Court
1989, Wurster, Bernardi & Emmons
Van Ness Ave. and Post St.

18. Japanese Cultural & Trade Center
1968, Minoru Yamasaki/Van Bourg Nakamura
Alas, this complex has none of the excitement of the Japanese architecture of the same time.

19. First Unitarian Church
1887-89, George W. Percy; add. 1967-79,
Callister, Payne & Rosse
1187 Franklin St.

17. Daniel Burnham Court

Thomas Starr King, famous preacher and civic leader of the 1860s, was associated with this congregation; his tomb is in the churchyard. The church is a mixture of Romanesque and Gothic Revival elements. The contemporary concrete and redwood buildings used for offices and the church school form a remarkably harmonious complex that holds its own amidst the asphalt roadways around it.

20. Castle Apartments
c.1920
825 Geary St.
Alhambra Apartments
1914, James F. Dunn
850 Geary St.
Two of the more exotic examples of local apartment house architecture. The ever-inventive Mr. Dunn here turns his hand to Moorish styling.

21. St. Francis Square
1961, Marquis & Stoller
Geary Blvd. bet. Webster and Laguna Sts.
The outstanding social success of Western Addition renewal, this project was sponsored and subsidized by the Longshoremen's Union and had an income ceiling for residents. Its internal garden courts are attractive, and its simple architecture has worn well.

22. Laguna Heights
1963, Claude Oakland
85 Cleary Ct.
Laguna-O'Farrell Apartments
1960, Jones & Emmons
66 Cleary Ct.
Two of the first center city projects by Joseph Eichler, a suburban developer famous for the architectural quality of his various housing tracts.

23. St. Mary's Cathedral
1971, Pietro Belluschi/Pier Luigi Nervi/
McSweeney, Ryan & Lee
Geary Blvd. at Gough St.
In 1960 after this site had been renewed with a supermarket, a fire completely destroyed the old cathedral on Van Ness Avenue. A quickly arranged trade demolished the year-old market, giving the Archdiocese a suitably prominent site in exchange for its Van Ness property. Four 190-foot hyperbolic paraboloids roof the 2,500-seat space over a base that houses various facilities including meeting rooms, a rectory, a convent, and, to the south, a parochial high school. The stained glass is by Gyorgy Kepes, the baldachino by Richard Lippold, and the organ was designed by Father Robert F. Hayburn.

20. Castle Apartments

21. St. Francis Square

23. St. Mary's Cathedral

24. St. Mark's Lutheran Church
1894, Henry Geilfuss
1111 O'Farrell St. bet. Franklin and Gough Sts.

A High Victorian Romanesque-Gothic church in red brick by an architect mostly known for his houses.

25. Moderne apartments
c.1925
1050 Franklin St. at O'Farrell St.

The medium-sized freestanding apartment house, richly ornamented and painted white, is a hardy building type that enriches many of the city's older neighborhoods.

26. Cadillac Showroom
1923, Weeks & Day
1000 Van Ness Ave.

27. Former Packard Showroom

An elegant automobile palace adorned with docile bears, California's official animal.

27. Former Earle C. Anthony Packard Showroom
1927, Bernard Maybeck/Powers & Ahnden
901 Van Ness Ave.

The queen of the Van Ness Avenue automobile palaces, built for one of Maybeck's great clients. The red marble columns have unfortunately been painted white.

28. Fillmore Center
1991, DMJM
Fillmore, Turk, Steiner, and Geary Blvd.

28. Fillmore Center

The latest and most impressive of the projects designed for the Western Addition Redevelopment Area, built about thirty years after the land was cleared, contains over 1,000 apartments and 74,000 square feet of retail space. In the blocks to the east of the Center are a number of smaller housing projects built in the 1970s by various architects.

29. Family Service Agency
1928, Bernard Maybeck
1010 Gough St.

Maybeck's personal stamp on this Mediterranean-style building is evident in the handling of such elements as the spiral fire escape in its slot, the fenestration on the west facade, and the fence motif.

29. Family Service Agency

30. St. Paul's Lutheran Church and Rectory
1894, Julius E. Krafft
Gough and Eddy Sts.
Apartment building
951 Eddy St.

A version of Chartres Cathedral in wood and an unusual apartment house with a sandstone base and an interesting balcony on its front.

30. St. Paul's Church

31. F. C. Stadtmuller house
1880, P. R. Schmidt
819 Eddy St.

A fine Italianate survivor of a time when this was a palm-lined street of single houses.

32. House
c.1875
807 Franklin St.
Another lonely Italianate.

33. German Association
1913, Frederick H. Meyer
601 Polk St.

More or less straight from old Munich, the building even has a rathskeller in the basement.

34. Opera Plaza

34. Opera Plaza
1982, Jorge de Quesada/Warnecke Assoc.
Golden Gate Ave. bet. Franklin St. and Van Ness Ave.
A luxury condominium development that brought high-density housing to the avenue.

35. McDonald's
1980, Whisler-Patri Assoc.
Van Ness and Golden Gate Aves.
The first venture into golden-archless contemporary design for this famous chaln.

35. McDonald's

36. Federal Office Building
1959, Albert F. Roller/Stone, Marraccini & Patterson/John Carl Warnecke
450 Golden Gate Ave.

A lackluster blockbuster expressing all too well the contemporary scale of government.

37. Motion picture studio
1930, Wilbur Peugh
125 Hyde St.

A fine Art Deco facade. See also two former film depots of 1930 by the O'Brien Brothers at 245-51 and 255-59 Hyde. This area was once the center of the city's film industry.

38. Hastings College of Law
1950, Masten & Hurd; add. 1967, Gwathwey,
Sellier & Crosby
198 McAllister St.
Law Center
1980, Skidmore Owings & Merrill
200 McAllister St.
Of this campus of modern buildings, the Law Center by
SOM is the most recent and the most distinguished.

39. William Taylor Hotel & Methodist Church
1929, Miller & Pflueger/Lewis P. Hobart
100-20 McAllister St.

40. Friendship Village
1971, Buckley & Sazevich
Fillmore St. to Webster St., McAllister St. to Fulton St.
Former Holy Virgin Russian Orthodox Cathedral
1880
858-64 Fulton St.
Several 19th-century facades are integrated into an
interesting and varied site plan, with sympathetic shingled
units around interior courts. On the same block is a
several-times-recycled Gothic Revival church taken over
by the Russians in 1930.

41. State Bar Association (two buildings)
1962, Hertzka & Knowles
601 McAllister St.
555 Franklin St.
1979, Hertzka & Knowles
San Francisco Ballet Center
1984, Beverly Willis
Franklin and Fulton Sts.

42. The Civic Center
1915-1981
Franklin St. to McAllister St., Market St. to Hayes St.
The Civic Center is not only a crowning achievement of
City Beautiful Movement design in this country (along with
the Washington Mall and the great turn-of-the-century

37. Motion picture studio

38. Law Center

*40. Former Holy Virgin Russian
Orthodox Cathedral*

117

fairs), but also the only really first-rate example of French High Baroque Revival carried out in detail and with loving care. The City Hall itself is the jewel, inside and out—don't miss the rotunda. Although the other buildings are Depression products they do not show it. The Opera House is modeled on Garnier's Paris Opera and has a circulation system nearly as impressive. The Veterans Building, erected without a clear program, was later occupied on the upper floors by the San Francisco Museum of Modern Art. It recently had its small auditorium restored as a recital hall. The other Civic Center buildings follow the general plan set forth by the advisory commission headed at first by John Galen Howard and later by Bernard Maybeck, and listing among its members Willis Polk, Ernest Coxhead, G. Albert Lansburgh, John Reid, Jr., Frederick H. Meyer, and Arthur Brown, Jr. The Civic Center has had a number of new additions over the years of varying quality; it continues to grow and to increase in vitality.

a. City Hall
1915 (competition 1912), Bakewell & Brown
b. Opera House
1932, Brown & Lansburgh
Opera House addition
1977, Skidmore Owings & Merrill
c. Veterans Building and Herbst Theatre/ San Francisco Museum of Modern Art
1932, Bakewell & Brown;
SFMOMA rem. 1971-72, Robinson & Mills
d. State Office Building
1926, Bliss & Faville
e. San Francisco Public Library
1916 (competition 1915), George Kelham
f. Civic Center Auditorium
1915, John Galen Howard, Fred Meyers & John Reid, Jr.; rem. 1964, Wurster, Bernardi & Emmons and Skidmore Owings & Merrill.

43. Federal Building
1936, Bakewell & Brown
Civic Center

44. United Nations Plaza Building
1980, Whisler-Patri & Assoc.
10 United Nations Plaza

42. Civic Center

44. UN Plaza

46. Orpheum Theatre

United Nations Plaza and fountain
1980, Lawrence Halprin

45. Site of the future Main Public Library
1995, James Ingo Freed/Simon Martin-Vegue Winkelstein Moris
101 Larkin St.

46. Orpheum Theatre
1925, B. Marius Priteca
1192 Market St.
Churrigueresque ornament prodigally applied over a very glassy curtain wall. The city and the owners each thought the other would pay to have the blank back wall finished to match the character of the Civic Center—neither did.

One Trinity Center
1989, Backen Arrigoni & Ross

46. One Trinity Center

47. Davies Symphony Hall
1981, Skidmore Owings & Merrill
S.W. cor. Van Ness Ave. and Grove St.
A thoughtfully done bridge between the French Classicism of the older Civic Center and the architecture of today.

48. New College of California
1932, Willis Polk
42-58 Fell St.

49. Former High School of Commerce
1927, John Reid, Jr.
135 Van Ness Ave.

47. Davies Symphony Hall

50. Former Masonic Temple
1910, Bliss & Faville
25 Van Ness Ave.

50. Former Masonic Temple

1. Amancio Ergina Village
2. Beideman Place
   Beideman Place town houses
3. Holy Cross Parish Hall
4. House 1825 Turk St.
5. House 1671 Golden Gate Ave.
6. Andreozzi house
7. Missionary Temple
   House row, flats and apts.
     1400 block Golden Gate Ave.
   Chateau Tivoli
8. Commercial-residential
   building 1801 McAllister St.
9. Public housing for the
   elderly
10. Apts. 1300 block McAllister
11. Houses 700 block Broderick
12. Houses 1201, 1255 Fulton St.
    Westerfield house
13. House 809-11 Pierce St.
14. Houses 900 block Steiner St.
15. Houses Steiner bet. Hayes
      and Fulton Sts.
    Houses 900 block Grove St.
16. Houses 800 block Fillmore St
17. Brahma Kumaris Meditation
    Center
18. House 1588 Fell St.
    House 301 Lyon St.
    Harkness Hospital
19. Ohloff house

20. Houses 400 block Shrader St.
21. Apts. 1899, 1907 Oak St.
22. House 400 Clayton St.
23. Phelps house
    Mish house
24. House 1901 Page St.
25. House 1777 Page St.
26. Houses 1542-48, 1550 Page
27. Houses 1478-80 Page St.
28. Haight Ashbury Children's
    Center
29. Apts. 1390-92 Page St.
30. Former telephone exchange
31. Houses 500 block Cole St.
32. Flats 1677-81 Haight St.
    1660 Haight St.
33. House row 1214-56 Masonic
34. House row 142-60 Central
35. Apts. 91 Central Ave.
36. Houses 1080, 1081 Haight St.
37. Apts. 135-39 Pierce St.
38. Hermann Garden Cottages
      and minihouses
39. Park View Commons
40. Houses 800 block Ashbury St.
41. Casa Madrona Apts.
42. Houses 1400 block Masonic
43. House 1526 Masonic Ave.
44. Floyd Spreckels Mansion
45. Apts. 555 Buena Vista W.
46. Cottage 439 Roosevelt Way

Alamo Square, the counterpart of Alta Plaza in Pacific Heights, is a focal point of the outer, or westerly part of the Western Addition. A high and empty plaza, it is a true breathing space, surrounded by a prime collection of the kind of late 19th-century houses that fill the blocks that make up the area in a steady progression westward to Golden Gate Park. South of the Panhandle is the once-notorious Haight-Ashbury district, no longer the haunt of flower children as it was in the late 1960s. The district grew up around the intersection of Haight and Ashbury streets.

Before the march of the streetcar suburbs began, these sparsely populated western lands were dairy farms and ranches. William Crocker, one of the so-called Big Four of the Southern Pacific Railroad, owned large tracts of land along with other wealthy citizens. After the Southern Pacific ran the first cable car line out Haight from Market to Stanyan in 1883, the area developed rapidly, partly because of the tourist traffic to Golden Gate Park and the Chutes, a typical 19th-century amusement park. As more streetcar lines were laid both on the flat streets and on the hills, more blocks were built up with houses. The disproportionate number of 1890s Queen Anne-style structures in the district testifies to the peak of the boom. As the area filled, apartment houses and flats were built in the transitional styles from Queen Anne to Colonial, and Classic Revival after the turn of the century. The enormous housing shortage after the 1906 disaster caused the conversion of many of the huge single and two-family houses to multiple-unit buildings. The more transient population brought about a decline in status for the area. As the single-family population got into their automobiles in increasing numbers and moved to the western suburbs, the area completely changed character. At the end of the post-World War II suburban expansion period it housed a mixture of members of the Beat Generation, blacks displaced by urban redevelopment in the nearby Western Addition, and others who had either been long-time residents or who had moved in to take advantage of the low rents. It seems unlikely that the district will return to its original state, but like the other former streetcar suburbs, it is closer to it today than it has been for years.

Because of limits of space it is not possible to present a comprehensive tour of the area here, but it is most walkable and full of possibilities for serendipity.

1. Amancio Ergina Village
1985, Daniel Solomon & Assoc.
Scott, O'Farrell, Pierce and Ellis Sts.
One of the best of the subsidized housing projects built in the Western Addition redevelopment area, this 72-unit cooperative is both contemporary and compatible with the late 19th-century neighborhood around it.

2. Beideman Place
c.1875-95
Eddy St. to O'Farrell St., Scott St. to Divisadero St.
Beideman Place town houses
1989, Daniel Solomon and Assoc./John Goldman
A mixed group of late l9th-century houses, three were moved here in 1976 and offered for sale by the Foundation for San Francisco's Architectural Heritage. The street also has a group of sympathetic contemporary town houses.

1. Amancio Ergina Village

3. Holy Cross Parish Hall
1854
1822 Eddy St.
The city's oldest church, on the exterior, is this simple frame building, formerly St. Patrick's. Originally built on Market Street where the Palace Hotel stands today, it was part of St. Ignatius College, founded by the Jesuits as the city's first institution of higher education. It was moved here in 1873 and remodeled in 1891 as a parish hall.

4. House
1895, Henry W. Cleaveland
1825 Turk St.
A Queen Anne house of noble proportions on a large lot.

7. Chateau Tivoli

5. House
c.1880
1671 Golden Gate Ave.
Moorish was stylish for firehouses and apartment buildings, but this seems to be the only Moorish house around.

6. Andreozzi house
1886, John W. Dooley, contractor
1016 Pierce St.
A representative 1880s house with fine decorative detail.

7. Missionary Temple, house row and apartments
1892-c.1900
1400 block Golden Gate Ave.
Flats
1884, John P. Gaynor
1400 block Golden Gate Ave.
Chateau Tivoli
1892-c.1900, William Armitage
1057 Steiner St.

7. Flats 1400 block Golden Gate Ave.

The Classic Revival building at 1455 resembles a branch library. Next to it are some amazing c.1890 castellated Queen Anne apartment houses and across the street there is a row of speculative flats built in 1884 for $30,000.

8. Commercial-residential building
c.1905
1801 McAllister St.
A tastefully refurbished example of a once standard building type that affords what Jane Jacobs calls "eyes on the street." Down McAllister at No. 1833 and around the corner at Nos. 623-29 Baker Street are some of the finest Queen Anne cottages in the city.

9. Public housing for the elderly
1974, Marquis & Stoller
1715-17 McAllister St.
A successful design, thoughtfully sited, with pleasant public areas for the residents to enjoy.

9. Public housing for the elderly

10. Apartments
c.1900
1300 block of McAllister St.
A splendid row of late chateauesque Queen Anne flats. Across the street at No. 1347 is one of James F. Dunn's elegant Parisian Belle Epoque designs. One wishes Mr. Dunn had had a block to himself somewhere. In any case, this is worth seeing for its complexity and contradiction.

11. Houses
1895, Cranston & Keenan, contractors
700-18, 701-11 Broderick St.
There is nothing like the Queen Anne style for bringing plasticity and rhythm to a streetscape. Plaster decorative motifs like those on 707 and 714 could be ordered by the piece from various catalogs of architectural decoration.

10. 1347 McAllister St.

12. Houses
1255 Fulton St.
c.1895
More Queen Anne to delight the eye of the visitor.
1201 Fulton St.
c.1895, Edgar Mathews
A cottage inspired by the English Arts and Crafts Movement, which drew inspiration from medieval building types like the Cotswold cottage.

Westerfield house
1889, Henry Geilfuss
1198 Fulton St.
Geilfuss's style is particularly marked by a linear or modular organization of the elevations emphasized by

12. Westerfield house

vertical decorative wood strips. This so-called San Francisco Stick or Strip style is a variation on the eastern style. Noted architectural historian Vincent Scully defined Stick as a more direct but complicated expression of the hidden structural frame as exterior decoration.

12. 1201 Fulton St.

13. House
1894, A. J. Barnett
809-11 Pierce St.
And another beautiful Queen Anne house.

14. Houses
910, 915, 921 Steiner St.
c.1895, Martens & Coffey
908 Steiner St.
1888
This was one of the first blocks in the area to be refurbished. In 1967 No. 908 became the first and most famous of a wave of super-colorful paint jobs. Since then taste has quieted down.

15. Houses
1890s
Steiner St. bet. Hayes and Fulton Sts.,
and 900 block Grove St.
A rich and varied stand of houses, some built on speculation and other designed for affluent clients. Nos. 710-20 Steiner (1894-95), developed by Matthew Kavanaugh, are among the city's most published "painted ladies." No. 940 Grove, on the corner of Steiner (1895, Pissis & Moore), had an addition in 1971 by Beebe & Hersey. No. 814 Steiner dates from 1895, and No. 850, by T. Patterson Ross, dates from 1899. The Koster mansion at No. 926 Grove (1897) is an imposlng early Classic Revival design. No. 975 Grove sports a California golden bear on the chimney, while No. 957 (1886) was designed by Samuel and Joseph Cather Newsom and cost all of $5,000.

15. 710-720 Steiner St.

16. Houses
1895, Martens & Coffey
820, 833-35 Fillmore St.
More examples of late Queen Anne exuberance.

17. Brahma Kumaris Meditation Center
c.1891
401 Baker St.
This former house is an unusually large Queen Anne with two towers and a notable profusion of plaster ornament.

*17. Brahma Kumaris
Meditation Center*

18. House
c.1895
1588 Fell St.
House
c.1895, William Curlett
301 Lyon St.
These two Queen Anne style houses are typical of the scale of residences in this prime location on the panhandle to Golden Gate Park. The Panhandle, as it was officially called, was landscaped in the 1870s under the park administration of William Hammond Hall. The eucalyptus trees are the park's oldest; they shaded a curving drive that was crowded with the carriages of the wealthy on Sundays. The park was private at first and fenced. The pretentious houses that lined the one-by-eight-block park are the measure of the streets' former status.

Harkness Hospital
c.1905; rehab., 1982, Lanier Sherrill Morrison
Baker and Fell Sts.
A fine Classic Revival building converted to 185 units of housing for the city's elderly.

18. 301 Lyon St.

19. Ohloff house
1891, Charles I. Havens
601 Steiner St.
Another fine Queen Anne house owned by the Episcopal Diocese of San Francisco.

20. Houses
c.1890
411-15, 426 Shrader St.
The first house dates from 1890 and was built by Cornelius Murphy; the second is a particularly fine work by Samuel and Joseph C. Newsom. It shows the influence of C.F.A. Voysey and other architects of the the the so-called English Domestic Revival Movement, which drew on medieval vernacular buildings and used such quaint detail as the rough-cast plasterwork in the gable ends that incorporates pouchlike swallows' nests.

20. 400 block Shrader St.

21. Apartments
c.1895
1899, 1907 Oak St.
A matching pair of beautiful apartment buildings.

22. House
1895, Coxhead & Coxhead
400 Clayton St.
Ernest Coxhead's manipulation of Classical ornament was so personal as to defy classification. He delighted in overscaling and intertwining traditional motifs and imposing them on plain, boxlike forms.

22. 400 Clayton St.

23. Phelps house
1850s; rest. 1976, The Preservation Group
1111 Oak St.
Mish house
1885, McDougall & Son
1153 Oak St.

23. Phelps house

The Abner Phelps house was long thought to have been prefabricated and shipped from New Orleans, but in the course of restoration it was found to be of local construction. Originally a farmhouse and probably built from a carpenter's plan book, it was moved more than once, ending up in the middle of this block, where for years it was invisible from the street. Now turned to face Oak Street and given a front yard, the house can be appreciated for its early Gothic Revival style, unique in the city. The Mish house next door is a grand Stick Style town house, also nicely restored in 1976 as part of this small office park called Phelps Place.

24. 1901 Page St.

24. House
1896, Edward J. Vogel
1901 Page St.

A transitional style, called Queen Anne because of its finely scaled plaster decorative detail, and Colonial Revival for its Georgian form. Novelist Kathleen Norris once lived here.

25. House
c.1890, Cranston & Keenan
1777 Page St.

These designers spiced up their Queen Anne houses with unusual plaster ornament such as the owls used here.

26.1550 Page St.

26. Houses
1890s
1542-48, 1550 Page St.

The first houses (1891) are by Cranston & Keenan; the house at No. 1550 is either by them or by the Newsoms, and is very handsome in either case.

27. Houses
1899, Newsom & Myer
1478-80 Page St.

The Queen Anne style tamed as it merged with Colonial Revival at the century's end.

28. Haight Ashbury Children's Center
1906
1101 Masonic Ave.

A substantial Classic Revival house, typical of the time period and architectural type.

27. 1478-80 Page St.

29. Apartments
c.1900
1390-92 Page St.
Craftsman style apartment houses that look like the work of Edgar Mathews, but are not identified as such.

30. Former telephone exchange
1890
865 Page St.
San Francisco's earliest known example of the Mission Revival building style.

29. 1390-92 Page St.

31. Houses
c.1890, Cranston & Keenan
500-06, 508-16 Cole St.
The first house is an interesting switch in scale of the usual components of the Queen Anne house: a small tower is squeezed between two large gables. Typical of most, they were clearly trying to get their money's worth out of this large corner lot.

32. Flats
c.1910, James F. Dunn
1677-81 Haight St.
Parisian style flats.

31. 500 block Cole St.

Commercial building
1907
1660 Haight St.
A rare Art Nouveau storefront; there is one other at 225 Frederick Street, designed by August Nordin (1912), which is not so dramatic as this.

33. House row
1896-97, Cranston & Keenan
1214-56 Masonic Ave.
Another wonderful row of Queen Anne houses—note especially No. 1226—by these contractors, who were particularly active in the area at this time.

32. 1660 Haight St.

34. House row
1899, Daniel Einstein
142-60 Central Ave.
The towers have been fused with the bays so that the houses look as though they were wearing helmets.

35. Apartments
1904, James F. Dunn
91 Central Ave.
An extraordinary Classic Revival facade embellished with wonderful plaster heads.

34. 142-60 Central Ave.

35. 91 Central Ave.

38. Hermann Garden Cottages

39. Park View Commons

36. House
1896, Fred P. Rabin
1080 Haight St.
House
1894, John J. Clark
1081 Haight St.
The Haight is introduced appropriately at this edge of the park by towered Queen Anne houses, perhaps the most typical—and certainly the most spectacular—building type in the area. In the next block is the Third Church of Christ, Scientist, 1918, by Edgar Mathews, very like the one at California and Franklin streets.

37. Apartments
c.1907, Charles J. Rousseau
135-39 Pierce St.
Combination Mission Revival and Art Nouveau.

38. Hermann Garden Cottages and minihouses
1983-85, Donald MacDonald & Assoc.
279-89, 380-84, 388-398 Hermann St.
498 Duboce St.
San Francisco has been having a cottage revival produced mostly by one architect, Donald MacDonald, who believes passionately that this house type offers the best solution to the problem of affordable housing in the Bay Area. Although these minihouses contain only about 600 square feet, they have complex spaces such as loft bedrooms and high ceilings that add a feeling of spaciousness.

39. Park View Commons
1990, David Baker Assoc.
Frederick and Willard Sts.
An exemplary development designed to integrate 114 units of affordable housing into the older fabric of the Haight-Ashbury district using three-story buildings containing both flats and two-story houses.

40. Houses
1908-12
806, 821-25, 857-61, 880 Ashbury St.
A wonderful potpourri of early 20th-century styles: No. 806 is a squeezed Classic Revival villa; Nos. 821-25 show French influence; No. 833 (1908), by Beasley & Beasley, is planned around a pleasant inner court; No. 857-61 is Elizabethan Revival enriched with plaster male faces; No. 880 (1908), by A. A. Cantin, is vintage Mission Revival. Mixed in are Colonial Revivals and other styles that defy description or easy categorization.

41. Casa Madrona Apartments
c.1920
110-16 Frederick St.
An unexpected oasis of Spanish Colonial Revival style apartments with a pleasant courtyard. Just down the block at 130 Frederick is an apartment block of 1919 by A.H. Larsen, who did the much larger Clay-Jones Apartments on Nob Hill. And at No. 191 Frederick is the Crossways, a vaguely Mediterranean apartment block.

42. Houses
c.1900
1430, 1450, 1482 Masonic Ave.
Three remarkable houses in the same block. No. 1450 (1891) is by A. J. Barnett; No. 1482 is an unusual shingled Queen Anne with a corner dome.

40. 800 block Ashbury St.

43. House
1910, Bernard Maybeck
1526 Masonic Ave.
A subtle composition in staggered roof planes and voids where the balcony and entrance stair occur. Maybeck's deft touch in a modest shingled house.

44. Floyd Spreckels Mansion
1897-98, Edward J. Vogel
737 Buena Vista Ave. West
A more imposing Queen Anne-Colonial Revival house than Vogel's other work in the neighborhood, but also with literary associations: both Ambrose Bierce and Jack London stayed here. Up the hill at No. 595-97 Buena Vista West is a pair of flats (c.1950) by Henry Hill, one of the post-World War II generation of Modern architects.

41. Casa Madrona Apartments

45. Apartments
c.1925, H. C. Baumann
555 Buena Vista Ave. West
One of Baumann's many neo-Churrigueresque apartment blocks to be found in the city.

46. Cottage
c.1910
439 Roosevelt Way
Anchored to the shelf of the hill by a grand porch with Corinthian columns, this house is larger than it appears because it steps down the hill behind.

43. 1526 Masonic Ave.

9
West Mission

1. Zen Center
   Dietle house
   Houses 273, 287 Page St.
   House 251 Laguna St.
   House 395 Haight St.
2. Nightingale house
   Apt. house 201 Waller St.
3. St. Francis Hospital
4. St. Francis Lutheran (St. Angsar) Church
5. California Volunteers' Memorial.
6. House 102 Guerrero St.
7. Baha'i Center
8. Levi Strauss Factory & Playground
9. Juvenile Courts & Detention Home
   S.F. Social Services Building
10. St. Nicholas Russian Orthodox Cathedral (former St. Luke's German Evangelical Church)
11. Church Street Terrace
12. Tanforan cottages
13. Valencia Gardens
14. St. John the Evangelist Episcopal Church
15. Armory
16. Everett Middle School
17. Mission San Francisco de Asis (Mission Dolores) Mission Dolores Basilica
18. Former Notre Dame School St.Mark's Lutheran Church
19. Duggans Funeral Service
20. Mission Plaza
21. Shop and flats 4200 17th St.

22. Apts. 4600 18th St.
23. Nobby Clarke's Folly
24. Castro Condominiums
25. Commercial building 4248 18th St.
26. Castro Theatre
27. Corner houses 437, 451 Noe
28. Mission High School Houses 3874 18th St.
29. Mission Neighborhood Center
30. Flats 96, 98 Cumberland St. Ascension Lutheran (Mission Park Congregational) Church
31. Russian Orthodox Convent of Our Lady of Vladimir
32. El Capitan Theatre
33. Houses 4100 block 20th St.
34. Moderne apts. 741 Noe St.
35. House 3851 20th St.
36. House 3755 20th St.
37. House 827 Guerrero St.
38. Liberty St. houses
39. Houses 700 block Castro St.
40. House 4015 21st St.
41. House 3833 21st St.
42. Casa Ciele House 3616 21st St.
43. Edison School
44. House 68 Fair Oaks St.
45. Hill St. houses
46. Firehouse No. 44
47. Houses 2-6, 22-24 Vicksburg
48. Bank building
49. St. John's Lutheran Church
50. House 160 Vicksburg St.
51. House row 1000 block Dolores St.
52. House 200 Fair Oaks St.
53. Collegio de la Mission (former S. Gompers High School)
54. Houses 703-09, 731-65 Capp
55. Horace Mann Middle School Mission Branch Library Houses 3300 block 23rd St.

9

West Mission

The Mission district, one of the city's largest, has two fairly distinct sections. Although the eastern part (covered in section 10) has always mixed industrial and residential uses—and originally large farms—the inner or western Mission grew in a more urban and residential way as a streetcar suburb. The mission itself, founded in 1776, was well sited on the banks of the Laguna de Manatial, which roughly covered the city blocks now bounded by 15th, Guerrero, 23rd, and Harrison streets. The lake was fed by the Arroyo de Nuestra Señora de los Dolores. In time the mission acquired the name of the stream. The wisdom of the Franciscan padres, who founded the mission in the most benign part of what they regarded as a generally bleak and unfriendly peninsula, was ignored by the early Yankee settlers, who located their buildings by the cold and foggy bay because their ties were to trade, not agriculture. Although the mission's long decline following the Secularization Act of 1834 freed a great deal of land, the area was so remote from the new city center that it preserved its pastoral quality until the streetcar era began in the 1860s. Mission Street, originally the plank road that linked the mission with downtown, served as the main development channel. Once the streetcars began to run, the pleasure seekers discovered the balmy climate. Roadhouses and an elaborate entertainment park called Woodward Gardens at Mission and Duboce responded to their needs. From about 1870 to the early 1900s, the area filled up with a rich variety of single- and multi-family dwellings, many of which survive. Several small hills add variety to the relatively flat terrain. Dolores Park is a welcome green open space stretched along Dolores Street by John McLaren's march of palms, planted in the median strip after the fire in preparation for the 1915 Panama-Pacific Internaitonal Exposition. Mission Street itself is one of the most colorful and lively of the city's major neighborhood shopping streets. Although it is slowly showing signs of gentrification, it is distinctly multinational Latin and wonderfully untidy—so far.

Noe Valley, named for a tract laid out in the 1850s by José Noe, extends roughly west of Sanchez Street to Douglass and from Market to about 30th Street. The neighborhood has two thriving shopping streets, 18th and 24th, on either side of the hill that rises up in the center. Of all the South of Market districts, this one gentrified most rapidly during the 1970s. Not only is it the heart of the city's internationally known gay community, but it is also home to a mixed professional and working-class population that has contributed to the neighborhood identity.

1. 251 Laguna St.

1. 273 and 287 Page St.

2. Nightingale house

1. Zen Center
1922, Julia Morgan
300 Page St.
Dietle house
1888, Henry Geilfuss
294 Page St.
Houses
273 and 287 Page St.
c.1875
251 Laguna St.
c.1885
395 Haight St.
c.1885
This cluster is well worth seeing; it offers one of Julia
Morgan's most gracious small institutional buildings,
originally designed as the Emanuel Sisterhood; a noble
Stick Style mansion by Geilfuss; and a varied group of
other Victorian structures.

2. Nightingale house
1882
201 Buchanan St.
Apartment house
201 Waller St.
A sprightly corner-bayed Stick Style cottage—perfect for a
witch with a small family. Across the street at 201 Waller
is a fine Mediterranean Revival apartment house.

3. St. Francis Hospital
1970, Stone, Marraccini & Patterson
Castro St. and Duboce Ave.

4. St. Francis Lutheran (St. Angsar) Church
1905-07
152 Church St.
This stern Gothic church built for a Danish congregation.

5. California Volunteers' Memorial
1903, Douglas Tilden, sculptor; base, Willis Polk
Dolores St. at Market St.
A superior equestrian statue by the city's greatest outdoor
sculptor, this is perfectly placed at the head of Dolores's
stately row of palms, although the surrounding buildings
don't give it much help. Gilbert Stanley Underwood's
mighty fortress for the U.S. Mint (1937) destroyed the
scale of this important intersection.

6. House
1873, Henry Geilfuss; rest. 1980, Roy Killeen
102 Guerrero St.
One of Geilfuss's most refined facades. The slender
colonnettes that divide the windows are unusual.

7. Baha'i Center
1932, Harold Stoner
170 Valencia St.
This remarkable facade is tucked under the curve of the
freeway. It was designed for the Woodmen of the World.

8. Levi Strauss Factory & Playground
1906; rest. 1970, Howard Friedman
250 Valencia St.
The starting place for all those blue jeans.

9. Juvenile Courts & Detention Home
1914, Louis Christian Mullgardt
San Francisco Social Services Building
1980, Garo Dorian
150 Otis St.
A high-rise version of the bungalows that Mullgardt
designed in the East Bay; the wall articulation was well
ahead of its time. The monolithic mass of the new welfare
building is, alas, a fitting expression for the bureaucracy. It
is ironic that, architecturally at least, the newer structure
has made the older one seem more humane.

10. St. Nicholas Russian Orthodox Cathedral (former St.Luke's German Evangelical Church)
c.1903
2005 15th St.
A Carpenter Gothic church converted to orthodoxy by the
addition of a cocktail-onion dome on its spire.

11. Church Street Terrace
1981, Stephen Allen Roake
350-60 Church St.

12. Tanforan cottages
c.1853
214, 220 Dolores St.
Two very early small cottages, one with a carriage house
behind, preserve the look of the early Mission district.

13. Valencia Gardens
1943, William W. Wurster & Harry Thomsen;
sculptor, Beniamino Bufano
15th, Valencia, and Guerrero Sts.

5. California Volunteers' Memorial

10. St. Nicholas Russian Orthodox Church

11. Church Street Terrace

One of the real landmarks of public housing from the days when that was far from a derogatory term; this simple group has had its ups and downs. Across the street at 224-26 Guerrero Street is the 1906 Sheet Metal Workers Hall, now converted to an artist's studio.

14. St. John the Evangelist Episcopal Church
1909
1661 15th St.
English country-parish Gothic done in shingles.

15. Armory
1909, Woollett & Woollett
14th and Mission Sts.
A clinker-brick bastion.

17. Mission Dolores

16. Everett Middle School
1925, John Reid, Jr.
Church St. bet. 16th and 17th Sts.
Although the design has some elements of the Mission Revival style, it also speaks strongly of the Moorish-Byzantine mode. The lavishness of the decorative detail shows how important urban public schools once were as neighborhood cultural institutions.

17. Mission San Francisco de Asis (Mission Dolores)
1782; rest. 1918, Willis Polk
Mission Dolores Basilica
1913
16th and Dolores Sts.
These two make an eloquent pair. With its powerfully crude, stumpy columns marching up and down the gable, the humble mission and the overwhelming Mission style basilica next door bespeak altogether different institutions. The interior of the mission should be seen, but that of the basilica is disappointing. At the rear the peaceful, time-worn cemetery with its lush vegetation blurs the harsh existence of the original mission population: 5,000 Indians were buried here. The original cemetery extended beyond what is now Dolores St.

18. Former Notre Dame School

18. Former Notre Dame School
1907
347 Dolores St.
This graceful building, which housed the city's first girls' school, has a composite style that may be the result of the rebuilding of an already modified older structure. Its scale is complementary to the old mission.

St. Mark's Lutheran Church
1901
3281 16th St.
A late Carpenter Gothic church.

19. Duggans Funeral Service
c.1900, Ernest Coxhead
3434 17th St.
Coxhead previewing the Postmodernists in this interesting distortion of Classical elements.

20. Mission Plaza
1981, Jorge de Quesada
Capp and Mission Sts.
A successful and contextual mixed-use residential and commercial development.

21. 4200 17th St.

21. Shop and flats
c.1890
4200 17th St.
The late 19th-century combination of commercial space and flats is one of the city's great vernacular building types. This is one of the best, with its residential box soaring off the hillside above an almost transparent base.

22. Apartment house
c.1900
4600 18th St.
An elegant late Queen Anne.

23. Nobby Clarke's Folly

23. Nobby Clarke's Folly
1892
250 Douglass St.
This imposing pile was built with the earnings of 30 years' service as clerk to the chief of police in the Vigilantes era. It originally had 17 more acres.

24. Castro Condominiums
1982, Dan Solomon and Assoc.
2425 Market St.
A skeletal entrance on Market St. marks this gleaming cluster of stepped boxes arranged on an awkward site.

24. Castro Condominiums

25. Commercial building
c.1900
4248 18th St.
An outstanding Victorian shop front.

26. Castro Theatre
1923, Timothy Pflueger
429 Castro St.
According to Steven Levin, movie theater historian, the Castro was the flagship of the extensive operations of the Nasser family, a pioneer motion picture family who built their first theaters in Noe Valley. For their young architect, Timothy Pflueger, this was the first of the seven movie palaces his firm was to design. Although it seats 1,800, it was not the largest neighborhood theater. Still, it was one of the most ornate. The Spanish Baroque style of the facade is carried out on the interior, but the auditorium is an extravaganza all by itself, with its ceiling cast in plaster to resemble a tent with swags, ropes, and tassels.

26. Castro Theatre

27. Corner houses
c.1890
437, 451 Noe St.
Two Stick Style towered corner houses show how to do streetscape on a domestic scale. Across the street, Nos. 460-76 were built by Fernando Nelson, local resident and prolific and well-known city builder.

28. Mission High School
1926, John Reid, Jr.; rehab. 1972-78, J. Martin Rosse
18th and Dolores Sts.
A Mission district landmark that competes in prominence with the Mission Dolores Basilica. The polychromed tile domes and expert Spanish Baroque detailing make this the most sumptuous of the city's public schools.

28. Mission High School

Houses
1990, Hood Miller Assoc.
3874 18th St.
A nicely varied project with six mid-block houses bracketed by apartment buildings on 18th and Dolores streets.

29. Mission Neighborhood Center
c.1900, Ward & Blohme
362 Capp St.
A residentially scaled Craftsman community center.

30. Flats
c.1900
96, 98 Cumberland St.
An unusual pair of gambrel-roofed flats.

Ascension Lutheran Church (Mission Park Congregational Church)
c.1900
19th and Dolores Sts.

29. Mission Neighborhood Center

31. Russian Orthodox Convent of Our Lady of Vladimir
1914
19th and Capp Sts.
The blue and white color scheme, appropriate to the
Russian Church, heightens the festive quality of this
decorated box built for the Emanuel Evangelical Church.

32. El Capitan Theatre
c.1930
2361 Mission St.
The scale of this combination theater and hotel with its
abundant ornament testifies to the importance the Mission
district had attained by the 1930s as a self-sufficient
suburb with all the conveniences of downtown.

33. Houses
1898-99, Fernando Nelson
4100 block 20th St.
Nos. 4100-38 and 4119-41 were built by Nelson in two
styles, which he called simply A and B, to give variety to
the block and some choice to the client.

34. Moderne apartments
c.1940
741 Noe St.
White stucco boxes stepping down the hillside.

35. House
c.1910
3851 20th St.
This chaste Classic Revival box with a Corinthian
columned side porch looks like a transplant from the
Pacific Heights section of the city.

36. House
c.1880
3755 20th St.

37. House
1881; rem. 1890, Samuel Newsom
827 Guerrero St.
The original house was enlarged and transformed by
Newsom into a rather ponderous but inventive version of a
Queen Anne, with a gambrel roof and exotic touches like
the "moon gate" entrance, a Newsom hallmark.

31. Our Lady of Vladimir

32. El Capitan Theatre

37. 827 Guerrero St.

38. Liberty Street houses

40. 4015 21st St.

38. Liberty Street houses
23-25 Liberty St.
1877
27 Liberty St.
1898, R. H. White
31 Liberty St.
1892, Julius E. Krafft
37 Liberty St.
c.1875
49 Liberty St.
1870
58 Liberty St.
1876
70 Liberty St.
1870
109 Liberty St.
1870
159 Liberty St.
1878

One of the Mission's best groups of Italianates and one imposing Queen Anne line a street that was obviously a choice place to live from early on. The houses on the south side are set high on the hill to catch the view.

39. Houses
701 Castro St.
1897, Fernando Nelson
712 Castro St.
c.1890
740-46 Castro St.
1894, Charles Hinkel

Two of the city's leading late 19th-century builders lived on this block. No. 701, Nelson's own house, was originally on the back lot and was moved forward over the garages that had been added later. By that time Nelson had moved to his fashionable new development, Presidio Terrace. Builder Hinkel lived in No. 740.

40. House
1952, Wurster, Bernardi & Emmons
4015 21st St.

A fine example of the kind of informal, yet clearly defined house designed in many variations by this firm from the 1930s through the 1950s.

41. House
1892, Charles Rousseau
3833 21st St.
An ornate Queen Anne-Italianate, to be compared with 835 South Van Ness, also by Rousseau.

42. Casa Ciele
1930
3698 21st St.
Built by the famed Mayor "Sunny Jim" Rolfe, this secluded English cottage in the pines has a superb view of the downtown San Francisco area.

House
1966, Lanier & Sherrill
3616 21st St.
A well-sited house that fits nicely into the neighborhood.

42. Casa Ciele

43. Edison School
1927; 1974, Eden & Eden
3531 22nd St. at Dolores St.

44. House
1888, A.R. Denke
68 Fair Oaks St.
A Stick Style house with an unusual porch with flat-sawn balusters, looking more like an eastern farmhouse than a city house. Fair Oaks has many interesting Victorians along its five-block length; note No. 92, for example.

45. Hill Street houses
14-28, 30 Hill St.
1878, The Real Estate Assoc.
25 Hill St.
1883, Charles Geddes
49 Hill St.
1885
77 Hill St.
1883
83-91 Hill St.
1884, T. J. Welsh
Another fine group: Italianate on the even side and Stick Style on the odd as a visual foil.

44. 68 Fair Oaks St.

45. Hill St. houses

46. Firehouse No. 44
c.1910; rem. 1962, Lanier & Sherrill
3816 22nd St.
A Mission Revival firehouse elegantly happy to have been remodeled into an artist's studio.

47. Houses
2-6 Vicksburg St.
1875
22-24 Vicksburg St.
c.1910
No. 2-6 is a lofty Italianate; No. 22-24 is a California Craftsman double house.

48. Bank building
c.1910
22nd and Valencia Sts.
One of several exemplary Classic Revival banks found throughout the Mission district.

48. Bank building

49. St. John's Lutheran Church
c.1895
3126 22nd St.
A simplified, even naive Carpenter Gothic facade, like a child's drawing of a Gothic cathedral.

50. House
1907
160 Vicksburg St..

51. Dolores St. house row
1000 Dolores St.
1889, Percy & Hamilton
1010 Dolores St.
1883
1037 Dolores St.
1887, Samuel & Joseph Cather Newsom
1041 Dolores St.
1904
1074 Dolores St.
1885, Schmidt & Havens
1083 Dolores St.
1890
A vintage block from the Mission's heyday as a suburban "zone of better residence," as the real estate brochures so confidently used to advertise.

49. St. John's Lutheran Church

52. House
1886
200 Fair Oaks St.
A Stick Style house, handsomely painted.

53. Collegio de la Mission (former Samuel Gompers High School)
1939, Masten & Hurd
22nd and Bartlett Sts.
This former high school has a streamlined Moderne rear elevation facing Valencia Street, with unusual rounded glass-block stair towers.

54. Houses
1889, T. J. Welsh
703-09, 731-65 Capp St.
Fifteen Stick Style houses, all by the same hand, 10 of which are as yet unaltered.

55. Horace Mann Middle School
1924, John Reid, Jr.; 1976, Hardison & Komatsu
3351 23rd St.
Another school by John Reid.

Mission Branch Library
c.1910
24th and Bartlett Sts.
This branch of the San Francisco Public Library is in the form of a small Italian Renaissance palazzo.

Houses
3350 23rd St.
1877
3336 23rd St.
1882
3330 23rd St.
1886
3326 23rd St.
1877, John Hinkel
A fine group of late 19th-century houses that span a decade but keep the same architectural style. The Hinkels may actually have done them all.

50. 160 Vicksburg St.

53. Collegio de la Mission

1
Union Square

Convention Center

7
Civic Center

10
South of Market

10
East Mission

10
Potrero Hill

1. Hills Plaza
2. Union Oil Co.
3. Bayside Village & South Beach Marina
4. Delancey Street Center
5. Pacific Telephone Building
6. South Park
7. S. F. Fire Department Pumping Station
8. Warehouses 100 block Townsend St.
9. Warehouses 600 block Third St.
10. Industrial buildings 200 block Townsend St.
11. China Basin Building
12. Warehouses 300 block Townsend St.
13. Senior Activities Center
14. Dettner Printing Co.
15. California Casket Co.
16. SoMa Community Recreation Center
17. Ukrainian Orthodox Church of St. Michael
18. Hallam St. cottages
19. Brain Wash
20. Koret of California
21. Magrun & Otter Co.
22. New Langton Arts
23. Warehouses 6th & 7th Sts. Baker & Hamilton Warehouse
24. Jewelry Mart
25. The Galleria Showplace Square
26. McGuire Warehouse
27. More Paper Co.
28. St. Joseph's Church
29. People's Laundry
30. Le Du Building Foremost Dairy Building
31. Far West Labs
32. House 573 S. Van Ness Ave.
33. St. Charles School
34. Pioneer Square Anchor Brewing Co.
35. House 19th & Florida Sts.
36. House 610 Rhode Island St.
37. Adams house Richards house
38. Crowell house
39. Streetscapes 500-600 block Arkansas St., 500 block Connecticut St.
40. Victoria Mews
41. Potrero Hill Neighborhood House
42. Town house duplex 782 Wisconsin St.
43. S.F. General Hospital
44. Houses & apts. 900-1000 block S. Van Ness Ave.
45. Double house 772-74 Shotwell St.
46. Apts. 1201 S. Van Ness Ave.
47. Houses 2733, 2735 Folsom
48. Galleria de la Raza
49. House 1348 S. Van Ness Ave. House 1381 S. Van Ness Ave.
50. House row 1100 block Shotwell St.
51. House row 1200 block Treat
52. Former fire station
53. Former Irving Scott School
54. Potrero Hill Police Station American Can Co.

When Jasper O'Farrell gave the city its first formal survey in 1847, he decided that the existing street grid north of Market was too confining, and so he made the blocks south of Market roughly four times as large—too large, in fact, for residential development. This decision consigned the area's flatlands to light industry beginning in 1851, when several foundries and shipyards were established along the shore beyond First Street. The city's first working-class neighborhood occupied the vale between the sandy hills on Market and Howard, euphemistically called Happy Valley. Looming over Happy Valley was Rincon Hill, where the rich lived until the late 1860s when Second Street was cut through, fracturing the hill and abetting the industrialization of the area. A reminder of its fashionable history is the remnant of South Park. When the cable car made Nob Hill accessible, the social climbers left Rincon for good. The hill itself departed when it was cut down to serve as the springing point for the Bay Bridge, completed in 1936, linking San Francisco with the East Bay.

Potrero Hill, former pastureland as the name implies, rises out of the flats south of Market Street. Though surrounded by freeways and industrial areas, the hill quickly becomes residential as it rises. A few early settlers such as Captain Adams, whose house stands at 300 Pennsylvania, saw the advantages of this secluded hill and its fine weather. They settled on the bay side in the 1860s and 1870s. In the 1880s when the Union Iron Works, now Bethlehem Steel, moved to the base of the hill, it was known as Scotch Hill because of the many Scots who lived and worked there. After 1905 Russians were the largest immigrant group and remained so until the 1930s. Potrero Hill is still something of a backwater. While most of the houses, both old and recent, are relatively small and unpretentious, the views of downtown and the bay are spectacular. The industrial belt adjacent to the waterfront and stretching south and east of the freeway is a treasure trove for fanciers of industrial architecture.

1. Hills Plaza (former Hills Bros. Coffee Factory)
1933, George Kelham; 1991-92, Whisler-Patri
Spear and Harrison Sts.

No longer an olfactory landmark for those crossing the Bay Bridge, this has become a much larger visual landmark with the addition of another building to create a mixed-use complex. Inside is the Gordon Biersch Brewery created by Interim Architects.

2. Union Oil Co.
1940, Lewis P. Hobart
425 1st St.

The Union Oil Company digital clock tower, another landmark for Bay Bridge traffic, was designed as a billboard to advertise the company's products to the crowds attending the Golden Gate International Expo of 1939-40 on Treasure Island. The Sailor's Union building next to it is a post-Moderne design of 1950 by William G. Merchant.

3. Bayside Village and South Beach Marina
1990-91, Fisher-Friedman Assoc.;
land. arch., Anthony Guzzardo
Bayside Village Place

High density rental housing in the SoMa Redevelopment Area. Bayside Village has about 106 units per acre on an 8.6-acre site and is divided into three sections by a landscaped street and pedestrian mall. The interior circulation system gives a strong sense of a village within the surrounding urban context.

4. Delancey Street Center
1990-92, Backen Arrigoni & Ross
602 Embarcadero

A remarkable achievement by an organization famous for social rehabilitation, this is a live-work complex with a large interior court and a lively and gracious appearance.

5. Pacific Telephone Building
1972, McCue, Boone & Tomsick
611 Folsom St.

A well-detailed brushed-aluminum box for delicate and complex telephone switchgear. The program, which called for stringent environmental controls, resulted in the windowless paneled skin interrupted only by glazed sections for personnel circulation and lunchrooms.

1. Hills Plaza

2. Union Oil Co.

3. Bayside Village

6. South Park
1856, George Gordon
2nd St. to 3rd St., Bryant St. to Brannan St.
One of San Francisco's first upper-class residential developments, South Park was a speculative tract laid out by an Englishman with similar London developments in mind. Though a few of the town houses that were meant to encircle the elliptical drive were built, the whole project failed because of the declining status of Rincon Hill in the 1870s. The short row of London-style town houses has disappeared, but the mid-block park still sparks memories and plans for recapturing its former promise.

4. Delancey Street Center

7. S. F. Fire Department Pumping Station
c.1920, Frederick H. Meyer
698 2nd St.
Given the right paint job, this building could very easily pass as Postmodern.

8. Warehouses
1890s-1900s
100 block Townsend St.
A block of fine warehouses. Be sure to notice the buildings with scalloped parapets.

9. Warehouses
1880s, 1890s, 1900s
615, 625, 660 3rd St.

7. S. F. Fire Dept. Pumping Station

Another good collection of brick warehouses—the oldest in the vicinity. At 665 3rd Street on the fifth floor is the Cartoon Art Museum—it's worth a visit!

10. Industrial buildings
c.1930, c.1890
224, 264 Townsend St.

11. China Basin Building
1922, Bliss & Faville; rem. 1973, Robinson & Mills
185 Berry St.
The office conversion of this enormous warehouse building, originally built for the Pacific Steamship Company, started the now well-established trend in this area.

12. 300 Block Townsend, warehouses

12. Warehouses
c.1900
310, 350 Townsend St.
Tasteful conversions of brick warehouse buildings that have used a design approach that might now be called "conversion vernacular."

13. Senior Activities Center
1925
360 4th St.
A residentially scaled Spanish Colonial Revival building that is a surprise in this area, fortunately put to good use.

14. Dettner Printing Co.
1909, Coxhead & Coxhead
835 Howard St.
The architect's fondness for exaggerated detail appears here in the giant keystone over the entrance, perhaps the only opportunity afforded by the budget to add a little drama to a typically utilitarian building type. The metal-framed ground floor is handsome and well-proportioned.

15. California Casket Co. office building
1909, Albert Pissis
965 Mission St.
An appropriately dignified Classical facade.

15. California Casket Company

16. SoMa Community Recreation Center
1991, Marquis Assoc./Omi Lang
6th and Folsom Sts.
A much-needed and well-designed oasis!

17. Ukrainian Orthodox Church of St. Michael
1906, S. Ardrio
345 7th St.
With its lively twin-towered facade approached by a double-branching stair and flanked by palm trees, this is another oasis; it proves that the cultural institutions of strong ethnic groups can endure even when their residential context disappears.

17. Ukrainian Orthodox Church of St. Michael

18. Hallam Street cottages
End of Hallam St.
1991, Donald MacDonald & Assoc.
Infill residential development on a very small scale.

19. Brain Wash
1989, Kotas/Pantaleoni
1122 Folsom St.
A novel combination of a coffee bar and laundromat.

20. Koret of California
c.1935; rem. 1972, Beverly Willis & Assoc.
1130 Howard St.
With its almost playfully fortified parapet, sunburst entrance, and other detail, this decorated box has the swank associated with the Art Deco period.

20. Koret of California

21. Magrun & Otter Co.
1928, Bliss & Faville
1235 Mission St.
A fine display of the decorative possibilities of terra cotta.

22. New Langton Arts
1246 Folsom St.
A mainstay of the city's contemporary art world featuring avant-garde installations, musical performances, performance art, readings, and video works.

23. Warehouses
c.1890
650 7th St., 6th and Bluxome Sts.
Baker & Hamilton Warehouse
1905, Albert Pissis
700-68 7th St.
More noble brick storage palaces.

23. Baker & Hamilton Warehouse

24. Jewelry Mart
1990, Tanner Leddy Maytum Stacy
999 Brannan St.
A triangular jewelry case with glass brick walls.

25. The Galleria
c.1900; rem. 1973, Wurster, Bernardi & Emmons
101 Kansas St.
A spectacular joining of two brick warehouses by a large steel and glass atrium.

Showplace Square
1970s
Brannan St. bet. 7th and 8th Sts.
Two of the major buildings housing the showrooms of many local interior design firms.

26. McGuire Warehouse

26. McGuire Warehouse
1988, Kotas/Pantaleoni
530 10th St.

27. More Paper Co.
c.1910
1489 Folsom St.

28. St. Joseph's Church
1912, John J. Foley
1415 Howard St.
St. Joseph's imposing twin-towered Neo-Baroque facade looms over the loft buildings of this now largely industrial area, testifying to the staunch Italian neighborhood that was once here. The Templo Calvario next door is an older Carpenter Gothic church, which has lost half its spire.

28. St. Joseph's Church

29. People's Laundry

33. St. Charles School

36. 610 Rhode Island St.

29. People's Laundry
1906, J. Dolliver
165 10th St.
Originally the Lick Baths, this picturesque complex was built to serve those rendered bathless by the earthquake.

30. Le Du Building
c.1930
123 S. Van Ness Ave.
Foremost Dairy Building
c.1930
167 Howard St.
Two more Moderne style buildings that also testify to the heavy industrial growth of this area despite the beginning of the Great Depression.

31. Far West Labs
c.1900; rehab. 1972, Esherick Homsey Dodge & Davis
1855 Folsom St.
Another brick warehouse conversion, this time to offices and laboratories for educational research. Nearby, the 300 block of Shotwell has an almost intact row of 1880s houses on the even-numbered side.

32. House
c.1890
573 S. Van Ness Ave.
A grand and lonely Queen Anne house.

33. St. Charles School
c.1880
18th and Shotwell Sts.
A rare survivor of wooden Italianate school design.

34. Pioneer Square & the Anchor Brewing Co.
c.1915
Mariposa, Carolina, 18th Sts.
Industrial buildings, one converted to mixed use and one housing the city's most famous local brewery.

35. House
1981, Jeremy Kotas
Near cor. 19th and Florida Sts.
In spite of a very tight budget the architect managed to give this house painterly Postmodern panache.

36. House
1991, Daniel Solomon & Assoc.
610 Rhode Island St.
This intentionally gritty design, with its black asphalt shingles, alludes to the industrial area down the hill. Its exposed metal fireplace box and flue express the bi-axial symmetry of this quite formal house for two musicians.

37. Adams house
1868
300 Pennsylvania St.
Richards house
1866
301 Pennsylvania St.
Captain Adams bought this 13-acre tract in the 1860s and built his home here probably from a carpenter's plan book from the east. The older Richards house seems, in comparison, very simple and chaste, having lost its entrance porch and its octagonal cupola, from which there must have been a fine view of the bay.

38. Crowell house
c.1870
400 Pennsylvania St.
Similar to the Adams house.

39. Streetscapes: cottages and houses
559-609 Arkansas St.
1885
512-26 Connecticut St.
1885

40. Victoria Mews
1979
20th and Wisconsin Sts.
Movie-set Victorian well done but best viewed from a distance, where the general mass merges with the older row housing in the hillside.

41. Potrero Hill Neighborhood House
1922, 1925, Julia Morgan
953 De Haro St.
This neighborhood house was established in 1919 by the Presbyterian Church to serve the Russian immigrants who had been settling on the hill since 1905. Morgan's reputation for designing successful small institutional buildings won her this job, which she executed with her usual concern for context in the informal design of this rustic shingled building with a welcoming entry and lobby areas.

42. Town house duplex
1991, Kotas/Pantaleoni
782 Wisconsin St.
Painted schoolbus yellow, the design of this back-to-back set of town houses makes a statement about its great view of the San Francisco bay.

37. Adams house

38. Crowell house

40. Victoria Mews

42. 782 Wisconsin St.

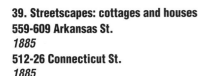

155

43. San Francisco General Hospital
1909-15, Newton Tharp, city architect; John Galen Howard/Frederick H. Meyer/John Reid, Jr.;
1976, Stone, Marraccini & Patterson
1001 Potrero Ave.

A huge campus of hospital buildings designed over a 50-year period. The progression from a rich selection of materials and a relatively small scale to the inhuman scale of modern medical technology in concrete is obvious.

43. San Francisco General Hospital

44. Houses and apartments
c.1890-1900
919, 920, 943, 959, 989 & 1080-86 S. Van Ness Ave.

A varied group of late 19th-century buildings, some of them very imposing, such as No. 943. Note the very ornate plasterwork on No. 959.

45. Double house
c.1875
772-74 Shotwell St.

The twin-bay Italianate at its best—a classic San Francisco row house type. The block as a whole is representative of this era of tract housing.

44. S. Van Ness Ave., houses and apartments

46. Apartments
c.1885
1201 S. Van Ness Ave.

Another unusual corner apartment house, this one with heavy gable hoods. The second floor was restored by San Francisco Victoriana, the city's leading Victorian restoration firm, after a destructive 1976 fire.

47. Houses
1880s
2733, 2735 Folsom St.

48. Galleria de la Raza
2851 24th St.

The city's first exhibition space devoted to contemporary Hispanic art; a list of the many murals that enliven building walls in the Mission district is also available here.

46. S. Van Ness Ave., apartments

49. House
1886, Seth Babson
1348 S. Van Ness Ave.

One of the state's first professionally trained architects designed this great Stick Style pile for Frank M. Stone, a prominent San Francisco lawyer. The richly detailed interior is apparently intact.

House
1884, Charles I. Havens
1381 S. Van Ness Ave.

50. House row
c.1885
1110-28, 1136-38, 1140-42 Shotwell St.
A fine and fancy row. At the corner of 26th Street and South Van Ness Avenue is an outstanding Craftsman apartment house of c.1910 in clinker brick and shingles.

51. House row
1890 and c.1885, John McCarthy
1200-02, 1232 and 1256 Treat St.
The first two buildings were built by an owner-developer who apparently wanted something fireproof for himself and so built this unusual brick Italianate. No. 1256 has some very fine ornament.

52. Former fire station
1917
2501 20th St.
Moorish Romanesque Revival—San Francisco has fire stations in almost every imaginable style. The open space in this bend of Potrero Avenue is the Knudsen-Bloom Park, designed by Esherick Homsey Dodge & Davis, whose offices are nearby at 2789 25th Street. There is an entry plaza off Utah Street.

53. Former Irving Scott School
1895
1060 Tennessee St.
The old wooden school building is a particularly choice piece of old Potrero Hill. The 1100 block of Tennessee Street has a fine row of 1880s cottages.

54. Potrero Hill Police Station
c.1910
3rd Ave. and 20th St.
A box wrapped in the Mission Revival style.

American Can Co.
c.1905
3rd Ave. bet. 20th and 22nd Sts.
A two-block-long concrete-frame industrial plant built from stock company plans used across the country, now converted to mixed use.

49. 1348 S. Van Ness Ave.

50. 1100 block Shotwell, house row

54. Potrero Hill Police Station

Presidio

1. Army Museum
2. Funston Ave. officers' quarters
3. Pershing Hall
4. Montgomery St. barracks
5. Former cavalry barracks and stables
6. Fort Point and the Golden Gate Bridge
7. Artillery gun emplacements
8. Fort Winfield Scott
9. Kobbe Ave. officers' quarters

Sea Cliff/Richmond

10. Scenic Way houses
11. House 850 El Camino Del Mar
12. House 895 El Camino Del Mar
13. Palace of the Legion of Honor
14. House 726 34th Ave.

Golden Gate Park

15. Beach Chalet, Dutch & Murphy Windmills
16. The Music Concourse
17. M. H. de Young Memorial Museum, Brundage Wing
18. Japanese Tea Garden
19. California Academy of Sciences
    Planetarium, Aquarium, Hall of Science
    Cowell Hall
    Whales Fountain
20. Conservatory
21. McLaren Lodge
22. Alford Lake Bridge
23. Children's Playground, Sharon Children's House

Outer Sunset

24. Shriners Hospital
25. San Francisco Conservatory of Music
26. "Doelger City"
27. San Francisco Zoological Gardens
28. Sigmund Stern Grove and Trocadero Inn
29. San Francisco State University, Student Union Building

St. Francis Wood

30. House 98 St. Francis Blvd.
31. House 30 St. Francis Blvd.
32. House 67 San Leandro Way
33. House 195 San Leandro Way
34. House 44 San Benito Way

Forest Hill

35. Erlanger house
36. House 35 Lopez Ave.
37. Young house
38. House 2 Clarendon Ave.
39. Moffitt house
40. 2 Glenbrook Ave., house
41. 150 St. Germain Ave., 175 & 176 Palo Alto Ave.
42. Twin Peaks Viewpoint

Diamond Heights

43. Red Rock Hill town houses
44. Diamond Heights Village
45. Eichler houses
46. St. Nicholas Syrian Antiochian Orthodox Church
47. Village Square
48. St. Aidan's Episcopal Church
49. Gold Mine Hill

Outer Mission

50. Poole-Bell house
51. Laidley St. houses
52. St. Paul's Roman Catholic Church & School
53. Church St. commercial-residential buildings
54. Holy Innocents Church
55. Houses 1200 block Guerrero

*T*he outer areas of San Francisco lend themselves to driving, not walking, except within selected districts; therefore, the outer tour is organized in small pieces linked by a continuous route. A brief introduction to each district follows.

Presidio. This beautiful site occupying the northwest quadrant of the San Francisco peninsula and encompassing about 1,500 acres has been a military reservation since 1776 when it was first established by the Spanish. In 1847 an American garrison was established in this barren, sandy site, and by 1883 a forestation plan began the extensive landscaping which justifies San Franciscans' regard for the Presidio as a public park, so everyone will applaud its official conversion to a part of the Golden Gate National Recreation Area in 1995.

Sea Cliff/Richmond. Mark Daniels, who also laid out Forest Hill, planned Sea Cliff in 1912. Streets follow the contours and afford a few places for panoramic views even though the houses are very close together. The architecture is blandly Mediterranean for the most part and the ambience redolent of privacy.

Golden Gate Park. Although Frederick Law Olmsted pronounced the prospective park site of miles of sand dunes hopeless, William Hammond Hall created one of the world's more verdant parks. After Hall's resignation, John McLaren spent more than 60 years completing the park and dominating the city's landscape.

Outer Sunset. Formerly occupied by horse racing, farming, dairy ranching, and gunpower production, the Sunset was not developed until linked to transportation to downtown work places. Residential tracts were laid out near the steam line in 1887, and in other areas in 1905 and 1911, but it was not until 1918 with the opening of the Twin Peaks Tunnel, which made rapid transit available to downtown, that building activity significantly increased. Most of the houses in the Sunset were built in the decades after World War II by the Gellert Brothers, the Stoneson Brothers, the Doelgers, Chris McKeon, or Ray Galli.

St. Francis Wood. Laid out in 1912 as a lush suburb-in-a-garden, St. Francis Wood was developed by the Mason McDuffie Co., a major realtor and investment company in the East Bay. The Olmsted Brothers planned the central boulevard and fountains, and the gates, terraces, and fountains were designed by John Galen Howard and Henry Gutterson, 1912-13. The tour is a selection of houses representing the range of styles and works by major architects.

Forest Hill. Another garden suburb, more formal than nearby St. Francis Wood, planned by Mark Daniels. Here, also, a neighborhood association maintained tight controls on architectural standards for structures as well as covenants restricting home ownership to Caucasians.

Outer Mission/Diamond Heights. Just south of Twin Peaks, Diamond Heights is a steep and windy ridge which, because of its inaccessibility, remained largely undeveloped until the 1950s. Single-family houses by Eichler and others gradually filled the western slopes, and by the 1970s the southern portion saw the development of town houses and apartments. East of Diamond Heights lies Noe Valley; its southern edge is the ridge that separates the inner and outer Mission.

Presidio

Although the Presidio was first established by the Spanish in 1776 as the military counterpart of the Mission, it was a sorry excuse for a fort, consisting of a small compound with a few structures of adobe. In 1847 an American Presidio garrison was established and the Spanish barracks and the coastal battery were repaired. However, in 1855 the five buildings were described as "unsightly mud enclosures." The Civil War increased the importance of the Presidio, and in 1862 the Army built twelve wooden cottages for officers along the eastern side of the original parade ground. Originally they faced west but were later turned around to present those coming from the city with a more attractive visual introduction to the base. The post hospital was built in 1863 along with some other wooden structures and a stone magazine. The Main Post continued to expand during the 1880s and 1890s, but equally important was the forestation plan that Major William A. Jones prepared in 1883 in which he proposed to plant the Presidio's three ridges with trees and leave the valleys treeless so that they would appear larger than they were and the ridges higher. The main post was to be the focal point of a composition with a background of forest overlooking extensive grassy stretches. No other military base in the country had such a landscape plan; even San Franciscans joined in the subsequent landscaping campaigns such as one that called for planting 60,000 Monterey pines by 1896. The Presidio also benefitted from the expertise of an army engineer, Major William W. Harts, who created a master plan for the reservation in 1907. Whether Harts consulted Daniel H. Burnham (who prepared the famous but unimplemented 1904 plan for San Francisco), whom he knew, or whether he simply drew on Burnham's planning ideas, Harts's plan has elements of the City Beautiful Movement's approach to civic design. Beside the main post, the other architecturally notable campus is Fort Winfield Scott, built on a ridge on the west side of the reservation from about 1910 to 1912. Major Harts was again involved, calling for buildings designed in "the old Spanish style," now known as the Mission Revival style. Although the style was already popular in California, this was the first use of it for military buildings.

A good starting point is the former Post Hospital (**1**), now the Army Museum, built in 1863. With its simple but elegant three-story galleries it is also one of the handsomest of the Presidio's buildings. Behind it along Funston Avenue is a row of Classic Revival/Italianate officers' quarters of 1862-64 (**2**), which originally faced the first parade ground. At the head of Funston is Pershing Hall (**3**), a Classic Revival brick building of 1904. Along Mont-

1. Army Museum

2. Officers' quarters

5. Barracks

gomery Street, facing the present parade ground, is a fine group of brick barracks (**4**) from 1895-97. Driving along Lincoln Boulevard toward the Golden Gate Bridge, you pass a white wooden Classic-Revival building of 1902 with a two-story veranda (**5**) which was built as barracks for the Cavalry division. Below the road are five handsome brick stables, each for 102 horses. A turnoff to the north slightly farther on leads to Fort Point (**6**) a polygonal brick coastal-defense fort of 1853-61, now a museum. As one of the finest surviving examples of a group that includes Fort Sumter in Charleston Harbor it is well worth a visit and has a wonderful view of the bay from beneath the Golden Gate Bridge.

4. Montgomery St. barracks

Continuing westward along Lincoln Boulevard past the bridge, you come to a string of abandoned coastal artillery gun emplacements facing the Pacific (**7**). Inland, Ralston Avenue loops around Fort Winfield Scott (**8**), a fine stand of Mission-Revival buildings built from 1908 to 1912. Along Kobbe Avenue is a handsome row of Classic-Revival officers' quarters (**9**), built around 1910.

5. Stables

1. Army Museum (former Post Hospital)
1863

2. Officers' quarters
1862-64
Funston Ave.

3. Pershing Hall
1903
Funston Ave.

4. Barracks
1895-97
Montgomery St.

6. Fort Point and the Golden Gate Bridge

5. Barracks and stables
1902
Lincoln Blvd.

6. Fort Point
1853-61
Golden Gate Bridge
1937, Irving Morrow, consulting architect;
Joseph Strauss, chief engineer
The 4,200-foot clear span was, until 1959, the longest in the world. The great achievement of placing tower foundations in the swirling currents of the Golden Gate, the superb setting, and the orange-red color of the bridge make it one of the landmarks of bridge building. The Moderne detailing, remarkably adapted to heavy steel construction, expresses its time.

7. Artillery gun emplacements
Lincoln Blvd.

8. Fort Winfield Scott
1910-12
Ralston Ave.

9. Officers' quarters
c.1910
Kobbe Ave.

9. Kobbe Ave. Officers' quarters

Sea Cliff/Richmond

The houses listed for this planned development of 1912 are a sampling of those by better known architects.
Visitors driving or walking around this special enclave will also be rewarded with fine views of the Golden Gate.

10. Houses
1914, Willis Polk & Co.
9, 25, 45 Scenic Way
Polk's late Classical style exhibits none of the idiosyn-crasies of his early work.

8. Fort Winfield Scott

11. House
1958, Wurster, Bernardi & Emmons
850 El Camino Del Mar

12. House
1963, Esherick Homsey Dodge & Davis
895 El Camino Del Mar
There are few contemporary houses in the area because it was rapidly built up in the 'teens and '20s, leaving only a few lots. These two houses reveal the evolution of Modern architecture over half a decade.

10. Scenic Way houses

13. Lincoln Park
Palace of the Legion of Honor
1916, George A. Applegarth
34th Ave. and Clement St. or El Camino Del Mar
Lincoln Park occupies the top of the Point Lobos Head-land. Like Lone Mountain, it once had a cemetery (aptly called the Golden Gate) where the golf course is now. Near the first tee an arch from a Chinese tomb commemorates this piece of the past. Matchless views of the Golden Gate Bridge, the Marin Headlands, and the city to the east delight those who walk along the north edge of the park. The California Palace of the Legion of Honor, an art museum devoted largely to 16th- to 18th-century Euro-

11. 850 El Camino Del Mar

pean painting and a Rodin sculpture collection, was given to the city by Adolph and Alma de Brettville Spreckels as a memorial to the W W I dead. The building is a modified copy of the Parisian palace of the same name, here given a country rather than a city setting.

14. House
1905, Willis Polk
726 34th Ave.
A modest but interesting shingled cottage that suggests a much different lifestyle than that of its neighbors, which were built in the 1930s.

13. Lincoln Park

Golden Gate Park

To create one of the world's more verdant parks out of miles of shifting sand dunes is no mean achievement. To do so in the face of parsimonious budgets and endless political intrigue is even more impressive. This was the task of William Hammond Hall, the man responsible for Golden Gate Park, now such a beloved and well-used part of the city that most residents take it for granted. The idea of the park began in the 1860s. Frederick Law Olmsted, creator of New York's Central Park, was invited by the Outside Lands Commission to give his advice. He pronounced the prospective site hopeless, but, happily, his advice was ignored. In 1871 Hall, an ex-Army engineer, was appointed the park's first superintendent. In five years, in spite of inadequate support, he had designed the park, figured out how to anchor the sand dunes by planting imported sand grass, and how to make the trees grow, and had begun, at the east end, to landscape the barren waste. But he was no politician and, after struggling vainly against budget cuts, resigned in disgust. Five years later he was wooed back, but accepted only long enough to hire his successor, the famous "Uncle John" McLaren, who is now widely and erroneously assumed to have designed Golden Gate Park.

The facts are remarkable enough. McLaren was superintendent from 1886 to 1943, when he died in office at the age of 96. Sage, tyrant, superb gardener, and adroit politician, he completed the park, landscaped the Panama-Pacific International Exposition, planted Dolores Street's parks, and generally dominated the city's landscape for 60-odd years. The park that Hall designed and McLaren built is one of the great monuments of romantic landscape design. Long and narrow, it provides maximum green

13. Palace of the Legion of Honor

frontage to the city on either side and, thanks to careful grading and planting, a great variety of sheltered and secluded areas. Because of the fog the lawns survive intensive use far better than do the lawns of eastern parks. Since much of the vegetation is not deciduous, the park is perennially green. Major museums occupy the park along with monuments and notable works of architecture. But above all it is, as all great urban parks are, a piece of the country in the city.

15. Beach Chalet.

15. Beach Chalet
1921, Willis Polk

A hipped-roof pavilion, which houses a remarkable set of WPA murals by Lucien Labaudt executed in 1936-37 illustrating recreational activities in San Francisco. Polk was also the architect for the Portals of the Past on Lloyd Lake, an Ionic colonnade that originally graced a Nob Hill mansion he designed. It burned in 1906.

Dutch Windmill & Murphy Windmill
1903, 1905
West end of the park

These two great windmills were built to pump irrigation water for the park.

15. Dutch Windmill

16. The Music Concourse

The sculptural rhythm of the pollarded plane trees makes this great formal space a perfect contrast to the surrounding lush, romantic landscape. The focus is the Music Pavilion, given by Claus Spreckels and designed by the Reid Brothers in 1899.

17. M. H. de Young Memorial Museum
1916, Louis Christian Mullgardt; rem. Arthur Brown, Jr.
Brundage Wing
1965, Gardner Dailey & Assoc.

De Young, founder of the *San Francisco Chronicle*, insisted that the museum he gave to the city be modeled on Mullgardt's Court of the Ages at the 1915 Panama-Pacific Exposition. The elaborate Spanish style ornament that originally encrusted the museum walls had to be removed for seismic safety, leaving its form in the nude. Arthur Brown then remodeled it in his late stripped Spanish mode, like Stanford's Hoover Tower. While neither the original museum nor the more recent Brundage wing are distinguished architecture, the art is well worth a visIt.

16, Music Concourse

18. Japanese Tea Garden
1874, George Turner Marsh

This Victorian idea of a Japanese garden, designed by an Australian who was the country's first Oriental art dealer, attracts a major share of the park's visitors—it is definitely a must. Originally built for the 1894 Mid-Winter Fair, the park's first major public event, the garden proved so popular that it was preserved. From 1907 to 1942 one family, the Hagiwaras, ran the concession, inventing fortune cookies along the way. In 1942 they were deported. In 1978 Ruth Asawa, who was a victim of the World War II Japanese relocation program, designed a bronze plaque honoring the Hagiwaras, which is located near the entrance. The Japanese Tea Garden has many special features, which are marked for visitors.

19. California Academy of Sciences
1915-31, Lewis P. Hobart
Planetarium, Aquarium, and Hall of Science
1951, Weihe, Frick & Kruse;
Cowell Hall
1968, Milton Pflueger
Whales Fountain
1939, Robert Howard
S. side of the Music Concourse
A successful integration of old and new buildings.

18. Japanese Tea Garden

20. Conservatory
1878, Hammersmith Works, Dublin, Ireland
John F. Kennedy Dr. opp. 4th Ave.
James Lick died before the magical greenhouse he had ordered for his San Jose estate could be erected. Leland Stanford and others bought it for the park. The building, its setting, and its contents marvelously preserve the ambience of the 19th century.

20. Conservatory

21. McLaren Lodge (Park Headquarters)
1895, E. R. Swain
N. of John F. Kennedy Dr. at east entrance
Rusticated sandstone with a tile roof; the Romanesque Revival style is reminiscent of H. H. Richardson's work and of Stanford University.

22. Alford Lake Bridge
1889, Ernest Ransome
Pedestrian underpass
Kezar Dr. opp. Haight St.
The first reinforced concrete bridge in the U. S., although the design does its best to conceal the fact. Instead, the material mimics stones dripping with mossy stalactites.

21. McLaren Lodge

23. Children's Playground
Sharon Children's House
1886, Percy & Hamilton
Kezar Dr. near 1st Ave.

23. Sharon Children's House

The playground occupies the site of a lake filled by the leveling of a nearby hill.The precedent for a children's playground came from New York's Central Park; the concept was typical of the social planning of the time and gathered great popular support. The Children's House, which holds all manner of child-oriented delights, is the city's purest surviving example of Richardsonian Romanesque. Heavily damaged in the 1906 earthquake, as were other masonry structures in the park, it was rebuilt within the year. The carousel dates from c.1892. In 1978 Michael Painter & Assoc. redesigned the playground.

Outer Sunset

The Sunset was originally part of the San Miguel Rancho, granted in 1839 to Jose Noe. In the 1850s the ranchlands lay in the path of the city's southwestern expansion. John Horner, an entrepreneurial sea captain, bought the 4,500-acre ranch in 1854, but he was mainly interested in the area now called Noe Valley. Horner lost the land to the Pioche family, from whom Aldoph Sutro acquired his estate about 1879. Sutro continued the planting of eucalyptus trees, which George M. Greene began in what is now Stern Grove in the early 1870s to ward off the invading sand dunes. The history of the Sunset, like that of the rest of the "Outside Lands," was tied to the development of transportation. Even with an acquired taste for living in the fog, the prospective buyer still looked for affordable property near transportation to downtown work places. Consequently, before the Outside Lands were tamed by municipal improvements, the sandy spaces were occupied by horse racing, farming, dairy ranching, and gunpowder production. Miles of orderly blocks of well-tended homes followed the laying of streets and tracks.

In 1887 Aurelius E. Buckingham christened his residential tract, laid out near the steam line, the Sunset. The plat extended for two or three blocks south from 5th Ave. and along H Street (Lincoln Way). To aid construction, the developer hauled crushed rock from the Sutro quarry and spread a thin layer of it over the sand, which he also planted with oats, lupine, and mustard. There were hardly 20 houses between Stanyan and the ocean at the time. Nor was there any real impetus for development until the excitement of the 1894 Mid-Winter Exposition.

In 1905 William Crocker's Parkside Realty Company opened a promising tract near 21st and Taraval that ultimately became Parkside. Although Sutro died in 1898, his vast oceanside estate was tied up in a contested will until 1909. In 1911 the first of his Rancho San Miguel land was subdivided. The 725 acres, bought by the A.S. Baldwin Residential Development Company for $1.5 million, became Forest Hill, St. Francis Wood, Westwood Park, Balboa Terrace, and Monterey Heights. Still, the inaccessibility of these communities to the downtown business district was a problem. Though the United Railroad Company built a line out Ocean Avenue, the literal breakthrough was the Twin Peaks Tunnel, which made rapid transit available to downtown starting in 1918. Thereafter the communities west of Twin Peaks became popular for their remoteness from what many middle-class citizens regarded as urban chaos.

City Engineer Michael O'Shaughnessy, who fostered the tunnel, also blessed the area with another important link to downtown. This was Portola Drive, a scenic route that connected St. Francis Circle to the Twin Peaks exten-sion of Market Street. From the Circle, Sloat Blvd., also by O'Shaughnessy, completed the scenic tour to the ocean. The major north-south arterial, 19th Avenue, was asphalt-ed in 1924, and Sloat defined an entrance to Sigmund Stern Memorial Grove, given to the city by Mrs. Stern in 1932 as a place of natural and cultural refreshment through the medium of the summer music festival. Off the beaten path is the former Trocadero Inn, built by George M. Greene— after he planted the eucalyptus trees—to accommodate the racing crowds. It is now the park headquarters and has been restored.

As the streets and car lines multiplied, the blocks filled with houses. The major builders in these early tracts are familiar names from other parts of the city: Fernando Nelson & Sons in West Portal Park and Merced Manor; Joseph Leonard and his Urban Realty Company in Balboa and Ingleside Terrace; and Mark Daniels, who planned Forest Hill after he laid out Sea Cliff. Numerous small contractors and builders contributed to the activity by developing a lot or two at a time. But if the names change, the basic building design does not. Builders borrowed and stole from each other, keeping a weather eye out for what was selling. In the hilly areas the topography influenced house plans and orientation to some extent, but in the flatlands, despite the studied variation in facade treatment, it is architectural homogeneity that is most impressive.

By far the greatest number of houses in the Sunset were built in the post-World War II decades. Most were products of the Big Five: the Gellert Brothers, the Stoneson Brothers, the Doelgers, Chris McKeon, and Ray Galli, who began building in the 1920s and 1930s. Soon they were caught up in the boom in middle-income housing created by the lending policies of the Federal Housing Administration, established in 1934. Soon miles of bare land in the Sunset were carpeted with homes, some of them completed by Henry and Frank Doelger at the rate of two a day. So-called Doelger City, located roughly between 27th and 39th Avenues and Kirkham and Quintara Streets, suggests the magnitude of the Doelgers's operations. In fact, from 1934 to 1941 they were the largest single home builders in the country.

24. Shriners Hospital

Although methods of rationalizing the mass production process varied, the Doelgers's approach was similar to that of other builders. A potpourri of styles—English Cottage, French Provincial, Regency, Colonial, and International Style Modern or Modernistic—provided variations on the general theme of homes uniformly scaled and placed on 25-by-100-foot lots. Henry Doelger professed a strong commitment to building well for the average family. The Doelgers used redwood for the house frame and worked with their team to create the best possible plan for prospective buyers, who soon responded in droves. The last step was "putting on the architecture." Elevations of the various facades were pinned on the wall individually and shifted about until a satisfying composition resulted, which was then drawn up and built. Neighborhood planning was not left out of the process. From the beginning the Big Five put utilities underground and located commercial strips for which they made an effort to attract merchants. After World War II the Veterans Administration GI loan program created an unprecedented housing boom. The Sunset blocks developed in the post-war decades show the effect of increased costs for labor and materials. Traditional styles, still in demand, become attenuated, appearing like cardboard cut-outs compared to the earlier models. The transition to modern architecture is evident in the variations on the ranch house theme that replace some of the period revival styles.

25. San Francisco Conservatory of Music

24. Shriners Hospital
1923; new building, 1970
1701 19th Ave.

A major landmark that, because of its luxurious ornamental detail and human scale, provokes a comparison with the contemporary behemoths that hospitals have become.

25. San Francisco Conservatory of Music
1928, Louis C. Mullgardt
1201 Ortega St. at 19th Ave.
An important cultural institution designed by an architect of considerable reputation and talent who had few building commissions in the city.

26. "Doelger City"
1932-c.1945, Doelger Bros.
Ortega St. to Kirkham St., 27th Ave. to 39th Ave.
Although not exclusively developed by the Doelger Bros., their many years of building activity in this area prompted the name Doelger City.

27. San Francisco Zoological Gardens
c.1925, Lewis P. Hobart; 1976, Esherick Homsey
Dodge & Davis
Sloat Blvd. and Zoo Rd.
The Mothers' Building
1925, George W. Kelham
Gorilla House, Wolf House, & Tule Elk House
1980, Esherick Homsey Dodge & Davis
Small Primates Complex
1983, Marquis Assoc.
Marquis Assoc. designed the Primate Discovery Center and refurbished the 1936 WPA Lion House. This firm is also remodeling the outdoor grottos with Royston, Hanamoto, Alley & Abey, landscape architects.

28. Sigmund Stern Grove and Trocadero Inn
1892
19th Ave. and Sloat Blvd.

29. San Francisco State University, Student Union Building
1980, Paffard Keatinge Clay
Following the acquisition of land for the campus from the Spring Valley Water Company in 1937, the State Architect's Office prepared a master plan. However, the building program did not begin until the late 1940s. The OSA was responsible for the design of the buildings erected up to 1970, when the office ceased to be the official planners. The most architecturally interesting building on campus is the 1980 Student Union, a neo-Corbusian structure dominated by two pyramidal elements, one of which serves as an outdoor amphitheater. The lobby serves also as a diagonal street entered through a pivoting enameled-steel slab door borrowed from Le Corbusier's Chapel at Ronchamp in France.

29. San Francisco State Student Union

26. Doelger City

28. Stern Grove and Trocadero Inn

St. Francis Wood

1912-1950s, Frederick Law Olmsted, Jr./John Galen Howard/Henry Gutterson/Louis C. Mullgardt
Entrance gates Junipero Serra Blvd. Boundaries: Portola Dr., Santa Clara Ave., Monterey Blvd., Manor Dr., and Ocean Ave.

As the most prestigious tract west of Twin Peaks, St. Francis Wood featured 50-by-100-foot lots, underground utilities, a boulevard with a landscaped median strip, and tree-lined streets separated from sidewalks by planting. Many of the trees came from the 1915 Panama Pacific Exposition's closing sale; they were mature enough to give a proper garden-suburb appearance. The Olmsted Brothers laid out a central boulevard punctuated midway by a circle with a fountain and terminating in another fountain and terrace at the top of the rise. The gates, terraces, and fountains were designed by John Galen Howard and Henry Gutterson and installed in 1912-13. Three model homes designed by Louis C. Mullgardt and Henry Gutterson were built in 1914-15 on San Benito Way. Their simplified Mediterranean styling struck a nice balance between historicism and modernism. Building proceeded slowly until the 1920s, when prosperous times and the effect of the Twin Peaks Tunnel connection to downtown brought the tract close to completion. The largely Irish population seems to have come from the Mission district and other areas of the inner city where accelerating development threatened that suburban ambience. Those who moved to the Wood were not urbanites. They enjoyed the remote, near-wilderness quality of this outer fringe area where hunting small game was still a major diversion. A strong neighborhood association controlled architectural design and enforced the racial convenants, which were not broken until the 1950s. Architecturally, St. Francis Wood is a period piece of revivalism. Despite the fact that a number of notable architects contributed their talents, homogeneity of scale, color, and style—achieved through the controls—is the dominant effect. The outstanding achievement, and one that distinguishes St. Francis Wood from the rest of the city's residential areas, is the lushness and continuity of the landscaping, which is integrated with the general plan. Following is a selection of houses that attempts to cover the range of styles and to present designs by major architects. The reader will not find it comprehensive, but will, we hope, be led on to make personal discoveries.

Entrance to St. Francis Wood

30. 98 St. Francis Blvd.

31. 30 St. Francis Blvd.

St. Francis Wood houses:

30. 98 St. Francis Blvd.
1917, Henry Gutterson; rem. 1929, Masten & Hurd

31. 30 St. Francis Blvd.
1927, Masten & Hurd

32. 67 San Leandro Way
1921, Julia Morgan

33. 195 San Leandro Way
1917, Julia Morgan

34. 44 San Benito Way
1913, Louis C. Mullgardt

35. 270 Castenada Ave.

Forest Hill

1913, Mark Daniels, planner
Main entrance on Pacheco St.off Dewey Blvd.
As in Daniels's other subdivision, Sea Cliff, streets were laid out to follow the contours of the hill. Between the branching streets before Magellan, a triangular plot of lawn with a monumental urn suggests—but fails to create—a formal entrance like that of St. Francis Wood. Forest Hill is blessed with two houses by Bernard Maybeck, in addition to his 1919 Tudorish clubhouse for the Forest Hill Association at 381 Magellan Street. Houses of various sizes and styles line the curving streets. Do explore and enjoy the view from the vest-pocket park at the end of Mendosa.

36. 35 Lopez Ave.

35. Erlanger house
1916, Bernard Maybeck
270 Castenada Ave. at Lopez Ave.
The clients wanted a medieval English manor house, but the product resists classification. The design reveals Maybeck's compositional skills and his ability to manipulate eclectic elements with originality.

37. 51 Sotelo Ave.

36. House
1915, Glenn Allen
35 Lopez Ave.
A Prairie style house with Sullivanesque ornament by an architect whose best known work is in Stockton. Another good Prairie style house is at 343 Montalvo.

37. E. C. Young house
1913, Bernard Maybeck
51 Sotelo Ave.
An intriguing play on the half-timber, with some features (the pulpit-like corner balcony with quatrefoils and the half-timber supergraphics) that are architectural puns.

From Forest Hill the tour crosses Twin Peaks and proceeds to this ridge that rises above Golden Gate Park and has a splendid view north to the Golden Gate. Here are several good examples of 1950s houses more visible than most of the vintage houses of this period, which are often hidden from view by dense foliage.

38. 2 Clarendon Ave.

38. House
1955, Anshen & Allen
2 Clarendon Ave.

39. Moffitt house
c. 1920-40
30 Mountain Spring Ave.

The owner, a furniture maker/woodworker, designed and built this Craftsman house as a home and workshop.

40. 2 Glenbrook Ave.

40. House
1948, John Funk
2 Glenbrook Ave.

41. House
1958, George Rockrise
150 St. Germain Ave.
House
1959, Campbell & Wong
175 Palo Alto Ave.
House
1959, Charles Warren Callister
176 Palo Alto Ave.

41. 175 Palo Alto

42. Twin Peaks Viewpoint
On clear days you can see the city spread out like a carpet densely woven in a pattern of buildings that ripples over the hills or that, like the central downtown stand of towers, creates a garden of forms.

42. Twin Peaks Viewpoint

Diamond Heights/Outer Mission

Diamond Heights is a steep and windy ridge just south of Twin Peaks. It remained undeveloped long after the rest of the city because of its foggy weather and the fact that it had originally been platted in the standard gridiron plan, which here finally met its limit—many of the lots were inaccessible. For this reason it was declared a redevelopment area in the 1950s, even though it was open land. Vernon DeMars did a street plan that followed the site's contours, and a competition was held in 1961 for the first phase of development. From the winning design by Cohen & Leverson only one group of town houses,which was to have high-rise towers on the hilltop and the north slopes, was ever built. Single-family houses by Eichler and others gradually filled the western slopes; an elementary school, a shopping center, and several churches were built by the early 1960s; the 1970s saw the development of the southern portion of the site with town houses and apartments. The general architectural level is undistinguished and does not compare favorably with older parts of the city. South and west of Diamond Heights, Glen Canyon Park is a wild and secluded stretch of open space in the heart of the city. East of Diamond Heights lies Noe Valley; its southern edge is the ridge that separates the inner and outer Mission. This area was generally built up with much smaller Victorian cottages than the northern Mission, and even today it has a more suburban flavor.

42. Twin Peaks Viewpoint

41. 176 Palo Alto Ave.

43. Red Rock Hill town houses
1962, Cohen & Leverson
Diamond Heights Blvd. and Duncan St.
The only built portion of the competition-winning scheme.

44. Diamond Heights Village
1972, Gensler Assoc./Joseph Esherick & Assoc.
Red Rock Way
A well-sited Shingle group where the high-rise buildings of the original plan were supposed to go.

44. Diamond Heights Village

45. Eichler houses
1962-64, Jones & Emmons/Anshen & Allen
1000 block Duncan St.
Eichler's suburban plans were adapted here for city lots, but these are still good examples of the work of a developer who brought contemporary architect-designed houses into the Bay Area tract home market.

45. Eichler home

46. St. Nicholas Syrian Antiochian Orthodox Church
1963, William F. Hempel
Diamond Heights Blvd. and Duncan St.
A reasonably convincing contemporary concrete version of the traditional domed plan.

47. Village Square
1972, Morris & Lohrbach
E. side Diamond Heights Blvd. bet. Duncan and Valley Sts.
Good site planning and landscaping make this is one of the more attractive developments on the Heights.

48. St. Aidan's Episcopal Church

48. St. Aidan's Episcopal Church
1963, Skidmore Owings & Merrill
101 Gold Mine Dr.
An irregular hexagon of white stucco, with an interior lit by a hidden clerestory and windows in the manner of Southwest missions. The mural painting is by Mark Adams.

49. Gold Mine Hill
1967, Fisher-Friedman
Gold Mine Dr. and Ora Way
One of several groups of town houses by this firm in the Heights. Others are on Carnelian Way on the north slope.

51. 123 Laidley St.

50. Poole-Bell house
c.1872
196-98 Laidley St.
Built by Cecil Poole, an attorney, this imposing Mansard-roofed house was bought about 1900 by Mammy Pleasant, a famous madam, for the widow of Thomas Bell.

51. Laidley St.Houses
1981-1991
102 Laidley St.
Kotas Pantaleoni
123, 135 Laidley St.
Jeremy Kotas
134 Laidley St.
Shaffer and Kotas
140 Laidley St.
Kotas and Shaffer
Rarely do architects have a chance to transform a street one house at a time and thus try out new ideas, but Jeremy Kotas and Skip Shaffer have managed and produced a series of sometimes funky and always adventurous houses (and a garage at 128 Laidley) in the process.

51. 140 Laidley St.

52. St. Paul's Roman Catholic Church and School
Church and Valley Sts.
A rare local example of a Gothic Revival style, more common east of the Mississippi, that combined a monumental towered stone facade with an interior dimly lit by stained glass and punctuated by attenuated columns supporting plaster vaults.

53. Commercial-residential buildings
c.1890
1500, 1544 Church St.
Two unusually fine examples of this once common type.

54. Holy Innocents Episcopal Church
c.1900, Ernest Coxhead
Houses
400 block Fair Oaks St.
In his early practice Coxhead was one of the great masters of the undulating shingled wall, and here, tucked away on this quiet street, is his surviving local example. Also in this block is a wonderful collection of Victorian and Craftsman houses, and at the south end on 26th Street is a very nice little Mission Revival hall.

55. Houses
1200 block Guerrero St.
Guerrero is virtually lined with Victorian houses, and this block has an outstanding group. Note especially the towered mansion built by an Austrian immigrant at 1286, two double houses at 1259-65 with their original iron fences, the in- and-out facade of 1257, an elegantly consistent Stick-Eastlake at 1253, and a fine corner commercial-residential building at 1201.

51.102 Laidley St.

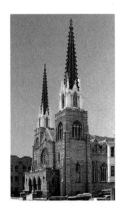
52. St. Paul's Catholic Church

55.1236 Guerrero St.

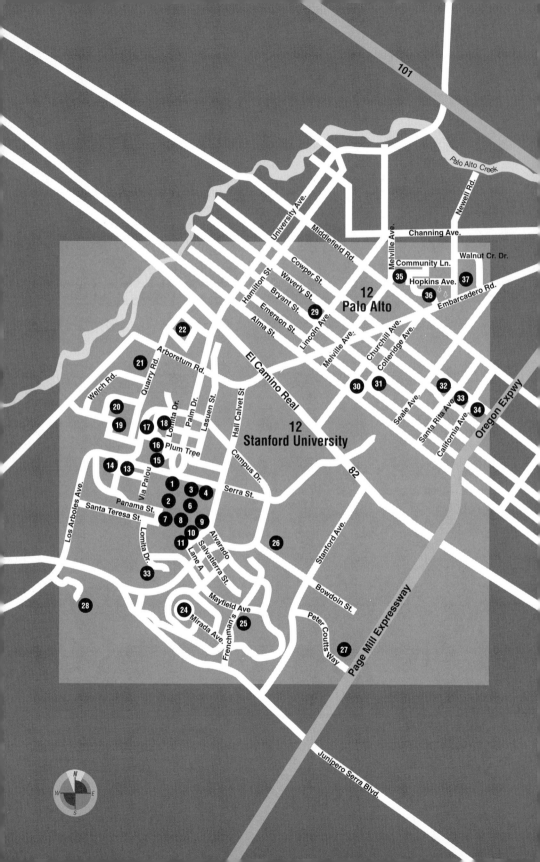

Stanford

1. The Quadrangle
2. Memorial Church
3. Art Gallery
4. Hoover Tower
5. Encina Hall
   Encina Commons
6. White Memorial Plaza
7. Former Student Union
8. Post Office & bookstore
9. Center for Research &
   Development in Education
10. Law School
11. Braun Music Center
12. Terman Engineering Center
13. Center for Integrated Systems
14. Central Energy Facility
15. C. H. Gilbert Biology Building
16. Chemistry building
17. Parking Structure
18. Art Museum
19. S. U. Hospital
20. Children's Hospital
21. Stanford Barn
    Stanford Shopping Center
22. Child Care center
23. The Knoll
24. Hoover house
25. Hanna house
26. Rains student housing
27. Peter Coutts Village
28. Center for Advanced Study in
    the Behavioral Sciences

Palo Alto

29. Kellogg house
30. Mendenhall house
31. Haehl house
32. Stern houses
33. House 2101 Waverly
34. Raas house
35. Lucie Stern Community
    Center
36. Rinconada Park
37. Cultural Center
    Former Main Library

Stanford. The original buildings of Stanford University are among the few great academic complexes in this country. Because of Leland Stanford's dictatorial influence—he insisted that the buildings be on the plain in the form of a parallelogram—the campus plan is unusually formal for Frederick Law Olmsted. Although it lost some of its punch when the tower of the University Church and the triumphal arch were toppled by the 1906 earthquake, it is still a knockout as you drive the monumental axis up Palm Drive to the triple-arched main gate, a focal point of the great twenty-foot wide arcades that surround the original buildings. This is a cloister taken to new heights, widths, and lengths; visit Stanford if only to stroll in it. Conceived by easterners in response to Stanford's request for an architecture with a California character, the buildings recall the missions and are well suited to the site and climate. And, like the missions, they have been repeatedly damaged by earthquakes, including that of 1989, from which they have yet to recover. Fortunately they are highly enough regarded that they are being restored at great expense. The standard that they set has proved too high to maintain, as a visit to today's campus reveals. Still, it is instructive to stroll what is still a very handsome campus to see how the tradition has been carried on. What follows is a selective list that can be covered in an hour's time.

Palo Alto as a whole is surprisingly lacking in interesting architecture, but the neighborhood known originally as Professorville has a number of significant houses from the early days. Driving up and down its streets is a good way to get a feeling for the older Peninsula community, which was very different and much more southern Californian than Berkeley.

Stanford University

1. The Quadrangle
1891, Shepley, Rutan and Coolidge; land. arch. & master plan, Frederick Law Olmsted
Serra St. at end of Palm Dr.

1. The Quadrangle

The first master plan called for continuing the system of linked quadrangles laid down by these buildings. Although this did not happen, what was built is impressive enough that it still dominates and gives focus to today's sprawling campus. These buildings originally contained all of the academic and administrative functions of the University, as well as its spiritual center, the University Church. Their heroic scale is still evident outside and in the arcades, but has been somewhat blurred inside the buildings, many of which had an extra floor tucked into the twenty-foot height of the original classrooms.

A combined program of seismic reinforcing and renovation is progressing slowly. Its most notable achievements to date are the northeast or History corner and Building 120 just east of the main gate, both by Esherick Homsey Dodge & Davis in 1979 and 1982. The whole complex repays detailed study; note particularly how the arcade and roof systems tie together a considerable variety of building sizes and shapes, and how different sizes of outdoor space range in scale from intimate to monumental. In front of the entry portals, in the northwest corner court, and at the northeast corner are four of Rodin's great bronze figures of the *Burghers of Calais*.

2. Memorial Church

2. Memorial Church
1903, Charles Allerton Coolidge;
reblt. 1913, C. E. Hodges
Quadrangle opposite main gate

Damaged heavily in 1906, when it lost its tower, and again in 1989, this earthquake-scarred veteran still has an interior with mosaics and stained glass of the period.

3. Art Gallery

3. Art Gallery
1917, Bakewell & Brown
Opposite the northwest corner of Quadrangle

A graceful variant on the original theme. Behind it in the court of the Cummings Art Building are sculptures by Joan Miró, Arnaldo Pomodoro, and Henry Moore.

4. Hoover Institution on War, Revolution and Peace (Hoover Tower)
1941, Bakewell & Brown,
Serra St.

By the time this was designed, the grace that distinguished the preceding entry was gone. As the campus campanile, the tower works best from a distance.

5. Encina Hall
1891, Shepley, Rutan & Coolidge
Encina Commons
1923, Bakewell & Brown
Serra St. west of the quadrangle
The dormitory for the original campus, now offices. The Commons behind is another of Bakewell & Brown's well-scaled and detailed variants on the original theme.

5. Encina Commons

6. White Memorial Plaza
1964, Thomas D. Church; fountain, Aristides Demetrios
Southwest of the quadrangle
A sucessful piece of place-making that marks the shift of the campus's center of gravity to the south.

7. Former Student Union
1915, Charles D. Whittlesey
West side of White Memorial Plaza
Romanesque Revival replaced Spanish Colonial Revival.

8. Post Office and bookstore
1960, John Carl Warnecke
East side of White Memorial Plaza
The original pair of buildings, excluding the later addition, is one of the most successful of recent efforts to reinterpret the original idiom of the campus.

8. Post Office and bookstore

9. Stanford Center for Research and Development in Education
1972, Skidmore Owings & Merrill
Alvarado Row at end of Galvez St.
With its arcade on the interior, this building is an abstraction and introversion of the original theme.

11. Braun Music Center

10. Law School
1973, Skidmore Owings & Merrill
Southeast of Center for Research, above
The same firm and the same exterior wall treatment as the Center, above, but different designers produce a very different building. (In the entry court is Alexander Calder's *Falcon* and in the inner court, Carla Lavatelli's *One-and-a-Half*. Behind the auditorium is Bruce Beasely's *Vanguard*.)

11. Braun Music Center
1984, Marquis Assoc.
North of the bend of Mayfield Ave.
An effective north gateway to the central campus.

18. Art Museum

19. Stanford University Hospital

20. Stanford Children's Hospital

21. Stanford Barn

12. Terman Engineering Center
1977, Harry Weese & Assoc.
Santa Teresa opp. Roble Dr.
Successful on its own terms, this makes no attempt other than the tile roof to follow the campus idiom.

13. Center for Integrated Systems
1984, Ehrlick & Rominger
Campus Dr. at Via Palou
Another recent abstraction of the original themes of arcades and tile roofs.

14. Central Energy Facility (COGEN)
1978, Spencer Assoc.
Campus Dr. and Ortega
Successful high-tech imagery, yet without violating the scale of the campus.

15. Charles H. Gilbert Biology Building
1991, Arthur Erickson
Serra opp. Via Crespi
As the programs and buildings get bigger, it becomes harder to cap them convincingly with a tile roof.

16. Chemistry building
1892, Shepley, Rutan & Coolidge
South end of Lomita Dr.
The only free-standing academic building of the original campus, this is a kind of companion-piece to Encina Hall.

17. Parking Structure
East side of Campus Dr. north of Roth Way
Parking structures almost never fit gracefully into academic campuses; this succeeds far better than most.

18. Leland Stanford Jr. Museum (Art Museum)
1892, Percy & Hamilton
Lomita at Museum Way
The only stylistic departure in the original group, this adopts a Schinkelesque Neoclassicism, based on the National Museum of Athens, that marks Jane Stanford's assumption of control after her husband's death. As of this writing it remains closed because of damage in the 1989 earthquake, but plans for its reconstruction are being prepared by William Turnbull Associates. In front is Arnaldo Pomodoro's *Cube,* and at the south end is the B. Gerald Cantor Rodin Sculpture Garden.

19. Stanford University Hospital
1959, Edward Durell Stone; exp. and moderniz.
1988, NBBJ
Campus Dr. opp. Roth Way

Stone's grille-wrapped confections with attenuated columns from the '60s have now acquired a certain period charm. This commission brought him to Palo Alto, where he grilled extensively thereafter. In front of the east entrance stands Jacques Lipchitz's *Song of the Vowels*.

20. Stanford Children's Hospital
1969, Stone, Marraccini & Patterson;
exp. 1991, Anshen & Allen
Welch Road west of Quarry

22. Child Care center

The terraced expansion is a graceful way of handling the always difficult massing of a low-rise hospital.

21. Stanford Barn
c.1870; rem. 1966
Welch Rd. at Quarry

The oldest building in the area, this was the barn to the Stanford farm that preceded the University.

Stanford Shopping Center
1957, Welton Becket; rem. 1977, Bull Field Volkman & Stockwell
El Camino Real at Quarry

23. The Knoll

North of the Barn spreads the very successful Stanford Shopping Center, designed originally by Welton Becket and extensively remodeled by Bull Field Volkman & Stockwell, with continuing remodeling by Field Paoli.

22. Child Care center
1989, Donald MacDonald
South of Palo Rd.

A child-scaled collection of gable-roofed cottages.

24. Hoover house

23. The Knoll
1918, Louis Christian Mullgardt
Lomita Dr.

This imposing pile was designed as the president's house. Less idiosyncratic than most of Mullgardt's work, it still seems alien to the character of the campus.

24. Hoover house
1919, Arthur B. Clarke and Birge Clarke
Cabrillo and Santa Inez

25. Hanna house

This very large, very Irving Gill-esque house was designed for Herbert Hoover with much advice from his wife. It now serves as the Stanford president's house.

25. Hanna house
1937, Frank Lloyd Wright
737 Frenchmen's Rd.
One of Wright's greatest houses, planned on a hexagonal grid, this was left to the University by its original owners. At this writing it is not open to visitors because of damage from the 1989 earthquake.

26. Rains student housing

26. Rains student housing
1988, Backen Arrigoni & Ross
North side of Bowdoin
The latest in a series of student housing groups. Others were by Campbell & Wong (high-rise) and Wurster Bernardi & Emmons (low-rise) in 1959, 1964, and 1966.

27. Peter Coutts Village
1982, Fisher-Friedman Assoc.
North of Peter Coutts Way
One of the most successful of this firm's many town house projects, this is laid out in two concentric rings around a central green.

29. Kellogg house

28. Center for Advanced Study in the Behavioral Sciences
1954, Wurster Bernardi & Emmons;
land. arch., Thomas D. Church
Los Arboles Ave. just south of Junipero Serra
This loosely grouped set of redwood and glass pavilions is a classic of the Bay Region style of the '50s.

30. Mendenhall house

Palo Alto

29. Kellogg house
1899, Bernard Maybeck
1061 Bryant St.
A rare early work of Maybeck's. The big gambrel roof gave this house the nickname of the "sunbonnet house."

31. Haehl house

30. Mendenhall house
1937, William W. Wurster
1570 Emerson St.
An unusual early Wurster in the Moderne style, now even more Moderne because of the recent addition of a rounded glass block stair tower.

31. Haehl house
c.1910, John Hudson Thomas
1680 Bryant St.
One of Thomas's Viennese Secession houses, on a more expanded plan than most of his Berkeley works.

32. Stern houses
1930, Birge Clarke
1950 & 1990 Cowper St.
A charming matched pair of Spanish Mediterranean Revival houses designed for two of Palo Alto's great benefactresses.

32. Stern house

33. House
1934, Carr Jones
2101 Waverly at Santa Rita
A slate-roofed, half-timbered Norman farmhouse in the middle of old Palo Alto, beautifully executed in the favorite mode of this exemplary "carpetect."

34. Raas house
1939, William W. Wurster
2240 Cowper St
Wurster's own Regency style used in a proto-ranch house.

33. 2101 Waverly

35. Lucie Stern Community Center
1935, Birge Clarke
Middlefield Rd. at Melville Ave.
A gracious building with a Mission patio forecourt.

36. Rinconada Park
1953, Eckbo, Royston & Williams
Embarcadero & Middlefield Rd.
This style of free-form landscape design has become so much a part of the California scene that one forgets how pioneering it was in the '50s.

35. Lucie Stern Community Center

37. Cultural Center (former City Hall)
1953, Leslie Nichols
Embarcadero Rd.at Newell Ave.
Former Main Library
1959, Edward Durrell Stone
1213 Newell Ave.
Two cultural period pieces. The former City Hall was an extraordinary civic concept when it was done (it was replaced by another Stone building downtown), while the library design by Stone's local representative, Lloyd Flood, is one of the most successful uses of Stone's hallmark, the perforated wall.

37. Former City Hall

187

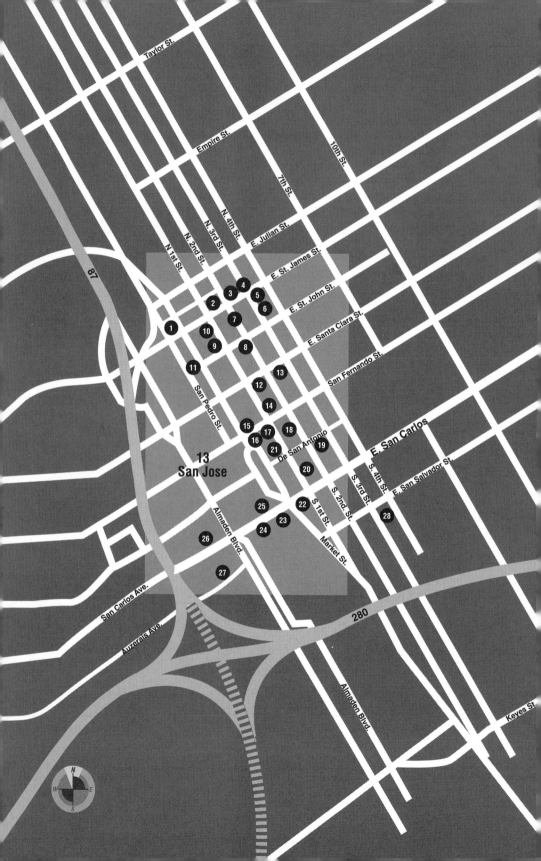

13

1. House
2. 1st Church of Christ, Scientist
3. Former St. Claire Club
4. St. James Place
5. Former Scottish Rite Temple
6. First Unitarian Church
7. St. James Park
8. Trinity Episcopal Church
9. U.S. Post Office
10. Santa Clara County Courthouse
11. Peralta Adobe
12. Bank of America Building
13. New Century block I.O.O.F. Building
14. Letitia Building
15. St. Joseph's Roman Catholic Church
16. San Jose Museum of Art
17. Office building
18. Retail center
19. State office building
20. U.S. Courthouse & Federal Building
21. Fairmont Hotel
22. St. Claire Hotel
23. San Jose Convention Center
24. Main Library
25. Former Civic Auditorium
26. San Jose Community Theater
27. Children's Museum
28. Rucker house

San Jose Tour

Founded in 1777, San Jose is California's oldest civic settlement and was briefly the state capital after the adoption of the first state constitution in Monterey on November 13, 1849. The first legislature convened in San Jose a month later in a two-story adobe and wood-frame building near the Plaza. Despite some hard work on the part of its members, it has passed into history's dustbin as the lesiglature "of a thousand drinks." The second legislature voted to remove the capital to Vallejo. For nearly two hundred years the seat of government was around the second site of the pueblo (the first site was subject to flooding from the Guadalupe River) between San Fernando and San Carlos Streets in the loop of Market Street. But beginning in 1959 with the completion of a new City Hall, a new civic center was built north of downtown. In the same period much of the central downtown was declared a redevelopment area, and a swath was cut across town to 4th Street that remained more or less barren until the 1980s. However, as of 1991 an impressive stand of new buildings now occupies the old wasteland with only a few holes waiting to be filled. A new light rail system runs along 1st Street with a transit mall designed by CHNMB that starts at San Carlos and runs north to St. James Street. An addition to the art museum, a convention center and the Children's Museum have also been completed in the central downtown area, creating a new civic center closer to the old heart of the pueblo. The Plaza has been re-landscaped and has a very successful fountain by George Hargreaves, who has also designed a new linear park for the Guadalupe River, now under construction west of downtown. When completed it will mitigate the damage to downtown wrought by the freeway, which runs north-south close by. In sum, a new downtown for San Jose is bursting out all over with old buildings being renovated as new ones are built.

Near downtown are 19th- and early 20th-century residential neighborhoods with blocks of fine buildings. North of Julian Street between 1st and 11th streets are more blocks of vintage houses and bungalows, and the blocks east and south of downtown on both sides of I-280 are rewarding to those interested in late 19th-century architectural styles. Southeast of I-280 is Keller Park, location of the Historical Society Museum and a collection of old buildings moved there to save them from bulldozers.

San Jose State University occupies several blocks east of central downtown and although not covered in this tour, it is certainly worth a visit. At this point in time, San Jose seems to be at last reaping the cultural benefits of being the major South Bay city and to be getting its share of the wealth produced by Silicon Valley. Having surpassed San Francisco in population, San Jose is now distinguishing itself in the fields of culture and architecture.

1. W. St. James at N. San Pedro

3. Former St. Claire Club

4. St. James Place

1. House
c.1870s
W. St. James and N. San Pedro Sts.
An exceptional Italianate house on a large corner lot.

2. First Church of Christ, Scientist
1905, Willis Polk
E. St. James and N. 2nd St.
An elegant Classic Revival design, the only one of its kind by this important San Francisco architect. The building also contributes, even in its currently abandoned state, to the civic dignity of St. James Park.

3. Former St. Claire Club
1893, A. Page Brown
65 E. St. James St.
A subtle design in the Craftsman mode that makes an unusually lavish use of brickwork as decoration.

4. St. James Place
1986, Daniel Solomon Assoc.
E. St. James and N. 3rd St.
A commendable attempt to design a much larger building to go with the older St. Claire Club.

5. Former Scottish Rite Temple
1924-25, Carl Werner
N. 3rd and E. St. James St.
An imposing Classic Revival temple by an architect based in Oakland. In 1981 the building was rehabilitated for the San Jose Athletic Club.

6. First Unitarian Church
1891, George M. Page
160 N. 3rd St.
This Romanesque Revival church interrupts the march of the Classic Revival mode down this side of the park. Next door is the Doric portico of the former Masonic Temple, now fronting for a recent high-rise behind it.

7. St. James Park
1848 survey by Chester Lyman
E. St. James, E. St. John, N. 2nd, N. 3rd Sts.
Part of Chester Lyman's 1848 plat of the city, this park became the focus of its civic aspirations in the latter part of the century. It was not landscaped until 1868 when the former courthouse was built in an attempt to attract the state capital back to San Jose. North 2nd Street was allowed to bisect the park in 1955, but today it is closed to automobile traffic and has been re-landscaped by Michael Painter. Having been spared major redevelopment in the post-war period, the scale of the park and its buildings is unusually harmonious.

8. Trinity Episcopal Church
1863, John W. Hammond
N. 2nd and E. St. John Sts.
The oldest church in San Jose; built in the Gothic Revival style by a sea captain who was a member of the parish. Originally constructed of redwood logged in Santa Cruz, the church was doubled in size and cut in half in 1876; the front half was moved to face N. 2nd Street. In 1887 the church was enlarged again, and the steeple added.

9. U. S. Post Office
1933, Ralph Wyckoff
N. 1st at E. St. John St.
A showpiece of the Depression-era WPA work with fine terra-cotta detail inside and out.

10. Santa Clara County Courthouse
1866-67, Levi Goodrich
N. 1st bet. E. St. John and S. St. James Sts.
A grand Classic Revival building that was even grander before it lost its upper story and dome in a 1931 fire; the present top is post-fire.

11. Peralta Adobe
c.1805; rest. 1976
184 W. St. John St.
The city's oldest Spanish colonial structure, which belonged to Luis Maria Peralta, Comisionado of the pueblo after 1807. It may be the oldest Bay Area adobe.

12. Bank of America Building
1925-26, H. A. Minton
S. 1st at E. Santa Clara St.
The major landmark of downtown for many years. A. P. Giannini, founder of the B of A, was a native son.

13. New Century block
1880
52-78 E. Santa Clara St.
The city's finest commercial palace of the time had two later additions and was renovated in 1984-85.

I.O.O.F. Building
c.1883, T. Lenzen
82-96 E. Santa Clara St.
A complementary building to the New Century block.

14. Letitia Building
1890, Jacob Lenzen
66-72 S. 1st St.
A business block in the now rare Romanesque Revival style once more common but usually built in stone and subject to earthquake damage as well as urban renewal.

8. Trinity Episcopal Church

10. Santa Clara County Courthouse

11. Peralta Adobe

12. Bank of America Building

16. San Jose Museum of Art

19. State office building

20. U.S, Courthouse and Federal Building

21. Fairmont Hotel

15. St. Joseph's Roman Catholic Church
1877, Hoffman & Clinch
Market at W. San Fernando St.
The first pueblo church of adobe was on this site; it was succeeded by two other structures before this grand edifice was built. Architect Brian Clinch was chosen for his erudition and his talent—he read the New Testament in Greek every day. The interior is equally grand.

16. San Jose Museum of Art
1892, Wiloughby Edbrooke; 1991, Skidmore Owings & Merrill
Market at W. San Fernando St.
Another Romanesque Revival building that has withstood earthquake damage in 1906 and 1989, as well as two changes of use. The recent addition by SOM is a handsome design in its own right that, happily, does not try to ape the style of the older building.

17. Office building
1989-90, Skidmore Owings & Merrill
Part of the new Silicon Valley Financial Center development planned and designed by SOM, which created the pedestrian mall from Market to 3rd Street.

18. Retail center
1989, Jon Jerde
San Antonio Mall bet. 1st and 2nd Sts.
A lively arcade of shops and restaurants designed by the southern California architect, who has made a specialty of shopping mall design.

19. State office building
1983, ELS Assoc.
E. San Carlos bet. 2nd and 3rd Sts.
One of a series of state buildings designed to conserve energy and provide a humane working environment with landscaped interior couryards

20. United States Courthouse and Federal Building
1984, Hellmuth, Obata & Kassabaum
S. 1st at E. San Carlos St.
Another building that makes a big display of energy conservation with a giant sunshade over the court.

21. Fairmont Hotel
1989, Hellmuth, Obata & Kassabaum
Market St. opp. the Plaza
Nothing if not monumental, this new luxury hotel has given a new importance to the old Plaza, which has been re-landscaped and has a fountain of walk-through jets designed by George Hargreaves.

22. St. Claire Hotel
1926, Weeks & Day
302 S. Market St.
A dignified and urbane building designed by the architects of other notable hotels such as the Mark Hopkins and the Huntington on Nob Hill in San Francisco.

23. San Jose Convention Center
1990, Mitchell/Giurgola
W. San Carlos at Market St.
A well-scaled civic design that attracts attention with a sprightly mural. Not the least of the convention center's contributions is that it has involved the main library next door and the old civic auditorium across the street in an urbanistic streetscape accentuated by the light rail station by Wallace Roberts Todd.

23. San Jose Convention Center

24. Main Library
1971, Norton S. Curtis
180 San Carlos St.
A period piece that used to look lonely and pretentious but has now been assimilated into a new cultural context.

25. Former Civic Auditorium
1934, William Binder & E. N. Curtis
145 W. San Carlos St.
A Spanish Colonial Revival building with a humanly scaled colonnade on the street. Also on the street is an entertaining Rube Goldberg-like artwork in a glass case that announces an exhibition space for high technology inside.

26. San Jose Community Theater

26. San Jose Community Theater
1972, William Wesley Peters
255 Almaden Blvd.
Late Wrightian design by the architect who headed Taliesin West after the master died.

27. Children's Museum
1991, Ricardo Legorreta
Technology Dr.
A sculptural composition in geometric forms and subtle colors that are the hallmarks of this noted Mexican architect, who also worked with Luis Barragan.

27. Children's Museum

28. Rucker house
c.1883
418 S. 3rd St.
This great Queen Anne villa offers a taste of San Jose's 19th-century residential neighborhoods. The blocks nearby on S. 5th and S. 6th are also worth exploring to see more fine houses. Try the 500 block of S. 6th Street.

28. Rucker house

14

1. Jack London Square
2. The Leviathan
3. Former Oakland Iron Works
4. Former Western Pacific
   Depot
5. Old Oakland Historic District
6. Preservation Park
   Pardee Mansion
   Remilard house
   Ginn house
   First Lutheran Church
   Green Library
7. City Center
   American President Co.
   Clorox Building
   Wells Fargo Building
   City Center Buildings & Mall
8. 1100 Broadway building
   Bank building
   Oakland Tribune Tower
9. City Hall
10. YWCA Building
11. Former Howden Building
12. Cathedral Building

13. Fox Oakland Theater
    and office building
14. Mary Bowles Building
15. Oakland Floral Depot
16. I. Magnin & Co.
17. Paramount Theater
18. Former Breuner Co.
19. Kaiser Center
    Ordway Building
    Kaiser Center Building
20. Oakland Hotel
21. Frank Mar Housing
22. Oakland Public Library
23. Scottish Rite Temple
24. Camron-Stanford House
    Museum
25. Alameda County Courthouse
26. Oakland Museum

Oakland Downtown Tour

Oakland Downtown Tour

Oakland's central downtown retains a rich diversity of architecture from its major periods of growth. The successive downtown centers lie along Broadway beginning at the waterfront with what is now called Jack London Square, the heart of the 1850s settlement. Over the next hundred years the city grew to the northeast away from the water, but now in the 1990s the heart of downtown is more or less where it was in the post-1906 boom period, mainly because large and important urban redevelopment projects have finally been completed giving the five-points intersection at 14th Street, Broadway, Telegraph and San Pablo avenues a new vitality.

Oakland was once part of the vast Rancho de San Antonio, granted to Luis Peralta, who lived out his life in a humble adobe in San Jose. A sharp and acquisitive-minded Yankee, Horace Carpentier, managed to lease land on the waterfront from the Peraltas and joined with two other Yankees to hire Julius Kellsberger in 1850 to map a town-site in a grid plan with streets 80 feet wide–except for Broadway, which was 110 feet wide–running through blocks 200 by 300 feet square. Seven blocks were allocated for public open space. In 1852 Carpentier got the state legislature to pass an act incorporating the settlement as Oakland, a fitting name at the time because the land was largely covered with oak groves. This "walking city" lasted until the railway era that followed the arrival of the transcontinental railroad at the Oakland Mole in 1868. In the 1870s railroad lines began to run along the lower east-west streets, and business and commercial interests moved up Broadway to the area around 9th to 11th streets, now called Old Oakland. Civic enterprises blossomed. Mayor Samuel Merritt presided over the creation of public libraries, a new city hall at 14th Street and San Pablo Avenue, and got the state legislature to create the first-ever wildlife refuge in North America on Lake Merritt in 1870. In the 1870s the city's wealthy and powerful citizens began to settle around the lake that bore the mayor's name and the central business district consolidated in the east-west blocks around Broadway from 10th to 14th Street.

The 1906 earthquake did less damage to Oakland than San Francisco and sparked another boom, which saw the business blocks transformed into skyscrapers from 1907 to about 1914. Even the new City Hall of 1912 was built as a skyscraper. The central retail district reached 17th Street during this period as Oakland became the focus of retail shopping for the surrounding East Bay towns. A civic center began to develop on Lake Merritt with the completion of a Civic Auditorium in 1914.

The impact of the automobile in the 1920s brought the creation of new suburbs in the areas north and west of downtown and sparked a new retail and entertainment district uptown around Broadway and 20th Street. By contrast the post-World War II suburban expansion had a minimal, even depressing, effect on downtown and brought declining real estate values, neglect and, ultimately, the federal bulldozer.

Today, as we noted in the first paragraph, downtown has a new, or renewed, look, but thanks to a strong preservation consciousness retains its historic diversity. Since most of it is quite walkable, it can be explored on foot. A number of public art works are disposed around downtown and Lake Merritt, which is a major scenic asset.

1. Jack London Square
Beginning of Broadway

The original waterfront, now transformed into a center for offices and tourism. Nearby is the warehouse district and the produce market developed in the 'teens and '20s. Many buildings have been rehabilitated for other uses, but the market still functions in the mornings in characterful buildings around 2nd and Franklin streets.

4. Former Western Pacific Depot

2. The Leviathan
1990-91, Ace Architects
330 2nd St.

A self-consciously outrageous design by architects who believe in exploiting the fanciful.

3. Former Oakland Iron Works
c.1880s; rehab. 1980s, Don Dommer Assoc.
2nd St. bet. Clay and Jefferson Sts.

An old industrial complex built over a period of time and nicely rehabiltated for a mix of uses.

5. Old Oakland Historic District

4. Former Western Pacific Depot
1909
3rd and Washington Sts.

A relic of the railroad era that until recently housed an important cultural center devoted mainly to jazz concerts.

5. Old Oakland Historic District
1868-1881; rest. 1970s-1980s, Storek & Storek
Broadway to Clay, 8th to 10th St.

A prime collection of 19th-century commercial buildings meticulously restored. Among them is the "lawyers' block" at Broadway and 10th, developed by Frederick Delger from 1880-85 and designed by Kenitzer & Raun, and Ratto's, 1876, designed by John S. Tibals, at Washington and 9th Sts. The latter building is a great food emporium.

5. 900 block Broadway

6. Preservation Park
Pardee Mansion
1868, Hoaglund & Newsom
672 11th St.
Peter Remilard house
1887
Frederick B. Ginn house
1890, A. Page Brown
First Lutheran Church
1890, Walter Matthews
14th and Castro Sts.
Green Library
1902, Bliss & Faville
14th St. and Martin Luther King, Jr. Way

6. Pardee Mansion

Most of these buildings were moved here out of the path of the adjacent freeway, although the first and last ones listed were always here. The Pardee house is a museum. Preservation Park is credible as a 19th-century neighborhood even if it is a bit make-believe.

7. City Center
American President Company Building
1991, Gensler Assoc.
1111 Broadway
Clorox Building
1976, Caesar Pelli
1345 Broadway
Wells Fargo Building
1974; Victor Gruen
1221 Broadway
City Center Buildings and Mall
1990, Ishimaru Design Group
11th to 14th Sts. & Broadway to Martin Luther King Way
Federal Building
1992, Kaplan, McLaughlin, Diaz
Jefferson to Martin Luther King, Jr. Way
Downtown's major new commercial and office complex, which has risen from land cleared for redevelopment about 25 years ago. The interior of the complex is a particularly attractive and successful work of urban design. A pleasant sculpture garden is located behind the American President Company Building.

6. Preservation Park

7. Oakland City Center

8. 1100 Broadway building
1911-12, Frederick H. Meyer
Bank building
1907, Charles W. Dickey; 1909,
1922-23, Reed & Corlett
1200 Broadway
Oakland Tribune Tower
1923, Edward T. Foulkes
13th and Franklin Sts.
The core of the post-1906 downtown, yet these were the mighty skyscrapers of their time, and the Tribune Tower is still *the* skyline landmark.

8. 1100 and 1200 Broadway

9. City Hall
1911-14, Palmer, Hornbostel & Jones
1 City Hall Plaza
A skyscraper with a Classical topknot lavishly decorated in white terra-cotta ornament depicting the state's fruits and flowers. The design was a competition winner.

22. Oakland Public Library

23. Scottish Rite Temple

24. Camron-Stanford House Museum

10. Y W C A Building
1915, Julia Morgan
1515 Webster St.
Morgan was the official architect for the YWCA and designed a number of its buildings in the west and in Honolulu. This one has an attractive interior court.

11. Former Howden Building
1915
17th and Webster Sts.
Built to advertise the owner's tile products, the interior is also richly decorated.

12. Cathedral Building
1913, Benjamin McDougall
Telegraph Ave. and Broadway
A chateauesque skyscraper with spikey ornament.

13. Fox Oakland Theater and office building
1928, M. I. Diggs, Weeks & Day
1815 Telegraph Ave.
An exotic Arabian nights movie palace.

14. Mary Bowles Building
1931, Douglas D. Stone
1721 Broadway
A small gem of Art Deco styling.

15. Oakland Floral Depot
1931, Albert Evers
1900 Telegraph Ave.
Another Art Deco jewel box; it was built by Capwell's to prevent a tall building from blocking the view.

16. I. Magnin & Co.
1931, Weeks & Day
20th St. & Broadway
Another box wrapped in Art Deco terra-cotta tiling.

17. Paramount Theater
1931, Miller & Pflueger; rest. 1976, Skidmore Owings & Merrill
2025 Broadway
Arguably the greatest Art Deco theater left on the west coast, the billboard-like exterior served its advertising-function superbly. The architects designed every bit of the interior and had talented artists, Ralph Stackpole and Robert Howard, create the relief sculpture and other decoration. Don't miss the ladies' lounge.

18. Former Breuner Co.
1931, Albert F. Roller
22nd St. and Broadway
Built for a furniture company, as the chair in terra-cotta relief over the entrance suggests.

19. Kaiser Center
Ordway Building
1970, Skidmore Owings & Merrill
Kaiser Plaza and 21st St.
Kaiser Center Building
1959; Welton Beckett & Assoc.;
Roof garden, Osmundsen/Staley
20th and Harrison Sts.
As the major property owner and most powerful local institution, Kaiser was initiated a new phase of office and commerical development by the lake.

20. Oakland Hotel
1910, Henry Janeway Hardenburgh, Bliss & Faville;
rest. 1981 and 1991, The Ratcliff Architects
270 13th St.
The post-1906 boom prompted this hotel, still a landmark, but now converted to housing for senior citizens.

25. Alameda County Courthouse

21. Frank Mar Housing
1991, Donald MacDonald
13th and Harrison Sts.
Affordable housing in a mixed format of low and highrise elements with varying numbers of units.

22. Oakland Public Library
1949, Miller & Warnecke
125 14th St.
Restrained Modern styling with a human civic scale.

26. Oakland Museum

23. Scottish Rite Temple
1908, O'Brien & Werner
1433 Madison Ave.
A particularly gutsy version of the Mission Revival style.

24. Camron-Stanford House Museum
1875, Samuel Merritt
1426 Lakeside Dr.
The last of the stately mansions that once lined the lake.

26. Oakland Museum

25. Alameda County Courthouse
1935, W. G. Corlett & James W. Plachek
13th and Fallon Sts.
The Public Works Administration's Monumental Moderne.

26. The Oakland Museum
1969, Kevin Roche, John Dinkeloo & Assoc.;
land. arch., Dan Kiley
Oak bet. 10th and 12th Sts.
A justly famous Bay Area building, this sunken museum houses Natural History, History, and Art and has a land-scaped courtyard framed by beautiful terraced gardens.

1. Berkeley Unified School District Building
2. Main Public Library
   Commercial building 2270 Shattuck Ave.
   United Artists Theatre
3. Tupper & Reed Music Store
4. Life Sciences complex
5. Genetics and Plant Biology Building
   Northwest Animal Facility
   Warren Hall
6. Hilgard Hall
   Wellman Hall
   Giannini Hall
7. Recreational Sports Facility
8. Former Unitarian Church
9. Sproul Hall and Plaza/ Student Union complex
10. Sather Gate
    Wheeler Hall
    Durant Hall
    California Hall
    Doe Library
    Bancroft Library
    Campanile
    South Hall
11. Hearst Memorial Gym
12. University Art Museum
13. Wurster Hall
14. Women's Faculty Club
    Senior Mens Hall
    Faculty Club
15. Hearst Memorial Mining Building
16. North Gate Hall
17. Foothill Student Housing
18. Graduate School of Public Policy
19. Freeman house
20. Oscar Mauer Studio
21. Maybeck Recital Hall
22. Rose Walk
23. Howard house
24. Greenwood Common
    Francis Gregory house
    Gregory house
25. Jackson house
26. La Loma Park/Maybeck land
    Lawson house
    Mathewson studio/house
    Maybeck "Sack house"
    Tufts house
    Wallen Maybeck house
    House 2753 Buena Vista Way
    Gannon house
27. Hume house
28. Thorsen house (Sigma Phi Fraternity)
29. First Church of Christ, Scientist
30. Julia Morgan Center

University of California / Berkeley Tour

*T*wo separate and distinct communities grew together to form the City of Berkeley, incorporated in 1878 with the waterfront community of Ocean View. The open fields that separated the University community from its industrial counterpart were gradually filled in with buildings, but unlike Oakland, Berkeley resisted urbanization and has remained a largely residential city with a small downtown.

The University got its start in Oakland in 1859 when the Reverend Henry Durant, founder of the College of Oakland, joined with members of an academic committee to purchase a 160-acre tract for the future location of the college, which they felt should be removed from the evil urban influences of Oakland. To help finance the purchase, a townsite of one-acre lots was platted in the typical gridiron plan and settlement began. The town was finally named after Bishop George Berkeley of Cloyne, whose line, "Westward the course of empire takes it way," seemed appropriate to the founding fathers. The College became the state university after the passage of the Morrill Land Grant Act of 1862. By the terms of the act each state got 30,000 acres of surveyed public land for each of its senators and representatives in Congress as apportioned by the 1860 census. Proceeds from the sale of the land were to be invested and the returns used to develop the campus buildings and grounds.

Just east of the center of downtown Berkeley, the main entrance to the University of California is at the end of University Avenue. The central campus is bounded on the west by Oxford Street, on the north by Hearst Avenue, and on the south by Bancroft Way. To the east the campus stretches up into the hills, but the central campus ends more or less at Gayley Way.

The University of California graduated its first class in 1873; the graduation ceremony took place in front of the first two buildings, North and South Halls, designed in 1873 by David Farquharson in the fashionable Second Empire style. (Only South Hall remains.) Between them the central axis of Frederick Law Olmsted's 1866 campus plan, now called Campanile Way, defined the visual path to the Golden Gate. Farquharson himself did a plan for the campus in 1873 that somewhat reflected Olmsted's, but it had hardly any effect on the siting of buildings when the University really began to grow in the 1880s. In the mid-1890s Mrs. Phoebe A. Hearst expressed an interest in funding a building for the College of Mining in memory of her husband, Senator George Hearst. Her subsequent involvement with the University resulted in an international competition for a master plan for the campus that was coordinated by Bernard Maybeck and judged by a distinguished jury of American and European architects in 1899. The winner, Emile Bénard, declined to serve as supervising architect, and the post was filed in 1903 by the fourth-place winner, John Galen Howard. As supervising architect for 22 years, Howard revised Bénard's plan and designed the buildings that comprise the central core of the campus. George Kelham followed Howard, then Arthur Brown, Jr., served as the last supervising architect. The post-World War II expansion filled the central campus with buildings, most of which are not up to the original standards set by Howard, yet the campus remains remarkably parklike.

Because several guides exist that cover architecture of the East Bay, we have limited our coverage to a brief mention of downtown buildings of interest, a selective walking tour of the University of California campus (cars are not allowed on campus), a tour of north Berkeley's famed residential architecture, and finally, three great architectural landmarks in south Berkeley that are not to be missed.

1. Berkeley Unified School District Building (former City Hall)
1908, Bakewell & Brown; rest. 1991
2134 Martin Luther King, Jr. Way
Beaux-Arts Classicism used to create an American version of a French provincial city hall, which the city outgrew some years ago, but has carefully restored.

1. Berkeley Unified School District Building

2. Main Public Library
1930; James W. Plachek
Shattuck and Kittredge Sts.
Commercial building
1914; rem. 1932
2270 Shattuck Ave.
United Artists Theatre
1932, C. A. Balch
2274 Shattuck Ave.
Three buildings in the Style Moderne; the first is the best.

3. Tupper & Reed Music Store
1925, W. R. Yelland
2277 Shattuck Ave.
Architecture from Mother Goose, delightfully dressed up.

4. Life Sciences complex
1930, George Kelham; 1993, MBT/Ratcliff Assoc.
Kelham's imposing building with fine sculptural detail by Robert Howard has been gutted and will receive new insides designed by the architects of the new building.

5. Genetics and Plant Biology Building
1990, Hellmuth Obata & Kassabaum
Hearst at Oxford St.
Northwest Animal Facility
1991, MBT
Warren Hall
1955, Masten & Hurd
The recent buildings–shoe-horned into a former parking lot–were planned to create a coherent, urbanistic precinct in this part of the campus.

6. Hilgard Hall
1917-18, John Galen Howard
Wellman Hall
1912, John Galen Howard
Giannini Hall
1930, William C. Hays
A harmonius complex in varied styles.

7. Recreational Sports Facility
1984, ELS Design Group
Bancroft Way

8. Former Unitarian Church
1898, A.C. Schweinfurth
Dana and Bancroft Way
A notable relic of the First Bay Region Tradition originally not part of the University.

9. Sproul Hall and Plaza/ Student Union complex
1941, Arthur Brown, Jr.; 1965, DeMars & Reay
Bancroft at Telegraph Ave.
Widely known as the site of student protests in the late 1960s, this is one of the most successful works of urban design in the Bay Area.

10. Sather Gate
1910, John Galen Howard
Wheeler Hall
1917, John Galen Howard
Durant Hall
1911, John Galen Howard
California Hall
1905, John Galen Howard
Doe Library
1907-1918, John Galen Howard
Bancroft Library
1949, Arthur Brown, Jr.
Campanile
1914, John Galen Howard
South Hall
1873, David Farquharson

10. Durant Hall

10. South Hall

Except for South Hall and the Bancroft Library, these core buildings of the early campus were designed by John Galen Howard, first supervising architect. Although they all employ the Classical language of architecture, their range of expression reveals what a rich language it was.

11. Hearst Gym

11. Phoebe A. Hearst Memorial Gymnasium
1925, Bernard Maybeck and Julia Morgan
N. side Bancroft Way near College Ave.
Morgan planned the building and Maybeck created the romantic architectural elements. The building was intended to be part of a larger complex with an auditorium, art gallery, and museum that was never built.

12. University Art Museum
1970, Mario Ciampi
S. side of Bancroft Way near College Ave.
A cubistic composition with a dramatic interior.

13. Wurster Hall/College of Environmental Design
1964, DeMars, Esherick, and Olsen
College Ave. at Bancroft Way
When built for the departments of design and planning, this was the world's largest prefabricated concrete building; it still overwhelms its surroundings.

13. Wurster Hall

14. Women's Faculty Club
1923, John Galen Howard
Senior Men's Hall
1906, John Galen Howard
Faculty Club
1902, Bernard Maybeck; 1903-04, John Galen Howard;
1914, 1925, Warren Perry; 1959, Downs & Lagorio
Along Strawberry Creek
An informal group of social buildings on Strawberry Creek, the first in the eastern Shingle Style and the second a monumental redwood log cabin. The last building stands at the end of Faculty Glade. Designed by Maybeck in a modified Mission Revival style, it has been enlarged several times, but the original main hall is intact.

14. Faculty Club

15. Hearst Memorial Mining Building
1902-07, John Galen Howard
The greatest building on the campus and one of California's architectural treasures, its generous budget made possible the elegant details, sculptures, and choice materials. Howard considered the design an evocation of California's Spanish missions, but it is a far cry from those rudimentary structures. The interior recalls the great Paris libraries of Henri Labrouste.

16. North Gate Hall/Graduate School of Journalism
1906-12, John Galen Howard; 1936, Walter Steilberg
The first building for the first department of architecture west of the Rockies, it was called the Ark (Howard was Noah) and was built as a temporary structure, hence its simple brown-shingled form and residential scale. The building grew around a pleasant courtyard. Uphill is the old Drawing Building, 1914, also by Howard.

14. Women's Faculty Club

17. Foothill Student Housing
1991, William Turnbull Assoc./Ratcliff Assoc.
Stern Hall
1942, 1959, Wurster, Bernardi & Emmons
A well-planned complex that incorporates an older dormitory; sensitively sited on difficult terrain.

18. Graduate School of Public Policy
1893, Coxhead & Coxhead; 1909, Bakewell & Brown
Hearst at LeRoy Ave.
Although somewhat altered, this is a good example of this first-generation Bay Region architect's work.

19. Freeman house
1904-06, Coxhead & Coxhead
LeRoy Ave. at Ridge Rd.
Another work by the Coxheads, this one a large Colonial Revival house of strong character in a suitable setting.

20. Oscar Maurer Studio
1907, Bernard Maybeck
1772 LeRoy Ave.
Beautifully sited by the creek and very inviting.

15. Hearst Memorial Mining Building

21. Maybeck Recital Hall/Alma Kennedy studio/house
1914, 1923, Bernard Maybeck
Euclid Ave. and Buena Vista Way
An idiosyncratic mix of Mediterranean and Gothic elements enhanced by vivid colors, the recital hall with attached home replaced a studio that burned in 1923.

22. Rose Walk
1913, Bernard Maybeck; 1925-36, Henry Gutterson
Rose bet. Euclid and LeRoy Ave.
A perfectly planned residential development compressed into one block. Maybeck designed the walk and the concrete retaining walls and light standards. After the 1923 fire, owner Frank Gray hired Henry Gutterson, Maybeck's protege, to design houses on the north side. The single and double houses were ingeniously sited to provide privacy and gracious living on a small scale.

21. Maybeck Recital Hall

23. Howard house
1912, John Galen Howard
1401 LeRoy Ave.
Designed in an L-shape to follow the lot frontage, this long, shingled house shows how much Howard's eastern-formality was modified by western informality. Julia Morgan added a library wing to the north end in 1927.

22. Rose Walk

24. Greenwood Common
1950s, Lawrence Halprin, land. arch.
W. side of Greenwood Terr.
William W. Wuster initiated this postwar development on property that belonged to his house, designed by John Galen Howard, which stands up the hill east of Greenwood

Terrace but is not visible. Like Rose Walk, this is an exemplary residential enclave, but from a different time. The Modern architects of the Second Bay Tradition are well represented in these modest houses, numbered from north to south around the common.

No. 1, 1955, Donald Olsen

No. 3, 1954, Joseph Esherick

No. 4, 1954, Harwell Hamilton Harris

No. 7, c.1920, R. M. Schindler and William W. Wurster

No. 8, 1953, Howard Moise

No. 9, 1954, Henry Hill

No. 10, 1952, John Funk

Francis Gregory house
1907, Bernard Maybeck
1476 Greenwood Terr.
A deceptively contemporary-looking house.

Gregory house
1912, John Galen Howard
1486 Greenwood Terr.
A sensitively sited Craftsmanly chalet.

24. Greenwood Common

24. 1486 Greenwood Terr.

25. Jackson house
1939, Michael Goodman
2626 Buena Vista Way
Early Modernism with a touch of the Regency style.

26. La Loma Park/Maybeck land
1915-1933, Bernard Maybeck
Buena Vista Way and La Loma Ave.
About 1900 the Maybecks purchased a large tract of land called La Loma Park with two friends and divided it up. The Maybecks' portion was built up mainly with family houses although some were designed for friends. Their large family house of 1909 was destroyed in the 1923 fire and replaced with a set of cottages that the family occupied in a somewhat nomadic fashion. Maybeck participated in the construction of most of the houses listed below; they embody innovative ideas and inventive handicraft.

Lawson house
1907, Bernard Maybeck
1515 LaLoma St.
Maybeck designed this innovative, poured-concrete house to withstand earthquakes and fire and to recall the houses of ancient Pompeii.

Mathewson studio/house
1915, Bernard Maybeck
2704 Buena Vista Way

Maybeck "Sack house"
1924, 2711 Buena Vista Way
Made of sacks dipped in Bubblecrete, a lightweight concrete, and hung on chicken wire.

26. Lawson house

Tufts house
1931, Bernard Maybeck
2733 Buena Vista Way

Wallen Maybeck house
1933, Bernard Maybeck
2751 Buena Vista Way

House
2753 Buena Vista Way
1914, William C. Hays
A small-scale Italian palazzo executed in the Shingle Style.

Gannon house
1933, Bernard Maybeck
2780 Buena Vista Way
Nearly a twin of Wallen's house adjusted for another site.

27. Hume house
1928, John Hudson Thomas
2900 Buena Vista Way
A romantic Spanish castle in concrete built around a court, its design was requested by the clients.

28. Sigma Phi Fraternity house (Thorsen house)
1909, Greene & Greene
2307 Piedmont Ave.
A rare and notable example in northern California of the work of this famous Pasadena firm.

29. First Church of Christ, Scientist
1910, Bernard Maybeck; 1927,
Sunday School add., Henry Gutterson
Dana at Dwight
Maybeck's masterwork and one of this country's most remarkable buildings. An amalgam of styles but a copy of none, the design demonstrates his genius for fusing structure with ornament as well as for making the most of a restricted piece of property. The church is open to the public after services on Wednesday night and Sunday morning. The interior is as magical at night as by daylight.

30. Julia Morgan Center (former St. John's Church)
1908-10, Julia Morgan
2640 College Ave.
Designed to fit into this early neighborhood.of brown-shingled houses, the building does not appear nearly as large as it is. The barnlike character of the interior was deliberate; its frankly expressed structural framework was enriched with handsome Craftsman lighting fixtures.Built at the same time as Maybeck's nearby church, it cost a quarter as much. The building is now used as a theater.

29. First Church of Christ, Scientist

30. Julia Morgan Center

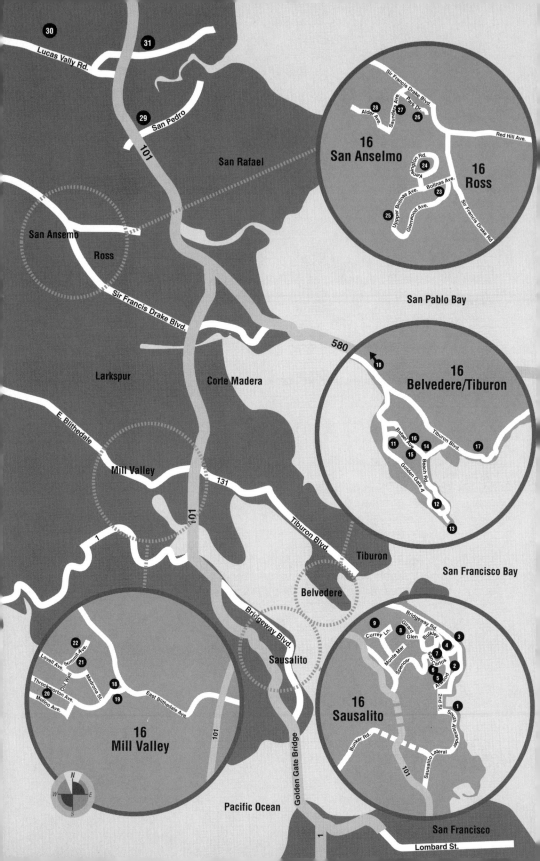

Sausalito

1. Dickinson house
2. House 60 Atwood Ave.
3. Sausalito Town Square
4. St. John's Presbyterian
   Church
5. House 39 Atwood Ave.
6. Sausalito Women's Club
7. Christ Episcopal Church
   Guild Hall
   Parish Hall
8. Gardner house
9. Curry Lane houses

Belvedere/Tiburon

10. Lyford house/Audubon
    Society
11. St. Stephen's Episcopal
    Church
12. Golden Gate Ave. houses
13. Blanding Lane houses
14. Belvedere Town Square
15. First Church of Christ
    Scientist
16. Belvedere City Hall
17. Point Tiburon

Mill Valley

18. Marin Outdoor Art Club
19. Depot Plaza and Cafe
20. Mill Valley Public
    Library
21. Evans house
22. Coffin house

Ross/San Anselmo

23. St. Anselm's Catholic
    Church
24. S.F. Theological
    Seminary
    Chapel
    Dormitory
25. Houses 40, 46 Upper Rd.
26. House 96 Park Dr.
27. House 206 Saunders Ave.
28. House 100 Alder Ave.

North of San Rafael

29. Marin County Civic
    Center
30. Lucas Valley
31. St. Vincent's School

Marin Tour

Marin Tour

Marin County is a scenic and architectural delight, but due to dense greenery, rugged terrain and the dwellers' insistence on privacy, is not easy to tour. The following list is designed to give a relatively manageable overview for the architectural sightseer.

Sausalito. William A. Richardson, English sailor and one of San Francisco's founding fathers, received Rancho Sausalito as the dowry of his Mexican bride. In 1869 1,000 acres were purchased by the Sausalito Land and Ferry Company, which subdivided the property as a speculative development, served of course by its ferry to San Francisco. Commuter settlement began in earnest in 1875 when the North Pacific Coast Railroad took control of the ferry, which until the opening of the Golden Gate Bridge, was the major northern entry to San Francisco. The town has evolved from fishing village to bohemian suburb to its present yuppified, congested but still picturesque state. Because of its precipitous terrain and narrow streets, driving is difficult, especially on weekends. On the other side of Route 101 is the portion of the Golden Gate National Seashore that includes the Marin Headlands and the old coast defense installations of Forts Baker, Barry, and Cronkhite. In addition to beautiful scenery and views, there are some fine old military buildings and artifacts.

Belvedere/Tiburon. The completion of the Northern Pacific Railroad from San Rafael to Tiburon in 1884 brought ferry service from Tiburon to San Francisco and created one of the world's most spectacular commutes. The first exurbanites settled along the harbor's edge largely in houseboats, a few of which survive as houses along Beach Road. In 1890 the Belvedere Land Company planted pine and eucalyptus on Belvedere "Island" (actually a peninsula), transforming the barren slopes into a Riviera-like paradise. Today most houses are barely visible, but it is worth driving around and climbing a few of the steep lanes to experience the ambience. The lagoon is a real estate creation of the 1950s, now so solidly lined with houses that it is difficult to get any sense of either the architecture or its relationship to the water. Most of these architect-designed houses are visible only from the water, so acess to a boat is necessary for a real view of them.

Mill Valley. A sawmill built on Cascade Creek to cut the then plentiful redwoods gave the town its name. In 1887 the land was acquired by a group of developers who connected it to the new railroad and by 1890 sold 3,000 lots, most of them for summer homes. But in 1903 electric rail service came to Mill Valley, linking it to the Sausalito ferry with a commute time as fast as today's and transforming it increasingly, like the rest of Marin, into a bedroom for San Francisco. In spite of this, and thanks in part to its setting, it has kept its character as a special place, more rustic and less yuppy than its neighbors. Here, too, houses are hard to see without trespassing.

Ross/San Anselmo. Nestled in a glen full of oaks in the heart of the peninsula, Ross was an early summer colony for the very wealthy. The best place to begin a tour is at Sir Francis Drake and Bolinas Avenue. Continuing up Bolinas past St. Anselm's and the Seminary to Upper Road, around on Upper to Glenwood and Fernhill avenues and back to Shady Lane will give a good picture of old Ross.

North of San Rafael. Off San Pedro Road in Santa Venetia is Frank Lloyd Wright's Marin County Civic Center. Farther north off Lucas Valley Road is the Eichler subdivision of Lucas Valley (turn off Lucas Valley at Mt. Shasta), an outstanding example of subdivision planning and design. At the Marinwood-St. Vincent's Road exit is the Spanish Colonial revival St. Vincent's School for boys, looking like old Mexico.

Sausalito

1. Dickinson house
1890, Willis Polk
26 Alexander Ave.
Straight ahead of you as you start around the sharp curve that brings you down into Sausalito, this dark shingle box is one of the oldest houses in town. A little beyond it on the left at 215 South Street is a Victorian Gothic cottage that is at least twenty years older.

2. 60 Atwood Ave.

2. House
1950, Joseph Esherick
60 Atwood Ave.
Best seen from below on Bridgeway, this remarkable house is built on the foundations of a castle started by newspaper magnate William Randolph Hearst.

3. Sausalito Town Square
Bridgeway at Excelsior Lane
Elephant lampposts, palms, and fountain wonderfully express the Mediterranean image Sausalito had of itself around the turn of the century.

4. St. John's Presbyterian Church

4. St. John's Presbyterian Church
1905, Coxhead & Coxhead
100 Bulkley Ave.
The interior of Coxhead's last Shingle Style church is much starker than his earlier ones, but is climaxed by the wonderful clerestoried tower.

5. House
1939, Gardner Dailey
39 Atwood Ave.
An inappropriate color scheme presently somewhat masks this classic example of early Bay Region Modernism.

5. 39 Atwood Ave.

6. Sausalito Women's Club
1916-18, Julia Morgan
Central Ave. at San Carlos
One of a series of Women's Clubs that Morgan designed around the Bay Area, this simple shingle building seems as right for its site and purpose today as when it was built.

7. Christ Episcopal Church
1882
Guild Hall
1889
Parish Hall
1967, Henrik Bull
Santa Rosa Ave. at San Carlos

6. Sausalito Women's Club

This harmonious group evolves from Carpenter Gothic origins through Shingle Style to Second Bay Region, of which the Parish Hall is an unusually fine example.

8. Gardner house
1869
Cazneau St. at Girard Ave.
A Carpenter Gothic cottage that is Sausalito's oldest essentially unaltered house.

9. Curry Lane houses
139 Curry Ln.
1958, John Funk
227 Curry Ln.
1955, John Hoops
244 Curry Ln.
1953, Roger Lee
250 Curry Ln.
1953, Charles Warren Callister
260 Curry Ln.
1956, John Hoops
290 Curry Ln.
1958, Henrik Bull
Most Bay Region Style houses of the 1950s are now so overgrown as to be invisible from the street. This is one of the rare groups that is still more or less visible, although some are best seen from Toyon Avenue below.

9. 139 Curry Ln.

9. 260 Curry Ln.

9. 244 Curry Ln.

Belvedere/Tiburon

10. Hilarita Reed Lyford house/Audubon Society
1874, rest. 1957, John Lord King
An Italianate villa perched on the edge of Richardson's Bay, this was originally built for the daughter of John Reed, owner of Rancho Corte Madera del Presidio and early settler of Mill Valley, on Strawberry Point.

11. St. Stephen's Episcopal Church
1954, 1959, Hansen & Winkler
Bayview and Golden Gate Ave.
This stark, reinforced-concrete church looks more European than American, but the interior is enriched by abstract stained glass.

11. St. Stephen's Episcopal Church

12. 416 Golden Gate Ave.

13. 6 Blanding Ln.

14. Belvedere Town Square

*15. First Church of Christ,
Scientist*

12. Golden Gate Avenue houses
304 Golden Gate Ave.
c.1900
332 Golden Gate Ave.
1903, Clarence Ward
334 Golden Gate Ave.
1904, Albert Farr
340 Golden Gate Ave.
1905, Daniel McLean
416 Golden Gate Ave.
1895; rem. 1906, Willis Polk
428 Golden Gate Ave.
1893, Willis Polk

This group is representative of the first wave of settlement on Belvedere, before it became fashionable to cling to the steep slopes craning for a view. Most of these houses are Shingle Style and, handsome as they are, could have been built anywhere. A notable exception is Polk's wonderful English Tudor Moore house at 416. The Blanding house at 440, also said to have been remodeled by Polk, was the manor house of an estate which once covered the entire southern tip of Belvedere. Other remnants are the former carriage house at 333 Belvedere and the gardener's house at 343 Belvedere Avenue.

13. Houses
6 Blanding Ln.
1972, Bull Field Volkman & Stockwell (John Field, des.)
End of Blanding Ln.
1972, Callister & Paine

These two give a good picture of the range of more recent designs: the first in a Bay Region adaptation of the International Style, and the second in Callister's more frankly woodsy Japanese-inspired manner.

14. Belvedere Town Square
1905, Albert Farr
Beach and San Rafael Ave.

Architect Albert Farr designed a masterpiece here for the Belvedere Land Company Offices, deriving the long horizontal banding and many gables from Voysey and clothing them in native shingles. Across the street are cottages and apartments by Farr and the Town Square Apartments of 1955 by Schubart & Friedman.

15. First Church of Christ, Scientist
1952, Charles Warren Callister
San Rafael Ave. at Laurel

Callister gracefully acknowledges here his debt to Wright and goes on to design his own prow-shaped church in redwood and concrete, fiting it neatly into its triangular site. A landmark of the Second Bay Region style.

16. Belvedere City Hall
c.1890, Albert Farr
San Rafael Ave. at Laurel
This former Presbyterian Church was moved here, minus its tower and spire, from Bayview and Laurel in 1950.

17. Point Tiburon
c.1988, Fisher-Friedman
Paradise Dr. bet. Point Tiburon and Mar West
Although its development had a long and controversial history, this town house and shopping group clustered around its own lagoon is among the most handsome of such recent developments, and a worthy successor to the work of the Belvedere Land Company in the early 1900s.

17. Point Tiburon

18. Marin Outdoor Art Club

Mill Valley

18. Marin Outdoor Art Club
1905, Bernard Maybeck
Throckmorton and Blithedale Aves.
The perfect gateway to Mill Valley and one of Maybeck's masterpieces, this simple hall gets its "architecture" from the inspired, if not altogether logical, projection of the trusses through the roof. A sort of rustic cousin of Mies van der Rohe's *Crown Hall* in Chicago.

19. Depot Plaza and Cafe

19. Depot Plaza and Cafe
c.1903; rest. c.1989
Throckmorton bet. Bernard and Madrona
This is the heart of town, and a very lively one it is. The former bus (and probably electric rail before that) depot has been refurbished as a bookstore-cafe fronting on the perfectly scaled and very popular plaza.

20. Mill Valley Public Library
1969, Wurster, Bernardi & Emmons
Throckmorton at Elma St.
Wurster's simple barnlike library set in the redwoods at the edge of the creek is a fiting companion piece to Maybeck's Outdoor Art Club on the other side of town. A swing down Cascade Drive (left on Laurel off Throckmorton after you pass the Library) behind the Library will give you a wonderful sense of Mill Vall-itude.

20. Mill Valley Public Library

21. Evans house
1907, Louis Christian Mullgardt
100 Summit Ave.
The downhill elevation of this chalet has been transformed by the sympathetic but recent addition of a projecting deck. It is one of Mullgardt's sadly few surviving houses.

22. Coffin house
1893, Emil John
15 Tamalpais Ave.
This remarkable Queen Anne was designed to look like a ferry boat. This, and the Evans house above, provide a sample of the many hidden in the woods hereabouts.

21. Evans house

Ross/San Anselmo

23. St. Anselm's Catholic Church
1907, Frank Shea
Shady Ln. at Bolinas Ave.
Frank Shea was one of a precious few Catholic architects of his time who did interesting churches. This free interpretation of Norman-English half-timbering is probably his finest work, and perfect for its setting.

23. St. Anselm's Catholic Church

24. San Francisco Theological Seminary
1892-97, Wright & Saunders
Seminary off Kensington Rd.
Chapel
Bolinas and Richmond Ave.
Dormitory
1958, John Carl Warnecke
One of the very few Bay Area examples of Richardsonian Romanesque, this does credit to the style. The chapel is by far the best of the group, but the setting of the other buildings on their little knoll is inspired. The reinforced concrete dormitory, on the north side off Mariposa, is also well worth seeing.

24. S. F. Theological Seminary Chapel

25. Houses
c.1900, John White
40, 46 Upper Rd.
Two redwood "cottages" by Maybeck's brother-in-law and sometime partner. A good picture of old Ross.

26. House
1904, Coxhead & Coxhead
96 Park Dr.

27. House
c.1890
206 Saunders Ave.

28. House
1910, Maxwell Bugbee
100 Alder Ave.
For those who wish to explore farther, this is an interesting trio quite close to one another. The Coxhead is a fine example of the tamer Shingle Style the firm adopted after the turn of the century. 206 Saunders is a rare if not unique local example of Victorian *Chinoiserie*, and Bugbee's house with its even more remarkable tower is completely *sui generis*. Apparently, it was designed for a man who was interested in Eskimos, so the house was known as the "Igloo House."

28. 100 Alder Ave.

North of San Rafael

29. Marin County Civic Center
1957-72, Frank Lloyd Wright
San Pedro Rd. at Civic Center Dr.
While this is very late Wright, completed after his death, and sometimes looks like a movie-set version of itself, the conception is so dazzling as to silence criticism. The first phase was the Administration Building, completed in 1962. Next was the Hall of Justice, completed in 1969. These two buildings bridge three hills, with auto access under the bridges. At the foot of the hill is the Post Office, the only U.S. government building ever designed by Wright. The separate Veterans Memorial Auditorium was designed by Taliesin Fellowship and completed in 1972.

27. 206 Saunders Ave.

30. Lucas Valley (Eichler subdivision)
1963, Claude Oakland;
land. arch., Royston, Hanamoto & Mays
Lucas Valley Rd. at Mt. Shasta
Better preserved than the earlier Eichler subdivision at Terra Linda, Lucas Valley is still an outstanding example of subdivision planning and design.

29. Marin County Civic Center

31. St. Vincent's School
c.1920
End of St. Vincent's Rd.
At the Marinwood-St. Vincent's Road exit and visible from the freeway is this remarkable Spanish Colonial revival group of school buildings. Unfortunately, it isn't quite as good close up, but considering how wide of the mark most such efforts are, it is still impressive.

Sonoma Plaza

15b 15a
13 14 15c 15d 1
West Spain
12 3 2
11 4
10 7 8 5
9 6

West Napa

Broadway

1st St. West
1st St. East

25

33
32
24
West Spain
31
West Napa
26
7
23
Curtin Ln.
5th St. West
3rd St. West
2nd St. West
1st St. West
Broadway
16 17
East Spain
22
21 20 19
18
East Napa
27
29
30
Andrieux St.
2nd St. East
Patten St.
4th St. East
1st St. East

17
Sonoma
France St.

West Mac Arthur
28
East Mac Arthur

N
W E
S

17

1. Mission San Francisco Solano
2. Blue Wing Inn
3. Vasquez (Hooker) house
4. Parmelee (Grinstead) Building
5. Sebastiani Theater Building
6. Duhring General Store Building
7. Sonoma City Hall
8. Former Carnegie Library
9. Leese-Fitch Adobe
10. Batto Building
11. Ruggles (Aquilon) Building
12. Salvador Vallejo Adobe
13. Sonoma (Plaza) Hotel
14. Swiss Hotel (Salvador Vallejo house)
15. Sonoma State Park
    a. Park Headquarters
    b. Indians' quarters and kitchen
    c. Toscano Hotel
    d. Barracks
16. Ray Adobe

17. Cooke house
18. Duhring house
19. Clewe house
20. First Baptist Church
21. Green (Nash-Patton) Adobe
22. Sassarini Elementary School
23. Andronico Vallejo Adobe and barn
24. Vallejo-Haraszthy house
25. Lachryma Montis (Mariano Vallejo house)
26. La Casita (Castenada Adobe)
27. McTaggart (Sebastiani) house
28. Burris house
29. Buena Vista (Haraszthy) Winery
30. Hacienda Vineyards
31. Temelec Hall
32. St. Andrew's Presbyterian Church
33. Wolf house, Jack London State Park

Sonoma Tour

Sonoma is the last and northernmost of the chain of Franciscan missions that extended up the California coast from what is now Mexico. It is also one of the few California towns that retains any significant imprint of Hispanic city planning according to the "Laws of the Indies" codified under Philip II in the late 16th century for the establishment of settlements in the New World. These dictated that towns should be laid out on a square grid with the principal public buildings around a central plaza. Thanks to the grandiose vision of Sonoma's founder, Commandante General Mariano Guadalupe Vallejo, its plaza is larger than the normal "Laws of the Indies" plaza (as indeed are all the original blocks) and there is an unusually wide boulevard leading into it from the south. What is more remarkable about Sonoma is that the Plaza influences town life to this day. Town life focuses on the Plaza; people meet there, eat there, celebrate there, hang out there — in short, behave more like Mexicans than Gringos. It is worth a trip to Sonoma just to spend a few hours in the Plaza, and many people do just that.

The mission was founded in 1823 just after Mexico became independent of Spain. Both the mission and the later town were established to head off the Russians, who were working their way down the coast from Alaska, having established a settlement at Fort Ross in 1812. As it turned out, the Russians were anything but a threat, even contributing to the building of the mission, and Sonoma had an amiable trading relationship with Fort Ross until the Russians gave up and went home in 1841.

Born into a military family in Monterey, Mariano Vallejo became Commandante of the San Francisco Presidio in 1833 at the age of 26. In 1834 he was made "Commisionado" in charge of the secularized holdings of the Sonoma Mission. He soon moved his family and most of his troops into the mission buildings, thus beginning a long and fruitful involvement in the affairs of the future town and its surrounding countryside. After several unsuccessful attempts to found settlements elsewhere, he laid out his grand plan for the present town in 1835. Although the pre-existing mission buildings doubtless influenced his decisions, the magnificent axis of Broadway, running due north from the Embarcadero at the head of navigation on Sonoma Creek to the Plaza cradled in its backdrop of hills, reveals the eye of a great urban planner. Of his buildings on the Plaza, only the Barracks and the Mission Chapel remain, his own Casa Grande with its four-story watchtower on the Broadway axis having burned in 1867. But reminders of the family are all around the Plaza, with two buildings by his brother Salvador and one by his brother-in-law Jacob Leese. While the Plaza gradually acquired a frame of buildings through the 19th century, the town of Sonoma grew slowly in comparison with its neighbors, Petaluma and Napa, and retains a charming small-town feel that, along with its incomparable Plaza, makes it a favorite tourist destination. Happily, it has largely resisted quaintness. Its unique array of architecture from the Mexican and early statehood eras is less well-known than it should be.

1. Mission San Francisco Solano

3. Vasquez (Hooker) house

5. Sebastiani Theater Building

1. Mission San Francisco Solano
1824-40
N.E. cor. Spain & 1st St. East

The entrance is through the remaining fragment of the original *convento*, or friars' quarters, on East Spain Street. The mission church, now gone, stood to the east; the present church is a later parish church built by Mariano Vallejo about 1840 and heavily restored. Tickets are sold here for the barracks across the street, the Vallejo home, and the Petaluma adobe, Casa Grande.

2. Blue Wing Inn
1840, James Cooper and Thomas Spriggs
125-129 East Spain

The basis for this structure was a modest two-room cottage built by the man first sent by Vallejo to look after the newly secularized mission. When two British seamen offered to buy the site Vallejo evicted his majordomo and the new owners built the present two-story adobe, which functioned as a hotel, saloon, and gambling hall. Guests included William Tecumseh Sherman, Joseph Hooker, Henry Halleck, and Sidney Longstreet, all of whom later won military fame in the Civil War.

3. Vasquez (Hooker) house
c.1850
129 East Spain (in court of El Paseo)

A prefabricated house from Sweden, bought by then Lt. Joe Hooker on the docks of San Francisco and erected originally on the southwest corner of the Plaza. It is now the headquarters of the Somoma League for Historic Preservation and is open to the public.

4. Parmelee (Grinstead) Building
1911
466 1st St. East

Now owned by Sonoma's leading amateur historian, this is a charming example of early 20th-century commercial building on a very small scale.

5. Sebastiani Theater Building
1933
476 1st St. East

While somewhat overwhelming in scale, this Mission Revival edifice is a local landmark, and in addition to a movie theater houses a fine French bakery and Sonoma's only nightclub.

6. Duhring General Store Building
1891
492 1st St. East
Damaged by fire in 1990, this one-story brick building with an octagonal corner cupola has just been restored. It was built by one of the town's pioneer merchants, a German immigrant who subsequently became one of its most prosperous residents, and whose family still owns it.

7. Sonoma City Hall
1906, H. C. Lutgens; rest. 1987, Gerald Tierney
Center of the Plaza
Although placing the City Hall in the middle of the Plaza would have violated "the Laws of the Indies," this stone Mission Revival block is a perfect termination for the grand axis of Broadway.

7. Sonoma City Hall

8. Former Carnegie Library Building
1913
1st St., E. side of Plaza
During most of the 19th century the plaza had neither buildings nor trees and thus had sites available for the early civic buildings of the American city.

9. Leese-Fitch Adobe
1836, Jacob Primer Leese
487 1st St. West
A remnant of a much larger building owned by a pioneer merchant, who was also a co-founder of Yerba Buena, later San Francisco. From 1849-53 it served as home for General Persifer Smith, Governor General of California.

9. Lees-Fitch Adobe

10. Batto Building
1912
457 1st St. West
A fine early 20th-century commercial building in brick.

11. Ruggles (Aquilon) Building
1860's
447 1st St. West
A simple frame building which housed Sonoma's first Chinese laundry.

10. Batto Building

12. Salvador Vallejo Adobe
1836
415-27 1st St. West
Built by General Vallejo's brother, who later extended it north on the site of what is now the El Dorado Hotel.

12. Salvador Vallejo Adobe

13. Sonoma (Plaza) Hotel
1872, Henry Weil, builder
110 West Spain St.
In atmosphere and furnishings, very much the country hotel of a century ago.

14. Swiss Hotel (Salvador Vallejo house)
1840, Salvador Vallejo
18 West Spain St.
Salvador's second building on the Plaza is a smaller version of the barracks down the street with a projecting second-story gallery.

15. Toscano Hotel and Barracks

15. Sonoma State Park
Center of north side of the Plaza

a. Park Headquarters (former boarding house)
1870
20 West Spain St.
Originally located where the Cheese Factory now stands.

b. Indians' quarters and kitchen
1835
to the left of Headquarters
The surviving outbuilding of General Vallejo's residence, which had a four-story flanking tower and stood on Spain Street astride the Broadway axis.

c. Toscano Hotel
1857-59
Spain St.
Furnished with period furniture by the Sonoma League for Historic Preservation, which provides guided tours.

d. Barracks
1840
1st St. East at Spain St.
Built by Mariano Vallejo to house his garrison and briefly in 1846 the headquarters of the Bear Flag Rebellion and capital of the Republic of California.

16. Ray Adobe

16. Ray Adobe
1849-50, John Ray
205 East Spain St.
The wooden section on 2nd Street East was built first; the adobe portion with its unusual two-story verandah was added after Virginian John Ray struck gold. One of the landmarks of early California architecture.

17. Cooke house

17. Cooke house
1852-57
245 East Spain St.
A wood-framed house built like an adobe with a continuous front porch off which the rooms opened.

18. Duhring house
1859; rem. 1928, Bliss & Faville;
Thomas Church, land. arch.
532 2nd St. East

An imposing Colonial Revival house that began as a simple frontier dwelling. Bliss and Faville were leading San Francisco architects, and Thomas Church later became California's most famous modern landscape architect. Not much remains of this early garden.

19. Clewe house
1876
531 1st St. East

This handsome Italianate was built by a cousin and sometime partner of the Duhrings across the street.

19. Clewe house

20. First Baptist Church
1870's
542 1st St. East

A simple Gothic Revival church that recalls New England.

21. Green (Nash-Patton) Adobe
1847, Henry Green
579 1st St. East

A typical adobe plan with two rooms downstairs on either side of a center hall, a large sleeping loft upstairs and a kitchen in the lean-to at the rear.

21. Green (Nash-Patton) Adobe

22. Sassarini Elementary School
1952, Mario Ciampi
652 5th St. West

Winner of a 1953 National AIA Design Award and a perfect period piece with a finger plan, large glass areas, bright colors and exposed bar joists. Thanks to good maintenance this building still has the fresh, high-tech look of the Americanized International Style.

22. Sassarini Elementary School

23. Andronico Vallejo Adobe and barn
1852, John Ray
700 Curtin Lane

The large gable roof of this adobe has a row of dormers to light the sleeping rooms. Ray sold the property to the General's wife, who gave it to her son.

24. Vallejo-Haraszthy house
1878
400 West Spain St.

23. Andronico Vallejo Adobe and barn

The intermarriage of two of Sonoma's first families resulted in this Italianate house, which duplicates the plan of Lachryma Montis.

25. Lachryma Montis (Mariano Vallejo house)
1852
North of West Spain St. at 3rd St. West
This beautifully restored and maintained complex testifies to the transition of General Vallejo—and Hispanic California—from a Mexican ranchero to a North American squire. Vallejo had a commodious house on the Plaza, but in 1852 he bought one of three "frames," as prefabricated houses were called, that had been shipped from Massachusetts around the horn on the San Francisco docks and at vast expense brought it to Sonoma. Using adobe to insulate the walls, he erected it on this lovely site along with a Gothic Revival carriage house, now gone, and summer house, as if to show that he was now a Yankee. The surviving "chalet" barn is also a prefab of sorts; its timber frame came from England. Only a little of the original garden remains.

25. Lachryma Montis

26. La Casita (Castenada Adobe)
1842-49, Salvador Vallejo
143 West Spain St.
One of several small adobes built by Salvador around the perimeter of his property and first occupied by Juan Castenada, Mariano Vallejo's secretary.

27. McTaggart (Sebastiani) house
1923, Samuele Sebastiani
400 4th St. East
A very grand Craftsman bungalow; humbler versions are further south along 4th Street.

27. McTaggart (Sebastiani) house

28. Burris house
c.1840-1860, Nicholas Burris
29 East MacArthur St.
Wood-framed houses are unusual this early because of the lack of sawmills. This one has the second-story gallery common in adobes of the period.

29. Buena Vista (Haraszthy) Winery
1857, Agoston Haraszthy
End of Vineyard Lane
Haraszthy, a Hungarian Count, is usually credited with starting California's wine industry. Recognizing that the climate and soil of the North Bay region were right for making fine wine, Haraszthy returned to Europe to collect root stocks and planted these vineyards. He and his descendants built the two stone wineries with limestone caves excavated in the hillside. Raise a glass to his memory in the tasting room of the older building!

29. Buena Vista Winery

30. Hacienda Vineyards (Haraszthy Villa)
1988; reconst. of the 1857 building, Victor Conforti
End of Castle Rd.

Hacienda Vineyards were originally owned by Haraszthy, whose villa overlooked them. Using the only known record, an engraving of the facade, owner Antonia Bartholomew and her architect rebuilt the villa with its unusual stepped-back facade. The interior consists of meeting rooms to serve the needs of the modern winery. Behind it is a pleasant Mediterranean Revival house of the 1920s that serves as the winery tasting room and offices.

31. Temelec Hall
1858, Granville P. Swift
Temelec Drive off Arnold

Now the clubhouse for a retirement community that surrounds it and bears its name, this large stone Italianate mansion with carriage house, barn, and Gothic Revival garden pavilions is a remarkable feat at such an early date. Swift, a Bear Flag rebel who later struck gold, built it with forced Indian labor.

32. St. Andrew's Presbyterian Church
1992, William Turnbull Assoc.
16290 Arnold Drive south of Sobre Vista Rd.

This newly completed church, school, and meeting hall building complex is grouped around a patio defined by a covered walkway.

33. Wolf house, Jack London State Park
1913, Albert Farr
London Ranch Rd., Glen Ellen

When London got rich from his writing, he bought this ranch and built his dream house, an enormous stone and timber pile he named Wolf house; it burned before he and his wife, Charmian, could move in. He died soon after, and she later built herself the "House of Happy Walls," where she lived until her death In 1959. Now a museum, It houses memorabilia of London. The ruins of Wolf house are some of the most evocative of their kind.

30. Hacienda Vineyards

31. Temelec Hall

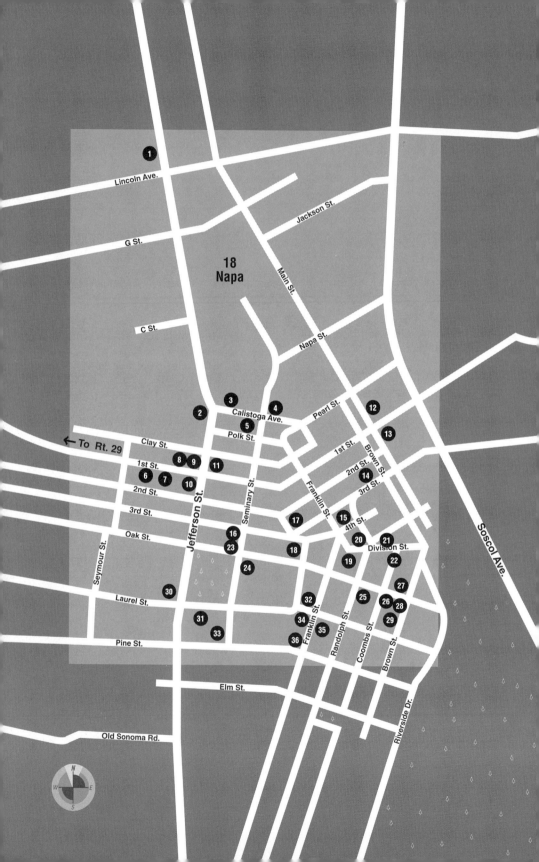

1. Napa Unified School District (former Napa High School)
2. House 1301 Jefferson St.
3. Cottages 1476, 1484, 1488 Calistoga Ave.
4. House 1386 Calistoga Ave.
5. Apts. 1556 Polk St.
6. House 2109 1st St.
7. House 1929 1st St.
8. House 1926 1st St.
9. House 1001 Jefferson St.
10. House 1801 1st St.
11. Noyes Mansion
12. Napa Opera House
13. Commercial building 942-48 Main St.
14. Napa County Courthouse
15. First Presbyterian Church
16. Andrews house
17. Nichols house
18. Migliavacca house

19. McClelland houses
20. First United Methodist Church
21. E.R. Gifford house
22. Goodman-Corlett house Hayman house
23. Houses 642, 705 Seminary St. Houses 1730, 1738 Oak St.
24. House 617 Seminary St.
25. George Goodman, Jr., house
26. Cedar Gables (former E. W. Churchill house)
27. George Goodman house
28. Churchill Manor (former E.S. Churchill house)
29. Manasse Mansion
30. William H. Corlett house
31. Turton house
32. Martin house Cottages 406, 436 Franklin St.
33. Yount house
34. Sawyer house Cottages 355, 361 Franklin St.
35. House row 356-86 Franklin St.
36. Apts. (Holden Mansion)

Napa and Petaluma have much in common. They were both founded around 1850 as river ports serving large agricultural areas; both have a collection of skewed street grids thanks to early rival developments; and both have fine collections of late 19th-century residential architecture. Both had an important local architect whose work can be seen throughout the old town; Napa's Luther Turton was somewhat older than Petaluma's Brainerd Jones. However, present-day Napa is considerably less coherent than West Petaluma, due to the loss of many fine old buildings downtown and some ill-advised urban renewal. Nonetheless, around the old downtown are a series of clusters of older houses that are well worth seeing; the most spectacular of them are on a grander scale than their Petaluma counterparts.

The original settlement and grid is that of Napa City, centered on 3rd Street and aligned with the river, which was once lined with steamboat wharves. South of this is the slightly later Napa Abajo, or Lower Napa, taking off at a different angle, with the break coming at appropriately named Division Street. This was where the steamboat captains built their stately mansions. To the west, yet another grid appeared with Brown and Walker's Addition and subsequent additions that developed into the area around Fuller Park, now one of Napa's handsomest residential neighborhoods. Northward from the park, Jefferson Street became the locus of more stately homes and evolved into the town's main north-south artery. With the notable exception of the old high school at Jefferson and Lincoln, virtually all of the architectural interest of Napa is in a roughly ten-block area centered on 1st and Seminary streets. As you continue north up the valley there are many great winery buildings, as well as the towns of Yountville, St. Helena, and Calistoga, but these are beyond the scope of this guide.

1. Napa Unified School District Headquarters (former Napa High School)
1922, W. H. Weeks
Jefferson at Lincoln St.

A splendid monument to the days when the local high school was a major cultural landmark, in a free and elegant combination of Beaux-Arts Classicism and Mediterranean Revival.

1. Napa Unified School District Headquarters

2. House (now offices)
c.1915
1301 Jefferson St.

A deceptively simple Craftsman bungalow with an asymmetrical entry porch, one of a group of handsome old houses converted into a mini office park. Across the street is an attractive garden apartment complex of c.1970.

2. 1301 Jefferson St.

3. Cottages
c.1885
1476, 1484, 1488 Calistoga Ave.

This matched row of Stick Style cottages is characteristic of early speculative development in towns like Napa.

4. House
c.1885
1386 Calistoga Ave.

Perhaps by the same builder as the cottages, but grander because of the corner lot. Diagonally across the corner is a Mission Revival apartment block.

5. Apartments 1556 Polk St.

5. Apartments
c.1885
1556 Polk St.

This neighborhood was apparently originally developed in the 1880s with a variety of housing at different scales.

6. House
c.1890
2109 1st St.

The verandahed bungalow done in the Stick-Eastlake style.

7. House
c.1875
1929 1st St.

With its Mansard roof and double-bayed front, this well-maintained house packs the maximum of Victorian grandeur into a small box.

7. 1929 1st St.

8. House
c.1900
1926 1st St.

The steep gable roof perpendicular to the street was popular around the turn of the century. Here the detailing combines elements of Colonial Revival, Queen Anne, and even Craftsman in the projecting beam ends on the porch.

9. House
c.1895
1001 Jefferson St.

Queen Anne houses gradually dropped the elaborate bracketing and strapwork of Stick-Eastlake for the simpler surfaces of the Colonial Revival, but kept the complicated massing. How they loved to turn a corner like this!

8. 1926 1st St.

10. House
c.1900
1801 1st St.

The strong horizontal banding of the windows and eave lines indicates that something new is happening amidst the Queen Anne jumble of forms.

11. Noyes Mansion
c.1905, attrib. to Luther M. Turton
1750 1st St.

Almost certainly by Napa's leading architect of the turn-of-the-century, this house shows the full flowering of the first Colonial Revival style, although the steep-gabled dormers and round central bay hark back to Queen Anne.

9. 1001 Jefferson St.

12. Napa Opera House
1879, Samuel & Joseph Cather Newsom/Ira Gilchrist
Main St. bet. 1st and Pearl Sts.

The long-awaited restoration of this cultural landmark is reportedly about to begin—as of this writing.

13. Commercial building
c.1910
942-48 Main St.

This handsomely restored block anchors the key corner of the old downtown, largely gutted by urban renewal west of here. South of it on Main at 902-12 is a charming little group of Art Deco shops.

10. 1801 1st St.

13. 942-48 Main St.

14. Napa County Courthouse
1878, Samuel & Joseph Cather Newsom/Ira Gilchrist
Brown St. bet. 2nd and 3rd Sts.
The Newsoms, later famous for their Carson House in Eureka, are here shown in their chaste civic mode. Gilchrist, the local man who probably got the job by saying he would bring in the eminent San Franciscans, did a number of houses around town, as well as collaborating on the Opera House. Across the street at 812-16 Brown is the rusticated stone Napa Law Center of around 1910.

14. Napa County Courthouse

15. First Presbyterian Church
1874, Daley & Eisen
3rd and Randolph Sts.
This spire is the major landmark of downtown. The church's sculptural ornament is a rich addition to this Gothic-Revival confection.

16. Andrews house
1892, Luther M. Turton
741 Seminary St.
Although Turton could do Eastlake with the best of them, he shifted to the Prairie style a quarter of a century later in his own house at 1767 Laurel.

17. Nichols house
1879, Ira Gilchrist
1562 3rd St.
A Stick Style house that looks like it might have been a reworking of an earlier Italianate.

15. First Presbyterian Church

18. Migliavacca house
1895, Luther M. Turton
1475 4th St.
This splendid Queen Anne house was moved here from where the new Library now stands on Division St.

19. McClelland houses
569 Randolph St.
1879
A Second Empire beauty that elegantly turns the corner where the grids collide with a rounded porch.
590 Randolph St.
c.1900, Luther M. Turton
A series of rounded bays pop out from the simpler main mass of this house.

18. Migliavacca house

20. First United Methodist Church
1916, Luther M. Turton
625 Randolph St.
Turton's masterwork, this reinforced concrete English Gothic church occupies a pivotal position in Napa both literally and culturally. Its conventional exterior encloses a wood-paneled quarter-circular sanctuary that is a fine example of the auditorium plan that swept the Protestant denominations in this country in the late 1800s. The congregation founded the Napa Collegiate Institute, active from 1870 to 1896, which then merged with what is now the University of the Pacific. As its extensive buildings indicate, it is still a major educational presence.

21. E. R. Gifford house
c.1890
608 Randolph St.
A lavishly bracketed Queen Anne house set in a garden that must be as old as the house.

22. Goodman-Corlett house
1882
1225 Division St.
Hayman house
c.1900
1227-29 Division St.
These well-maintained neighbors illustrate the evolution of taste at the end of the last century. The Italianate at 1225 Division was built by George Goodman, who founded Napa's first private bank and donated its first library, and was given to his son Harvey. It was updated with a round Queen Anne tower in the 1890s. The Hayman house has the complex massing and curved eaves of the Queen Anne style combined with fanlights and porch columns of the Colonial Revival style.

23. Houses
642 Seminary St.
c.1890
1730, 1738 Oak, 705 Seminary St.
c.1865
A group of three Stick-Eastlake houses and an earlier Carpenter Gothic cottage facing Fuller Park.

24. House
c.1905
617 Seminary St.
A gem of a Colonial Revival cottage with a swoop of Queen Anne in the porch.

20. First United Methodist Church

21. E. R. Gifford house

22. Hayman house

24. 617 Seminary St.

25. George Goodman, Jr., house
c.1890
492 Randolph St.

George senior built this Queen Anne house with all the trimmings for his obviously favorite son.

26. Cedar Gables (former Edward Wilder Churchill house)
1892, Ernest Coxhead
486 Coombs St.

Nearly identical to a house that Coxhead designed at the same time for David Greenleaf in Alameda, this Queen Anne house is one of Napa's great treasures; it displays the architect's skillful handling of shingled surfaces.

26. Cedar Gables

27. George Goodman house
1872-73, MacDougall & Marquis
1120 Oak St.

The senior Goodman's mansion, now unfortunately crowded by modern apartments, is in the Second Empire style with a Mansard roof. Oak and Brown was once Napa's millionaire's corner.

28. Churchill Manor (former Edward S. Churchill house)
1889
485 Brown St.

Originally Second Empire style, Napa's grandest mansion was updated to Colonial Revival in 1906. Its interiors are largely intact and can be visited by appointment.

28. Churchill Manor

29. Manasse Mansion
1886, William H. Corlett
443 Brown St.

Another ingenious updating was performed on this Stick-Eastlake around 1900, when it was given a colonial portico. Combined with the two angled corner gables, it gives the look of a house charging off in all directions.

30. William H. Corlett house
c.1916, William H. Corlett
507 Jefferson St.

Architect-builder Corlett's house, charming as it is, shows how much more conservative he was than his builder colleague Turton.

29. Manasse Mansion

31. Turton house
1915, Luther M. Turton
1767 Laurel St.

Although this is pretty tentative Prairie style, it is an amazing leap for a man who was immersed in the Queen Anne style only a few years before.

30. William H. Corlett house

32. Martin house
c.1890
409 Franklin St.
Cottages
c.1870
406, 436 Franklin St.
The Martin house is a two-story double-bayed Italianate that has had a Colonial Revival porch added. Across the street are two charming Gothic Revival cottages.

33. Yount house
1884
Seminary and Pine Sts.
A large Stick-Eastlake house built by the daughter of the founder of Yountville.

34. Sawyer house
c.1875
389-97 Franklin St.
Cottages
c.1880
355, 361 Franklin St.
This block of Franklin is marked by the extraordinary and perhaps not well-advised—as anyone who has tried to domesticate a redwood will know—use of redwoods as street trees. It also has a fine collection of houses. The Sawyers founded one of Napa's principal industries, The Sawyer Tannery, still active today at 68 Coombs Street. Next door to their double house is a charming pair of Eastlake cottages with curving porches facing each other.

35. House row
c.1885
356-86 Franklin St.
Five Stick-Eastlake houses obviously built as a speculative development. Some remodeling has taken place, notably at 376, which was transformed into the Shingle Style in the early 1900s.

36. Apartments (Holden Mansion)
c.1886
313 Franklin St.
At the south end of the block stands this fine Italianate mansion. Facing it across the street are a pair of California Bungalows from the early 1900s—an altogether remarkable block, rather shady but very nice!

32. Martin house

32. 406 Franklin St.

33. Yount house

34. Sawyer house

1. Petaluma Community Center
2. A. Agius house
3. House 421 E. Washington
4. Perkins house
5. Labor Administration Building (Phillip Sweed School)
6. House 319 Keokuk St.
7. Haubrich house
8. Bungalow 300 Kentucky St.
9. J. H. Gwinn house
10. Giovanni Canepa house
11. Schuckebier house
12. St. Vincent's School
13. Northwestern Pacific Railroad Depot
14. Sunset Line and Twine Mill
15. Herold Building
16. Sonoma County National Bank Building
17. Maclay Building (former Opera House)
18. Former Odd Fellows Hall
19. Former American Trust Co. Bank
20. Veale house
21. Masonic Hall 11-15, 19 Western Ave. Mutual Relief Building
22. McNear Building
23. Great Petaluma Mill (former Post Office)
24. Bungalow 500 Western
25. Cavanaugh Inn (Cavanaugh house)
26. School Administration Building (Lincoln Primary School)
27. Historical Museum (former Free Library)

28. Post Office
29. Stewart house
30. Evangelical Free Church (First Congregational Church) Petaluma Women's Club
31. St. John's Episcopal Church
32. Atwater house
33. House 300 4th St.
34. House 619 B St.
35. House 523 B St.
36. House 100 6th St.
37. E. D. McNear house
38. House 47 6th St.
39. Cottage 404 4th St.
40. Maclay house
41. House 625 D St.
42. House 112 7th St.
43. A. L. Whitney house
44. House 400 6th St.
45. J .E. Allen house
46. Fairbanks house
47. House 853 D. St.
48. Must Hatch Incubator Building
49. Brown house 901 D St.
50. Brown house 920 D St.
51. Scrutton house
52. House 1000 D St.
53. Casa Grande

Petaluma Tour

19

Petaluma Tour

Of all the older towns within easy driving range of San Francisco, Petaluma retains the most complete array of late 19th- and early 20th-century architecture. Settled in the 1850s, it became a farming and commercial hub for the North Bay since it was ideally situated on a navigable river in the middle of rich farmland. By 1858 it was a chartered city, the largest in the North Bay. Feeding booming San Francisco, and later sending eggs all over the world, it grew and prospered steadily for some 80 years. In 1918 it was the richest city of its size in the country; in 1926 it had a population of 7,000 and 2,000 chicken farms. Although the Depression more or less halted building, in 1940 Petaluma still supplied 32% of California's eggs. However, in 1958 the Poultry Producers' Cooperative transferred its headquarters to San Leandro, the Pioneer Hatchery went out of business, and it was clear that people, not chickens, would dominate Petaluma in the future.

Too many people, in fact—at least as Petalumans saw it. Route 101 had been upgraded to freeway status in 1956, opening the way for suburban commuters who came in steadily increasing numbers. In 1972 the city was horrified to discover that it had grown from 25,000 to 30,000 in just two years. Its response was to pass the first growth-control ordinance in the country, which was promptly taken to court by pro-development interests from all over, but survived and has become a model for other communities. Of course the city has grown, but while East Petaluma is all subdivisions and shopping malls, West Petaluma, the old town, has kept the scale, feel, and much of the architecture of the pre-automobile era, making it a favorite film set. Happily it is also a very real town, full of buildings both old and interesting, and well worth an extended visit. Here you will find the best set of cast-iron commercial fronts in the Bay Area, houses by Julia Morgan from every phase of her career, a life-time of building by a fine local architect, Brainerd Jones, and whole streets of Victorian houses. There is no better place to study the evolution of mainstream American domestic architecture from 1850 to 1930. The burghers of Petaluma did not go in for newfangled things; they built well and cared for what they built.

Petaluma Boulevard (formerly Main Street) more or less follows the west bank of the river. From it radiate the three main roads west: Bodega Avenue, which becomes Washington Street to the east, Western Avenue, and D Street. Each of these offers a spectacular drive to the coast. The village of Bodega, out Bodega Avenue, was the setting for Alfred Hitchcock's *The Birds*. It has an almost surreal cluster of old buildings—church, school, houses and barns. You can see why he chose it. On Spring Hill Road at Purvine, off Western Avenue, about six miles from downtown Petaluma, is an apparently original and unaltered Orson Fowler "Octagon House." Other old farms are scattered along all three routes.

The town is laid out on three more or less unrelated grids, the first being the one north of Western Avenue and west of the river, platted in 1852 by a squatter named Keller, after whom one of its streets is named. It contains the hub of the town at Washington and Petaluma Boulevard. The second, south of it on the flat, is easier to find your way around and equally full of interesting architecture. The third is East Petaluma, whose spine and orientation line is East Washington Street.

1. Petaluma Community Center
1988, Roland Miller Assoc.
N. McDowell north of Joan Dr.
A well-designed Postmodernish complex of meeting rooms set in a park. The large multi-purpose room is worth a look inside.

2. A. Agius house
1935, Julia Morgan
210 West St.
A good example of minimalist Mediterranean Revival.

3. House
c.1860
421 E. Washington St.
A Gothic Revival cottage straight from the pages of Andrew Jackson Downing.

4. Perkins house
1892
343 Keller St.
Queen Anne/Stick style stripped of some of its original ornament and so even stickier.

5. Labor Administration Building (Phillip Sweed School)
1927, Brainerd Jones
331 Keller St.
A late work by Jones, it has a portico with octagonal columns reminiscent of the work of Chicago architect George W. Maher.

6. House
c.1912, Brainerd Jones
319 Keokuk St.
Jones' version of the steep-gabled, Shingle/Colonial Revival style house common in the first decades of this century, and especially common in Petaluma. The bracketed window boxes and columned entry porch are details typical of his work.

7. Haubrich house
1891
200 Prospect St.
A monumental Queen Anne style house, built by the proprietor of the Crystal Saloon—evidently a profitable enterprise. It is said that his wife designed it.

1. Petaluma Community Center

2. A. Agius house

3. 421 E. Washington St.

6. 319 Keokuk St.

8. Bungalow
1900, Brainerd Jones
300 Kentucky St.
Jones has added personal touches to the California Bungalow such as the squat-columned side entry porch.

9. J. H. Gwinn house
1929, Julia Morgan
14 Martha St.
One of Miss Morgan's most graceful houses. The many-gabled roof is especially well handled.

8. 300 Kentucky St.

10. Giovanni Canepa house
1880
223 Kentucky St.
This double-bayed facade with a lacy two-story porch joining the two bays exemplifies the inventiveness of late l9th-century carpenter-architects.

11. Schuckebier house
c.1875
245 Howard St.
Greek Revival moving into Italianate style. Note the unusual side entry.

12. St. Vincent's School

12. St. Vincent's School
1888
Union at Howard Sts.
The sawed-off appearance here is due to the loss of the gable-roofed upper floor.

13. Northwestern Pacific Railroad Depot
1914
Lakeville Rd. south of E. Washington St.
As nice a Mission Revival station as you could ever see.

13. Northwestern Pacific Railroad Depot

14. Sunset Line and Twine Mill (former Carlson Courier; and former Belding Bros. and Belding Corticelli Silk Mill)
1892, Charles Havens; rem. 1922, Brainerd Jones
Jefferson at Erwin St.
Once one of the major manufacturers of silk thread in the country, whose silk came direct from China by ship, this great twin-towered brick mill looks like a transplant straight from New England.

14. Sunset Line and Twine Mill

15. Herold Building
1899
Kentucky and Washington Sts.
The candle-snuffer round bay was a favorite late 19th-century way of marking the corner.

16. Former Sonoma County National Bank Building
1926
Washington and Petaluma Blvd. N.
Built to be and still *the* landmark of downtown Petaluma, when banks thought of themselves as temples (to the disgust of Louis Sullivan).

16. Sonoma County National Bank

17. Maclay Building (former Opera House)
1870; rem. 1901, 1970, Brainerd Jones
149 Kentucky St.
A theater until 1900 (now shops and offices), the Maclay Building still has its original roof trusses and iron-and-sheet-metal facade.

18. Former Odd Fellows Hall
1871-78
107-113 Petaluma Blvd. N.
Built in two stages, this building replaced one of Petaluma's first hotels. The same cast-iron facade treatment and Mansard roof once extended south to the corner, with a sidewalk arcade sheltering pedestrians.

18.-19. Odd Fellows Hall (right), American Trust Co. Bank (left)

19. Former American Trust Company Bank
1926, Hyman & Appleton
101 Petaluma Blvd. N.
The counterpart of the Sonoma County Bank at the other end of the block, this is somewhat more imaginative Classic Revival and has elegant terra-cotta ornament.

20. Veale house
c.1900
115 Liberty St.
The inflated round corner bay encircled by a round porch mark this Queen Anne as moving into the 20th century.

21. Block of cast-iron-front buildings
Masonic Hall
1882
49 Petaluma Blvd. N.
11-15 Western Ave.
c.1882
19 Western Ave.
c.1885
Mutual Relief Building
1885
25 Western Ave.
This block, including the McNear Building around the corner, is the finest surviving group of cast-iron facades in the Bay Area. The Mutual Relief Building has elaborate cast-iron window surrounds framing stuccoed brick infill panels. Diagonally opposite it is a streamline Moderne department store building.

21. Cast-iron-front buildings

22. McNear Building

22. McNear Building
1886, 1911
15, 23 Petaluma Blvd. N.
The McNear family dominated Petaluma commerce for 50 years or so, and the name appears all over town. This building housed a National Guard Armory in Spanish-American War days and later a silent movie theater. The open space in front served as a parking area and turnaround for farm wagons.

23. Great Petaluma Mill (former Post Office)
c.1920, Brainerd Jones
22-34 Petaluma Blvd. N.
Now the facade for a complex of shops, this was once the Petaluma Post Office.

23. Great Petaluma Mill

24. Bungalow
c.1910
500 Western at Post St.
An unusually assertive bungalow, probably intended as Mission Revival, but now, having lost some ornament, looking more Viennese Secessionist.

24. 500 Western Ave.

25. Cavanaugh Inn (Cavanaugh house)
c.1902
10 Keller St.
The boxy massing and somewhat naive detailing of the early Colonial Revival style.

26. School Administration Building (Lincoln Primary School)
1911, Brainerd Jones
11 5th St.
An Ionic portico and other classical details are nicely combined with more daring clustered windows.

26. School Administration Building

27. Historical Museum (former Free Library)
1904, Brainerd Jones
4th at B St.
Easy to recognize as a Carnegie Library, this shows an interesting combination of rusticated masonry with more usual Classic Revival elements.

27. Historical Museum

28. Post Office
1932, James Wetmore,
supervising arch., Treasury Dept.
4th at D St.
Elegantly pared-down Mediterranean Revival.

28. Post Office

29. Stewart house
1865
6 6th St.
Greek and Gothic Revival styles sometimes came together, as in the lancet windows in the side gables of this otherwise Greek Revival house.

30. Evangelical Free Church (First Congregational Church)
1901, Harold Gregg
5th at B St.
Taking advantage of a corner site with lively eclecticism.

Petaluma Women's Club
1913, Brainerd Jones
518 B St.
As in other California cities during the Progressive era, the women's clubs always commissioned the most advanced architectural design.

31. St. John's Episcopal Church
c.1890, Ernest Coxhead
5th and C Sts.
One of the Bay Area's architectural landmarks and one of the finest of Coxhead's many Episcopal churches, this one displays his distinctive way of wrapping shingles around forms. The interior is as good as the exterior.

32. Atwater house
c.1875
218 4th St.
A large Italianate house facing Wickersham Park and built for one of the town's first citizens in both senses of the term. Unlike Sonoma's plaza, this park was an afterthought and looks it.

33. House
c.1894
300 4th St.
A beautifully maintained Queen Anne cottage with a Shingle Style corner turret.

30. Evangelical Free Church

30. Petaluma Women's Club

31. St. John's Episcopal Church

33. 300 4th Street

34. House
c.1907
619 B St.

A turn-of-the-century Colonial Revival box with an ornate entry porch and front dormer. A comparison of such houses with the aggressively picturesque Queen Annes that preceded them reveals some of the changes in American taste around 1900.

35. House
c.1860
523 B St.

Once an isolated farmhouse, this is a simpler version of the house by Jones at 319 Keokuk unmixed with Gothic.

36. House
1901
100 6th St.

To correct the asymmetry of this Colonial Revival house the builder-architect reintroduced the segmental doorway pediment over the windows on the left side, where it doesn't quite fit.

37. E. D. McNear house
1910, Julia Morgan
617 C St.

Miss Morgan's steep-gabled chalet form has a brown-shingled exterior and a broad two-story window bay as the focal element of the facade.

38. House
c.1925, Brainerd Jones
47 6th St.

Jones's handling of the Spanish Colonial Revival, while thoroughly competent, shows that he could not have been the architect of the Maclay house, below.

39. Cottage
c.1880
404 4th St.

A simple gabled box graced with very fanciful bracketing.

34. 619 B St.

35. 523 B St.

37. E. D. McNear house

39. 47 6th St.

40. Maclay house
c.1925
600 D St.

One of Petaluma's outstanding houses, thls is an elegant and sophisticated example of the Spanish Mediterranean Revival style which could only have been designed by one of a handful of architects practicing in California in 1925, but, alas, the name is unknown. Note especially the treatment of the patio wall and auto entry.

40. Maclay house

41. House
1925, Brainerd Jones
625 D St.

Compare with the house across the street, where Jones did a brick version of the Spanish Mediterranean style.

42. House
c.1885
112 7th St.

One of the best of Petaluma's remarkable collection of Queen Anne villas.

41. 625 D St.

43. A. L. Whitney house
1885
312 6th St.

The opulent portico and gables with sunburst motifs of this Queen Anne are reminiscent of the work of the Newsoms, designers of the Carson House in Eureka.

44. House
c.1865
400 6th St.

A rare Gothic Revival house with an Italianate bay perhaps added later to bring it up to date.

43. 312 6th St.

45. J. E. Allen house
1910, Julia Morgan
707 D St.

A less-convincing design of the same type as the house at 100 6th Street, perhaps because of later remodeling.

46. Fairbanks house
1890, Walter Cuthbertson
758 D St.

A San Francisco architect showing the locals how to do Queen Anne bigger, if not better.

44. 400 6th St.

47. House
c.1929
853 D St.
Another mystery house designed by an unknown but very sophisticated architect, this eastern transplant in Flemish brick is a cross between Bulfinch and Tidewater, Virginia.

48. Must Hatch Incubator Building
1927, Brainerd Jones
401 7th St.
A monument to the invention that made Petaluma the egg capital of the world.

47. 853 D St.

49. Brown house
1902, Brainerd Jones
901 D St.
Jones at the start of his career, doing a very eastern-like Colonial Revival for one of Petaluma's first families.

50. Brown house
1870
920 D St.
Another Queen Anne house with an exterior that reflects the interior even to the windows stepping down the stairs.

51. Scrutton house
1925, Julia Morgan
15 Brown Court
By 1925 the Colonial Revival had become a different and more literate style than it was around the turn of the century. One wonders if the shingles were always painted.

48. Must Hatch Incubator Building

52. House
c.1930, Warren Perry
1000 D St.
The last of a series of houses that shows that D Street was *the* street in Petaluma for 50 years or so. The elegant Georgian detailing seems somewhat ill at ease with the shingle siding, but otherwise this is a fine example of the literate Colonial Revival style of the '20s and '30s.

49. Brown house

53. Casa Grande
1834, General Mariano Vallejo
Adobe Rd. at Casa Grande
This huge two-story adobe originally surrounded a court and was a combination fort and ranch headquarters for Vellejo's extensive lands. It housed manufacturing and storage facilities for soldiers, ranch hands, and Indians, as well as accommodations for them all.

52. 1000 D St.

Names of architects, artists, builders, and landscape architects are followed by their guide sections and page numbers.

The San Francisco Downtown Walking Tour Map is located on the inside back cover of the guide. Each building entry is followed by the guide section and entry number.

1. Ferry Building
1895-1903, A. Page Brown/Edward R. A. Pyle, St. Dept. of Engineering
beginning of Market St. (2-46)

2. Audiffred Building
1889; 1980-81, William E. Cullen
1-21 Mission St. (2-43)

3. YMCA
1924, Carl Werner

Bayside Plaza
1986, Tower Architects
188 The Embarcadero (2-41)

4. Rincon Center
1939-40, Gilbert Stanley Underwood
99 Mission St.

Rincon Towers
1989, Pereira & Assocs.
88 Howard & 101 Spear St. (2-40)

5. Southern Pacific Building
1916, Bliss & Faville
1 Market St. (2-44)

6. S. F. Federal Reserve Bank Building
1982, Skidmore Owings & Merrill
l00 Market St. (2-38)

7. Pacific Gas & Electric Co.
1925, Bakewell & Brown
245 Market St.

Matson Building
1921, Bliss & Faville
215 Market St. (2-37)

8. M. Justin Herman Plaza
1971, Mario Ciampi/Lawrence Halprin & Assoc./John Bolles
beginning of Market St. (2-45)

9. Hyatt Regency Hotel
1973, John C. Portman
Davis St. at Market St.

The Embarcadero Center
1967-81, John C. Portman
bounded by Clay, Battery, Sacramento, Drumm, California and Market Sts. and M. Justin Herman Plaza (2-31)

10. 100 California St. building
1959, Welton Becket & Assoc.
Security Pacific Bank Building Art Gallery
1990, Frederick Fisher/David Ireland
50 California St. (2-34)

11. 101 California St. building
1982, Johnson/Burgee (2-35)

12. 388 Market St. building
1987, Skidmore Owings & Merrill (2-36)

13. Shaklee Terraces
444 Market St., 1982
Skidmore Owings & Merrill (2-28)

14. Industrial Indemnity Building
1959, Skidmore Owings & Merrill
255 California St. (2-29)

15. Tadich Grill
1909, Crim & Scott
240-242 California St. (2-30)

16. Crown Zellerbach Building
1959, Hertzka & Knowles/Skidmore Owings & Merrill
1 Bush St. (2-22)

17. Citicorp Center
1910, Albert Pissis; 1921, George Kelham; 1984, Pereira & Assoc.
1 Sansome St. (2-23)

18. Adam Grant Building
1908, c. 1910, Howard & Galloway
114 Sansome St.

Former Standard Oil Building
1912, 1916, Benjamin C. McDougall
200 Bush St.

Former Standard Oil Building
1922, George Kelham
225 Bush St. (2-21)

19. Shell Building
1929, George Kelham
100 Bush St.
Heineman Building
1910, McDonald & Applegarth
130 Bush St.

Mechanic's Monument
1894-95, Douglas Tilden, sculptor; Willis Polk, architect
Battery, Market, & Bush Sts. (2-25)

20. Pacific Coast Stock Exchange Trading Rm.
1915, J. Milton Dyer; 1930, Miller & Pflueger
301 Pine St.

Office Tower
1930, Miller & Pflueger
155 Sansome St. (2-20)

21. Royal Globe Insurance Co.
1907, Howells & Stokes
201 Sansome St. (2-19)

22. J. Harold Dollar Building
1920, George Kelham
341 California St.

California Center
1986, Skidmore Owings
& Merrill
345 California St.

Robert Dollar Building
1919, Charles McCall
301-33 California St. (2-18)

**23. Bank of California
and Tower**
1907, Bliss & Faville; 1967,
Anshen & Allen
400 California St. (2-16)

**24. Embarcadero West/
Old Federal Reserve**
1924, George Kelham; 1991,
Studios Architecture/Kaplan
McLaughlin Diaz
400 Sansome St. (2-15)

25. 343 Sansome St. buildings
c.1930, Hyman & Appleton;
1990, Johnson Burgee (2-14)

26. Alcoa Building
1964, Skidmore Owings &
Merrill
1 Maritime Plaza (2-32)

**Golden Gateway
apartment towers**
Wurster Bernardi & Emmons,
1961-63

Town houses,
1961-63, Anshen & Allen
Clay-Jackson-Battery-
Drumm Sts.

Condominiums
1981-82, Fisher-Friedman
Davis St.-Broadway (3-16)

27. U. S. Customs House
1906-11, Eames & Young
555 Battery St. (3-15)

28. Jackson Square
1850s-1860s
Jackson St. bet. Montgomery
and Sansome Sts. (3-17)

**29. Former Transamerica
Building**
1911, Salfield & Kohlberg
4 Columbus Ave. (3-14)

Transamerica Building
1971, William Pereira & Assoc.
600 Montgomery St.

Washington Montgomery Tower
1984, Kaplan McLaughlin Diaz
695 Montgomery St. (2-13)

30. Kohl Building
1904, Percy & Polk; 1907,
Willis Polk
400 Montgomery St.

456 Montgomery Building
1983, Roger Owen Boyer
Assoc./MLT Assoc. (2-11)

**31. Former Bank of America
World Hdq.**
1969, Wurster Bernardi &
Emmons/Skidmore Owings &
Merrill/Pietro Belluschi
555 California St. (2-9)

32. Security Pacific Bank
1922, George Kelham, rem.
1941, The Capitol Co.; int. rest.
1978, Baldwin-Clarke
300 Montgomery St.

Insurance Exchange Building
1913, Willis Polk
433 California St.

Merchants Exchange Building
1903, D. H. Burnham & Co./
Willis Polk
465 California St. (2-10)

33. Russ Building
1927, George Kelham
235 Montgomery St.

Mills Building and Mills Tower
1891, Burnham & Root; 1908,
1914, 1918, D. H. Burnham &
Co./Willis Polk; 1931
Lewis Hobart
220 Montgomery St. (2-7)

34. Hallidie Building
1917, Willis Polk
130-50 Sutter St.

French Bank Building
1902, Hemenway & Miller; rem.
1907-13, E. A. Bozio
108-110 Sutter St.

Hunter-Dulin Building
Schultze & Weaver
111 Sutter St., 1926 (2-6)

35. Hobart Building
1914, Willis Polk
582-592 Market St. (2-5)

36. Former Crocker Bank Hdq.
1983, Skidmore Owings &
Merrill; 1908 Banking Hall by
Willis Polk
1 Montgomery St. (2-4)

37. Sheraton Palace Hotel
1909, Trowbridge & Livingston;
1991, rem. Skidmore Owings &
Merrill/Page & Turnbull
633-65 Market St.

Monadnock Building
1906-07, Meyer & O'Brien
685 Market St. (2-1)

38. Sharon Building
1912, George Kelham
39-63 New Montgomery St.

Call Building
1914, Reid Bros.
74 New Montgomery St.

Rialto Building
1902, Meyer & O'Brien; 1910,
Bliss & Faville
116 New Montgomery St. (2-2)

**39. Pacific Telephone &
Telegraph Co.**
1925, Miller & Pflueger/
A. A. Cantin; rest. 1990
134-40 New Montgomery St.
(2-2)

40. Hearst Building
1909, Kirby, Petit & Green
691-99 Market St.

Central Tower
1938, Albert Roller; 1989 rem.
Kotas/Pantaleoni
703 Market St.

Lotta's Fountain
1875, Wyneken & Townsend
Kearny, Geary & Market Sts.

First Nationwide Bank
1902, 1906, William Curlett; add.
1964, Clark & Beuttler
700 Market St. (1-42)

41. Wells Fargo Bank
1910, Clinton Day
744 Market St.

Cable Car Clothiers
1919 Bliss & Faville
1 Grant Ave.

Phelan Building
1908, William Curlett
760-84 Market St.

Humboldt Bank Building
1906, Meyer & O'Brien
783-85 Market St. (1-37)

42. Marriott Hotel
1989, Anthony Lumsden
(DMJM)
777 Market St.

Jessie Street Substation
1905, 1907, 1909 Willis Polk
222-26 Jessie St.

St. Patrick's Church
1872; int. rem. 1907, Shea &
Lofquist
756 Mission St.

Aronson Building
1903, Hemenway & Miller
700 Mission St.

Yerba Buena Center/Gardens:
Center for the Arts
1993, Fumihiko Maki/Robinson,
Mills & Williams
3rd and Mission Sts.

Center for the Arts Theater
1993, James Stuart Polshek
& Assoc.
Third and Howard Sts.

Yerba Buena Gardens
1993, Mitchell/Giurgola
Mission to Howard St.

George R. Moscone
Convention Center
1981, addit. 1991, Hellmuth
Obata Kassabaum/ T. Y. Lin,
Structural Engineer
Howard to Folsom, 3rd
to 4th Sts.

S. F. Museum of Modern Art
1995, Mario Botta
3rd bet. Mission and Howard Sts.
(1-38, 1-39)

43. Macy's
1928, Lewis Hobart
101 Stockton St.

I. Magnin & Co.
1946, Timothy Pflueger
233 Geary St. (1-7)

Neiman-Marcus
1982, Johnson/Burgee
Stockton & Geary Sts. (1-6)

44. Union Square (1-1)

45. Circle Gallery (former V. C.
Morris Store)
1949, Frank Lloyd Wright;
restored 1983, Michele Marx
140 Maiden Lane (1-5)

46. Hyatt on Union Square
1972, Skidmore Owings
& Merrill
345 Stockton St.

Bullock & Jones store
1923, Reid Bros.
370 Post St.

Qantas Building
1972, Skidmore Owings
& Merrill
350 Post St. (1-3)

47. Commercial building
1910, D. H. Burnham & Co./
Willis Polk
278-99 Post St.

Gump's
1861, Clinton Day
246-68 Post St. (1-4)

48. Shreve Building
1905, William Curlett
201 Grant Ave.

Hastings Building
1908, Meyer & O'Brien
180 Post St.

Phoenix Building
1908, George Applegarth
220-28 Grant Ave.

Head Building
1909, William Curlett & Sons
201-09 Post St.

Rochat Cordes Building
1909, Albert Pissis
126-30 Post St. (1-36)

49. The White House
1908, Albert Pissis
255 Sutter St.

Hammersmith Building
1907, G. A. Lansburgh
301-03 Sutter St. (1-35)

50. W. & J. Sloane Building
1908, Reid Bros.
220 Sutter St.

Goldberg Bowen Building
1909, Meyers & Ward
250-54 Sutter St.

Bemiss Building
1908
266-70 Sutter St. (1-34)

51. Pacific Telephone &
Telegraph
1908, Ernest Coxhead
333 Grant Ave. (1-33)

52. S. F. Fire Station No. 2
1909, Newton J. Tharp
466 Bush St. (1-32)

53. Notre Dame des Victoires
1913, Louis Brouchoud
564 Bush St.

San Francisco
Environmental Center
1916, W. Garden Mitchell; 1982,
Storek & Storek
530 Bush St. (1-31)

54. Sing Chong Building and
Sing Fat Building
1908 T. Patterson Ross and A.
W. Burgren
717-19 California St.

Old St. Mary's Church
1853-54; 1907-09, Craine &
England; 1969, Welsh & Carey
Grant Ave. at California St.

Paulist Center of the West
1964, Skidmore Owings &
Merrill
600 California St.

St. Mary's Square
1960, Eckbo, Royston &
Williams, statue of Sun Yat-Sen
by Beniamino Bufano (3-3)

55. Nam Kue School
1925, Charles E. Rogers
765 Sacramento St.

Chinese Chamber of Commerce
1912 (3-10)

56. Building
c.1915
745 Grant Ave.

Soo Yuen Benevolent
Association
1907-19, Salfield & Kohlberg
801-07 Grant Ave. (3-11)

57. Portsmouth Square (3-13)

58. Bank of Canton (former
Chinese Telephone Exchange)
1909
743 Washington St. (3-12)

59. Waverly Place (3-8)

Chinese Baptist Church
1887, G. H. Moore; reb. 1908, G.
E. Burlingame
15 Waverly Pl. (3-9)

60. Methodist Church
1911, Clarence Ward
Grant Ave. at Washington St.

Gum Moon Residence
1912, Julia Morgan
940 Washington St.

Commodore Stockton
School Annex
1924, Angus McSweeney, rem.
1974-75, Bruce, Wendell
& Beebe
Washington at Stone St. (3-7)

61. Chinese Consolidated
Benevolent Association of the
U. S. (Six Companies)
1908
843 Stockton St., (3-8)

62. Donaldina Cameron House
1908, Julia Morgan; rem. 1940s;
add. 1972, E. Sue
920 Sacramento St. (3-5)

63. Former Chinatown Women's
YWCA Residence Hall
1932, Julia Morgan
940-50 Powell St.

YWCA Clay Street Center
1931, Julia Morgan
965 Clay St. (3-6)

64. Ritz Carlton Hotel
1909, LeBrun & Sons; 1913,
Miller & Colmesnil/Miller &
Pflueger; 1991, Whisler-Patri
Assoc.
600 Stockton St. (3-2)

65. Joice Street Steps (3-1)
66. Fairmont Hotel
1906, Reid Bros.; 1907, rest.
Julia Morgan; 1962, tower add.
Mario Gaidano
950 Mason St. (4-14)
67. Brocklebank Apts.
1926, Weeks & Day
1000 Mason St.
Park Lane Apts.
1924, Edward Young
1100 Sacramento St. (4-15)
68. Apartments
1916, Arthur Laib
1230, 1242 Sacramento St. (4-17)
69. Chambord apts.
1921, James F. Dunn
1298 Sacramento St. (4-17)
70. Grace Episcopal Cathedral
1911-1928, Lewis Hobart; 1964,
Weihe, Frick & Kruse
California bet. Taylor and
Jones Sts.
Cathedral House
1911, Austin Whittlesey
1055 Taylor St.
Dioscesan House
1912, Austin Whittlesey
1051 Taylor St.
Cathedral School
1965, Rockrise & Watson
1275 Sacramento St. (4-8)
71. Pacific Union Club
1886, Augustus Laver; 1908-
1912, Willis Polk; 1934,
George Kelham
1000 California St.
Huntington Park
1906
next to the Pacific Union Club
(4-12)
72. Huntington Hotel
1924, Weeks & Day
1075 California St.
Nob Hill Center Garage
1956, Anshen & Allen
1045 California St.
Town house
1911, George Schasty
1021 California St.
Morsehead Apts
1915, Houghton Sawyer
1001 California St. (4-10)
73. Town houses
1917, Willis Polk
831-49 Mason St. (4-11)
74. Mark Hopkins Hotel
1925, Weeks & Day
999 California St. (4-13)

**75. Dennis T. Sullivan
Memorial Home**
1922
870 Bush St. (1-27)
76. Apartments
1909, Frederick H. Meyer
980 Bush St.
Apartments
1914, Grace Jewett
972 Bush St. (1-26)
77. Apartments
1914, 1912
1086, 1060 Bush St. (1-25)
78. Metropolitan Club
1916, 1922, Bliss & Faville
640 Sutter St.
YWCA
1918, Lewis Hobart
620 Sutter St. (1-24)
79. The Family Club
1909, C. A. Meussdorffer
545 Powell St.
Town house
1911, C. A. Meussdorffer
535 Powell St.
Chesterfield Apartments
1911
560 Powell St.
Academy of Art College
1909, A. A. Cantin
540 Powell St. (1-28)
80. Sir Francis Drake Hotel
928, Weeks & Day
432-62 Powell St. (1-29)
81. First Congregational Church
1913, Reid Bros.
491 Post St.
Medico-Dental Building
1925, George Kelham/William G.
Merchant
490 Post St.
Elks Club
1924, Meyer & Johnson
450-460 Post St.
Chamberlain Building
1925, Arthur Brown Jr.
442-44 Post St. (1-23)
82. Bohemian Club
1934, Lewis Hobart
625 Taylor St.
Olympic Club
1912, Paff & Baur
524 Post St.
Pan-Pacific Hotel
1990, Portman Assocs.
Post and Mason Sts. (1-22)
83. Alcazar Theatre
1917, T. Patterson Ross
650 Geary St. (1-20)

84. Native Sons Building
1911, Righetti & Headman/E. H.
Hildebrand
414-30 Mason St.
San Francisco Water Dept.
1922, Willis Polk & Co.
425 Mason St. (1-21)
85. Geary Theatre
1909, Bliss & Faville
415 Geary St.
Curran Theatre
1922, Alfred H. Jacobs
445 Geary St. (1-18)
86. Cliff Hotel
1913, MacDonald & Applegarth;
1926, Schultze & Weaver
491-99 Geary St.
Bellevue Hotel
1908, S. H. Woodruff; 1993,
Roma Design Group
501 Geary St. (1-18)
87. St. Francis Hotel
1904-07, 1913, Bliss & Faville;
hotel tower, 1972, William
Pereira
301-45 Powell St. (1-2)
88. Commercial building
1933
200-216 Powell St. (1-8)
89. James Flood Building
1904, Albert Pissis
870-98 Market St.
Bank of America
1920, Bliss & Faville
1 Powell St.
Hallidie Plaza
1973, Lawrence Halprin & Assoc.
Powell St. BART Station
1973, Skidmore Owings &
Merrill (1-9)
**90. Former Hale Bros.
Dept. Store**
1912, Reid Bros., rem. 1989,
Whisler-Patri
901-19 Market St.
**Nordstrom/San Francisco
Shopping Center**
1989, Whisler-Patri
5th and Market Sts.
The Emporium
1896, Joseph Moore; 1908,
Albert Pissis
835-65 Market St. (1-10)